A DJ's SPIN

My Life in Radio

by
Dick Williams
"The Tall One"

Published By

Bettger Books

London, Canada, 2015.

Websites:
www.bettgerbooks.com
www.adjspin.com
www.dickwilliamsvoice.com
www.southernmostradio.net

Cover Design and Artwork:
Shane Rundle

Interior design and Layout:
Will Chapman - Good Bucket Productions

Library of Congress and Canadian Cataloguing in Publication Data
Williams, Dick, 1940
A DJ's Spin: My Life in Radio (First Edition)

ISBN 978-1-987812-03-9
1. Autobiography
2. Radio
3. Television
4. Humor
5. Nostalgia

Foreword

Like many kids of my generation, it was the transistor that first allowed me to connect to the wider world. More specifically, the transistor radio. I got my first one from my parents in 1962, and it became my constant companion. I listened on the way to school, during recess and lunch hour, and any time the teacher left the room. It set the pace for my walk home after school and in the evening providing the background music for doing my homework (when I managed to get around to it). Afterwards, it lulled me to sleep, playing quietly next to my pillow.

And, like most kids in London, Ontario, evenings meant the Tall One's Show with Dick Williams. He was the Big Daddy of local DJ's and his show was a must-listen for much of my early teens. Funny, irreverent, and playing the biggest hits on the area's biggest station, he was a larger-than life figure. I first met him at a station-sponsored teen dance in 1963, when he actually took the time to talk to a star-struck fourteen-year-old would-be broadcaster. I would go to his remotes and just hang around watching him do his thing, enthralled by the magic of it all and thrilled when he remembered my name.

As a listener I have vivid memories of many of the zany things he talks about in this book and I also remember him singing Long Tall Texan at some outdoor event with our late friend Johnny Stevens and his Sextet. He later MC'd a number of shows where my band was on the bill, and that was always a thrill for us.

The thing about Dick was that he was always approachable, always friendly and always accommodating. And we knew he was big time, too. Later in the evening we would listen to WLS in Chicago and especially WABC in New York City, rock powerhouses where the hottest DJ's in the business worked their radio magic. As good as they were, Dick always held his own. He never sounded small-town and his jokes and production bits were as good as anyone's. We were proud to belong to the Tall One's Club because it proved we weren't just hicks in the sticks, we had our own Boss Jock who was as groovy as anyone on the airwaves.

I temporarily lost touch with Dick, especially went he left radio for a few years, but I vividly remember being at a barbecue when someone announced The Tall One was coming back to the local airwaves. People actually clapped at the idea. That's the kind of fan appeal he had, and it has never left him.

Years later, when I was a radio veteran myself and he had 'officially' retired, he dropped by the station one day and sat in on my talk show. We had a great chat and afterwards I got a lot of positive feedback from listeners who shared pleasant memories of the days when The Tall One ruled the London airwaves.

I feel privileged to have been able to work with Dick on the manuscript for this book and serve as the senior editor for the project. His story is a fascinating peek behind the scenes of the golden age of rock radio, from a guy whose career paralleled the rise and lasted through the decline of the kind of pop music radio that helped define a generation and changed the role of music in our lives forever. And it is also a very personal and entertaining memoir of one man's journey through a career he loved so much that he will tell you even now that he never worked a day in his life.

Jim Chapman, CFPL-AM, CKSL-AM, CJBK-AM, CHRW-FM, Bettger Books.

"But first, these words!"

I'm writing this book in Key West, Florida, a sunny place filled with shady characters. It's the southernmost City in America, just ninety miles across the blue water from Cuba. I'm not the first 'writer in residence' here. There was a guy named Hemingway who sold a few books, and his battered typewriter sits in the Hemingway Home tourist attraction about a mile from my studio. His medium was the printed word, however, while mine has always been the spoken variety. This is my first serious effort to convert one into the other so please bear with me as I put a few things "on record."

More than half a century has passed since some of these stories happened. My memory may be slipping, or my imagination working overtime, but I've tried to make my reminiscences as accurate as possible.

You'll note I haven't mentioned people's full names in many of the stories that follow. It's a little like the intro to the old Dragnet radio show.

"The story you are about to hear is true- only the names have been changed to protect the innocent."

Innocent or not, many of the individuals I'll be talking about later in their careers went into more senior positions than when these events occurred. I wouldn't want to embarrass anyone by holding them accountable for the sins (and plain foolishness) of youth. Beyond that, many are friends of long standing and I truly respect their professionalism and the reputations they have built.

Other great people I've had the pleasure of working with are now doing air shifts in the Big Studio in the Sky, and I'm not about to soil their heavenly wings.

But that all said, let's tell the story.

Day to day, success in radio is measured by consistency of results. We all have good days and bad, but it is your overall performance that defines who you are in the business. And in spite of appearances in this book to the contrary, professional radio requires preparation, perspiration, concentration and focus. It takes *work*. Steady, hard work.

This is by way of saying the stories I am going to share are likely to focus on the highlights, (and some lowlights) of a lifetime in broadcasting more than the regular routine of a working jock. They may not have been what made my career, but they certainly made memories. And even though the wilder tales are the exception and not the rule, they give a real flavor to what it was like to be there.

You may notice throughout the book that I talk mostly about the guys I worked with. To put it bluntly, for much of my career there were few, if any, female radio announcers. And they generally found themselves marginalized by being slotted only into late-evening shifts and told to sound soft and sexy if they wanted to keep their jobs. It was years before I worked with my first female DJ.

If you are reading this book in an eBook format, you will see links throughout to various websites. They have been deliberately placed at points where I'm talking about a particular subject, and these links will allow you to hear, see, or explore it further before returning to the eBook. At the time of publication all the links are functional, but I can't guarantee they will always be that way.

Readers of print versions are invited to visit the websites, too, via computer, in order to access the same information.

Here is my You Tube Channel for "A DJ's Spin," with all of the aviation videos and off-air recordings of my shows over the years that you're going to read about in the book, or if you want to watch and listen from your home computer. Each clip is labelled with its own description. Here's the link: bit.ly/ADJsSpin (Case sensitive.) You might want to bookmark it in case you can't connect through an e-reader, or aren't in a wi-fi area. Also, the same list of pictures, audio and video can be found at the website for this book at www.adjspin.com Life in the computer age is such fun, isn't it?

So, with all that behind us, gentle reader, in the words of a fellow Disc Jockey so many years ago, "let's get this beguine begun!"

Track 1

"The radio craze ... will soon fade."
Thomas Edison, 1922

Now Playing: Yesterday Once More, by The Carpenters
"When I was young I'd listen to the radio, waiting for my favorite song."
Richard Carpenter ©A&M Records

"It's not true I had nothing on. I had the radio on."
Marilyn Monroe

It all began with sound. My first memory of putting on a set of headphones, or cans as they're frequently called in the business, happened around the age of seven. Our class was being given hearing tests to determine how sensitive our young ears were. I was fascinated by the sound as the testers raised the frequency of the test tones from the bottom threshold of hearing all the way up to where only dogs could make them out!

I was so entranced wearing this new gizmo that I forgot to tell them when I could hear the sounds coming from the plastic, cup-shaped earphones. My parents were given a note for me to report to an audiologist for further testing, and if necessary, some form of hearing aid. As it turned out, it wasn't necessary because I could hear just fine when I paid attention, but the memory is still with me. Like many of my peers, however, my hearing has now been impaired by decades of broadcasting my radio shows with the headphone volume turned all the way up to 'Blare.'

As a kid I would listen to the radio in the dark late at night. The sounds of distant stations from Chicago and New York City took me far away from my bedroom in Kitchener, Ontario, where I frequently listened to KOMA In Oklahoma City, Oklahoma. Little did I know that later in life I would get an offer to work at that powerhouse station in the late evenings!

Faint signals in the darkness brought me the voice of Franklyn MacCormack, a radio personality at WGN 720 in Chicago. His program was sponsored by Meister Brau beer, and aired from 11:05 pm to 5:30 am, six nights a week. It was also known as the Meister Brau Showcase.

It featured easy-listening music and a bit of jazz, and his melodious voice would segue oh so smoothly into a product endorsement.

"Have you ever held a beautiful woman in your arms, kissed her tenderly and then looked deep into her eyes? Well that's the same feeling you get when you take a long refreshing drink from an ice-cold Meister Brau beer."

At that time, naturally, I had no knowledge of either beer or women but I later learned the comparison was way off mark, no disrespect to the amber liquid.

One of MacCormack's loyal admirers was Gary Theroux, a radio personality, musicologist, author and producer who, among other things, was the Music & Entertainment Editor of Reader's Digest for twenty years.

"Like so many others growing up in the Midwest, I listened to a lot of radio, the medium that not only shaped a lot of my own career (as a broadcaster myself) but my perceptions of the world. I particularly grew to cherish the kind of radio you'd listen to in your car right up until the moment you pulled into your driveway and shut the ignition off. The motor would stop, but then you'd click the radio back on, because you were afraid that if you *didn't,* you'd miss something. Franklyn's broadcasts were like that. Compulsive radio that you simply could not turn away from for fear of missing a magic moment and breaking the spell."

That, my friends, is a description of old-time radio at its finest!

Fast-forward to age ten and I finally found myself in front of a real microphone for the first time. I attended church regularly at St. Andrews Presbyterian, where Reverend Findlay Gordon Stewart was our minister. A marvelous communicator and speaker, he had learned the persuasive power of radio early on. You'll hear more about him later in this story. (And that is the first tee-up, or teaser, in this book. It's a radio thing…tweak the listener's interest, hoping they'll stay tuned for an upcoming event).

Back to that ten-year-old kid. Some of the members of the Sunday school class were invited to a studio for a series of broadcasts which were recorded, or to use the technical term, transcribed, for later broadcasts. There was a group of kids like me, wide-eyed and almost overwhelmed, who were given scripts to read. We stood clustered around a big microphone mounted on a boom, in a carpeted room with floor-to-ceiling curtains to further muffle any ambient sound. It was incredible.

We read our lines and then, for the very first time, I was able to listen to a playback from the transcription we had just recorded. This was before the days of audio tape, so a sensitive needle riding over the surface of a spinning disc of acetate actually carved our words into the surface. I guess that made me officially a 'groovy guy' (sorry!), but I wasn't impressed at all with the high-pitched voice of the person I heard when the playback started. Like most people when they hear their own recorded voice for the first time, it was not what I expected. To say I was let down would be an understatement.

Unfortunately, the idea of syndicating our efforts to radio stations across the country apparently fell on deaf ears, and my first experience as an on-air performer came to a screeching halt after recording perhaps a half-dozen of these programs.

My Aunt Lillian was one of the first stewardesses for American Airlines, and had a lot of friends in various places. She knew of my budding love for radio and sometime around 1950 pulled some strings to get me inside my first bona fide radio station. WJBK-AM was a Detroit landmark, and Ed McKenzie was the then-famous on-air character, Jack the Bellboy. The name and theme song for the show were taken from a 1940 Nat King Cole and Lionel Hampton recording of the same name.

Ed was undisputedly the top radio disc jockey in Detroit and perhaps the country at that time. His gift of gab served him well and led to strong ratings, and in later years he also hosted his own TV dance party. His unique success was due in no small part to the music he played, and many of the performers he featured were black artists. Not everyone agreed with his playlists, but Ed (or Jack) had the last word.

"Music is music, and it doesn't matter who makes a good thing."

With that attitude, Jack the Bellboy made himself a hero to legions of younger fans, primarily teenagers, who felt the same way. What a thrill for me to sit spellbound in his big studio as he spun records that kept people in the Motor City glued to their radios! He was very kind and engaging to the young, skinny kid sitting with him at his console beside the turntables, and I hung on his every word.

Ed later moved to Detroit's WXYZ-AM, and retired when they switched formats to the then-new Top 40 formula. His last day on air at that station was March 16, 1959. His parting words addressed his reluctance to do tightly-formatted radio.

"I'd sooner dig ditches or sell hot dogs, because I can't do something I don't believe in."

Among the old-time big-voiced announcers who were his peers, he certainly wasn't alone in his thinking. Many of them were dismayed by the changes in radio. Suddenly they were thought of as dinosaurs, left behind by the rapidly changing evolution of radio.

Much more about this as we move on, but let me now take you to The Big Apple and my childhood exposure to the newly-emerging world of television.

During a school break around 1953, my parents hauled me along on a trip to New York City, where the search for a little entertainment led to a life-changing revelation. They got tickets to The Steve Allen Show at the Hudson Theatre. Though at that point it was a local show airing from 11:20 pm to midnight on WNBT-TV, New York, the local NBC affiliate, it moved to the full NBC network the next year as The Tonight Show and the first network episode aired on September 27, 1954.

The show's announcer was Gene Rayburn, a silky-smooth, telegenic guy you might know best as the twenty-two-year host and MC of TV's The Match Game.

Skitch Henderson's band provided live music, and a very young Steve Lawrence and Eydie Gormé were the head-over-heels-in-love young singers with the band.

Similar to most such programs then and now, Steve Allen handled his own pre-show warmup with the audience, reminding them that they were an important part of the show. He pointed out the huge Applause signs which hung out of the cameras' field of vision. When they lit up, triggered by the Floor Director's switch, the studio audience was supposed to burst into spontaneous applause. Being an active part of that show was one of the milestones of my young life. I somehow knew right then that TV was going to be part of my future, along with my first love, radio. How thrilling it was to be sitting in that huge theatre under the bright Klieg lights (huge carbon arc lamps used in filmmaking) and watching three or four monstrous studio cameras roam around the stage.

My particular favorite was mounted on a small crane, which could be lowered to the studio floor or elevated to about eight feet above the ground, to capture high-angle shots. The entire contraption was on four large rubber wheels, which allowed the camera to move silently around the set. Looking down on the entire set was a huge boom, which hung a microphone over the performers' heads. An operator stood on this rig, moving and dipping the microphone just out of the view of the camera's lens, and he was also able to turn it to and fro to capture all the interplay between performers on the set.

Of course, this was before the days of the TelePrompTer, the electronic device now so commonly used in TV for both newscasts and late-night shows, so as Steve did his monologue a stagehand crouched beside the camera constantly flipping and discarding cardboard cue cards with the script in large letters. A nice touch, I thought, was that Steve held Eydie's cue cards, with the lyrics spelled out on them, while she sang songs during the show. In return, she did the same for him.

All too soon, the show was over, the performers disappeared backstage and the stage lights dimmed. But walking out of that theatre I knew that one way or another, in front of or behind the cameras, I wanted to be a part of this exciting new medium.

A small RCA studio crane camera, which could be elevated to around 8 feet, or lowered to floor level for dramatic shots.

Track 4

During this same visit, I managed to talk Mom and Dad into a tour of the NBC Radio studios in 30 Rockefeller Center. One of the highlights of the tour was an explanation of how sound effects were produced by specialists in their craft, inside the sound-effects "booth." It was a real eye-opener to see what could be done with something as basic as a pair of hollowed-out coconut shells. They both had a handle and a man held one firmly in each hand. In front of him was a table filled with gravel and another with sand. He would recreate the sound of a horse's hoofs by plunging the coconuts into the dirt in the rhythm of a horse's gait. He would increase the tempo to a gallop, then 'jump' the horse by pausing for a long second before resuming the clopping after what sounded like a mighty leap into the air.

Thunder was created the same way it had been in the theatre for centuries. The sound man hit a hanging sheet of tin with a soft-headed mallet and presto, a pretty good roll of thunder. Cellophane from a cigarette pack, when rolled between his hands, simulated the sound of fire, or eggs sizzling in a frying pan. Try it yourself by putting some cellophane up to your ear and rubbing it between your fingers. Pure audio magic.

Another highlight of the tour was a look through studio 8H, which had just been converted to a large TV sound stage. It was once the largest radio studio in the world and is now the home of Saturday Night Live on NBC-TV. From 1937 to 1950 it was home to the NBC Symphony Orchestra.

Unlike today, when you turn to one station for news, another for music, another for sports and another for comedy, in those days individual radio stations had to be many things to many people. They were programmed in blocks and during the course of the day, or the week, various types of shows would air at particular times, each attracting its own specific audience.

But a new generation of popular music was being born. Very quickly, big-band stalwarts like the Dorsey Brothers and Glenn Miller and vocal groups like the Mills Brothers were being elbowed aside by younger artists who were arriving on the scene, sometimes almost overnight, catering entirely to the taste of teen-agers.

Bill Haley and the Comets' Rock Around The Clock, which hit the pop music charts in 1954, Little Richard's Tutti Frutti in 1955, and Elvis Presley's Hound Dog in 1956 were among the standout songs that popularized this new style. A whole new music market had been born, and it was filling with young fans eager to hear their new musical idols.

The music was so immediate and so intense, and its fans so fervid, that it revolutionized radio broadcasting forever. Stations across North America switched to what came to be known as the Top Forty format, including Toronto's CHUM, WHB in Kansas City, KLIF in Dallas, and Houston's KILT. Big stations with big audiences. Hundreds of smaller stations in lesser markets followed suit and a brash new breed of on-air personality burst onto the scene. In what seemed like no time at all, younger, more raw and exciting radio voices were being heard everywhere!

Stories and legends of its creation abound, but the idea for Top Forty is thought to have occurred when an inventive Program Director noticed that the juke boxes from which many teens got their music generally held about 40 of the most popular songs. This individual (or individuals) recognized that these records were played in a predictable pattern based on current popularity, and the more popular songs were played many times each day. What if you set up a playlist to duplicate that phenomena, and fed the audience what they most wanted to hear?

Todd Storz in Omaha and Gordon McLendon in Dallas (who was known as The Old Scotsman), developed and perfected a format that emphasised local DJs playing the most current and popular records, along with news and zany on-air contests. It became the paradigm for rock and roll radio stations and its popularity lasted for several decades. It was a format that was to be very kind to me.

Track 6

Announcer: *"Ladies and Gentlemen, we're on the air!"*

"I was the class clown, you know, that kind of thing, and I gathered around me a group of guys who also were silly. I wanted to be a radio announcer." Dick Van Dyke

"I dug it very much, just from the first go round." WJLB Detroit legend 'Frantic' Ernie Durham on his first time in radio.

"Be willing to starve for a couple of years." Well-known air personality Gene Taylor from CKLW-AM Windsor, CHFI-FM Toronto, and Oldies 104.3-FM in Detroit, on the harsh reality of starting a radio career.

"My existence went up about 12 levels of intensity." Wolfman Jack, describing his first radio job.

CKCR-AM Kitchener, 1956 Playlist:
"Heartbreak Hotel" Elvis Presley
"Don't Be Cruel" Elvis Presley
"Lisbon Antigua" Nelson Riddle
"My Prayer" The Platters
"The Wayward Wind" Gogi Grant
"The Poor People of Paris" Les Baxter
"Whatever Will Be Will Be" Doris Day
"Hound Dog" Elvis Presley
"Memories Are Made of This" Dean Martin

"Rock and Roll Waltz" Kay Starr
"Moonglow and Theme from "Picnic" Morris Stoloff
"The Great Pretender" The Platters
"I Almost Lost My Mind" Pat Boone
 "Canadian Sunset" Eddie Heywood and Hugo Winterhalter
"Blue Suede Shoes" Carl Perkins
"The Green Door" Jim Lowe
"No, Not Much" The Four Lads

Now Playing: Juke Box Baby, by Perry Como
"Jukebox baby, put a nickel in for 'Maybelline'
Jukebox baby, drop another one for 'Seventeen'
Jukebox baby, whisper to your daddy-oh
Three little love words, 'Ko-ko-mo'"
Noel and Joe Sherman © Sony/ATV Music Publishing LLC

My first real on-air performance had nothing to do with Top
Forty. It was in 1955 at a tiny 250-watt AM station in
Kitchener, Ontario. I was in grade ten in high school and
Mike Miller was a classmate of mine whose father owned a
radio and record store in the heart of town. If memory
serves, his dad was a sponsor on the station promoting his
store, and Mike was a born hustler who worked himself into
hosting a weekly half-hour show called High Time. In those
days the word high did not have the same connotation it does
now. I asked him if he would consider adding me to the
show in the role of school reporter. My plan was to clip out
the news printed in the local Kitchener Waterloo Record
relating to the two local high schools and present a two-
minute summary during the show. He agreed, and before I
knew it there I was, in the studio, sitting across the desk from
him.

I knew I had to be ready to say something when Mike cued me, but I wasn't ready for the speed with which he launched into it.

"Now, with High Time News and Views, here's Dick Williams!"

Suddenly, I was on the air. I was no stranger to talking, but it was very disconcerting to hear my voice coming back to me through the headphones. They were used so you could hear what was actually being broadcast. You see, as soon as the microphone is turned on in the studio, the monitor speakers there are automatically turned off, to eliminate the high-pitched squeal of feedback. A few seconds before the record ends, the operator of the show, in this case the Program Director of the station, cues the studio host and turns on the microphone. The music and program feed are fed directly into the on-air performer's headset, and it took me a moment or two to get past the novelty of hearing my voice as others heard it.

Ken McKinnon was the Program Director, and after the broadcast, he called me aside and complimented me on my delivery. After the second or third week on High Time, he asked me if I would be interested in learning how to become an announcer. You'll note I didn't say disc jockey or DJ, but announcer. That implied you spoke on the radio but to be truthful, that wasn't always the case. The actual job was often board operator or op, as they were known then and are now, someone to flip the switches and keep track of the broadcast logs. Not counting the janitor, it was the bottom rung on the broadcasting ladder.

You might have noticed I didn't make any mention of salary. That's because I didn't get one, but that was just fine with me. I said yes to the job and that began my initiation into all things radio.

The history of radio is mostly about the people who invented and re-invented it as a mass medium. And it certainly was people who helped me re-invent myself as a radio personality, my fellow workers and my instructors and mentors. I learned from them all, and most were generous to a fault. I prided myself on the fact I never made the same mistake twice, but I sure did make a lot of mistakes once. More on that later.

In today's politically-correct language, our morning man would be described as a little person. He stood about four feet, five inches at most and his name was Dick Austin. He billed himself on air as Radio's Big Little Man because, despite his diminutive size, his voice was powerful and robust. He was very patient teaching me the ropes and I learned a lot from him.

He had a developed several neat little ideas to draw in his listeners. He would encourage people around the city to call him with the morning temperature at their homes, and then mention them by name on the air. It may sound cornball now, but it was very popular in those days. His technical style was unique, as he worked standing up at the controls, which put the turntables at his shoulder level. But his skill on the board was outstanding.

Our newsman at the time was attracted to spirituous liquids, and would often have sampled a few wobbly pops before he came to the studios. I was walking down the street with my parents one day and saw him coming towards us. I was about to make the appropriate introductions when he stumbled and fell, doing a perfect face-plant almost at their feet. I had reason to suspect he had lots of practice. He wasn't exactly the best example of the broadcasting industry with which to impress my parents.

Another of our on-air staff was an announcer from Detroit named Don Haney. He had a smooth, mellow voice, knew his music inside and out, and was a polished performer. It never made any difference to me, but Don was black and at the time there were few, if any, black performers in Canadian radio. I learned a lot about delivery and pacing from watching and listening to him. Don continued to broadcast from Little Rock, Arkansas, until the time of his death. He hosted a program called Haney's Jazz. He was a witty and articulate host, and knew jazz music inside out. I was about to contact him for a quote for this book when I learned that he had just passed away. He was one of a kind.

A 1958 picture of the CKCR Control Room showing an unsmiling young DJ. Why the long face? Blame it on dental braces. The joys of adolescence!

Our sports guy was Don Cameron, and once I had learned the basics of broadcasting he and I frequently travelled to out-of-studio locations to cover baseball and hockey games. One winter trip we travelled two-lane highways for about five hours to get to a hockey game. It was an away date for our local team, and we made sure to arrive at the arena in plenty of time to get everything set up properly and ready to go for our broadcast. Don would be doing the play-by-play call of the game, and I was along to set up the control board, plug in the broadcast lines, monitor the levels of the outgoing signal back to our studios in Kitchener, and voice the scheduled live commercials. That was the plan, anyway.

As I set about hooking up the various cables involved in preparing a remote broadcast, I discovered we were short some important pieces of equipment. There wouldn't have been much of a game had the players all forgotten to bring their sticks, and there wouldn't be much of a broadcast without the microphones we had left behind. Since the town didn't have any radio station and we had less than an hour to game time, there was no way to find replacements. The worst part of all was that we couldn't even tell the listening audience why they wouldn't be hearing the game. After that embarrassing and disappointing experience, I became much more careful about what gear I had with me before I headed out of town. Don, to his credit, was gracious as could be about my forgetfulness, but it's hard to fire a guy who is dumb enough to work for nothing anyway, right?

I'm not a sports guy. I have no problem with people who like watching and playing games, it's just not my cup of tea. My knowledge of any sport is very limited, and that contributed to a memorable broadcast of a local baseball game being played in Victoria Park in Kitchener. This time, I had done my set-up homework and we each had a microphone. A definite improvement on that hockey game.

We sent test tones and microphone checks back through our system to the studio, got our watches synchronized, and were ready to go on air at least forty-five minutes ahead of the first pitch. Don was an experienced pro, and since it was a warm night, suggested he would go over to the Press Box and get a little refreshment for the two of us. He brought back a beer for me in a big cup, and I had a couple of tasty pre-game swallows. How much harm could that do, right?

We were soon live, on-air, and I learned quickly how much even a little alcohol could affect my on-air performance. A few minutes before the opening pitch, I opened the microphone and made my unforgettable introduction.

"Welcome to Baseball on CKCR! This is insert your name here!"

That's what the generic introduction script said, so that's what I read. I should of course have said "This is Dick

Williams" but somehow that eluded me. Not a great start, and it got worse.

The main sponsor for the game was an outfit that made Super Sash-less Side-slide Windows. Easy for them to say. You can imagine how the tipsy young announcer mangled that one, over and over again? It was only one beer, but for some reason it felt like I'd had a lot more.

Came the seventh-inning stretch, and Don handed things over to me.

"Now for a word from our sponsor from Dick Williams, and his comments to summarize tonight's game."

He then repaired to the Press Box for a quick snort, leaving me on my own. I was caught a bit off guard, but I read another commercial while I tried to decide how I was going to fill the time until he came back. I turned to look for him while I was speaking and saw him deep in conversation, cup in hand, with another sports reporter. Apparently I was on my own for a while yet. As the panic started to squeeze at my innards, I summarized the score then realized I didn't know enough about the game to fill any more time. Throw the ball, hit the ball, catch the ball. Beyond that, baseball was pretty much a mystery to me. Missing Don and desperate for something to say, I plunged into uncharted waters.

"Well, fans, it's a beautiful clear night here at the park, but it sure is hot! I'll bet those pitchers out there are struggling to deal with this ferocious heat wave tonight!"

I was mentally kicking myself: Is that the best you can do? Feeling more desperate by the moment, slightly fuzzy from the beer and the heat and at a loss for anything else to say, I continued to blather on about the temperature and the humidity and what I supposed was its negative effect on the opposing pitchers, until Don came racing back into the broadcast booth and grabbed the microphone.

"Well Dick, as I'm sure you realize, this is actually good weather for baseball. The heat keeps the players loose and limber. As you know, that's why the pitchers usually leave their jackets on when they're not on the mound, so their muscles don't tense up. Now back to you with another word from our sponsors."

He had heard my verbal distress on a nearby radio and rushed back to rescue me in the nick of time. I gratefully wrestled once again with Super Sash-less Side-sliding Windows, and Don took it from there. After a mercifully-brief two more innings the game was over, and not a moment too soon. I slumped into my chair, closed my eyes and let out a sigh of relief. I had learned the hard way that beer and broadcasting can be a dangerous mix. And if you're going to talk on the radio, it's a lot easier when you actually have something to say and know what you're talking about! Come to think about it, that's true off the air as well.

Track 10

For several months, I worked evenings and weekends on a part-time basis and my introduction to a radio station control board took place one step at a time. The workings of the various knobs, dials, meters and procedures had to be explained by the on-air people I soon got to know. In those days there were no community college radio courses that would lead to a degree in broadcasting after two or three years. This was front-line teaching, one on one, with an eye to getting right to the nitty-gritty reality of day-to-day broadcasting.

There were no workshops, intern programs or seminars, just a hands-on opportunity to learn the ropes, guided by radio grunts who may have had only a few years' experience themselves. There were no do-overs, because live radio is just that, live. Warts and all. What a way to learn!

We had a master control room, flanked on each side by a big glass window which looked into two studios, each with tables and sets of headphones and microphones. The operator would open and close (turn on and off) the studio microphones through the control board.

The control board itself sat between two large multi-speed turntables, and nearby were positioned a pair of reel-to-reel tape machines. The turntables were big bulky things and had not one, but two tone arms attached to them. One would play back songs recorded at 33, 45, or 78 RPMs. The other arm handled only ET's, the big Electrical Transcription platters on which pre-recorded programs were played back.

They were about twenty-four inches in diameter, roughly the size of a large pizza. The tone arms could play the programs from outside-in, like most record players, but many of the transcriptions were grooved so they played back inside-out! Each tone arm had to be set for playback of any particular record and the correct speed, so the possibility of playback at the wrong speed was always present, and very much to be avoided.

The first order of business was to learn how to cue a record. This consisted of selecting the playback speed, selecting the correct tone arm, and then physically dropping the needle and playing the record on a separate cue circuit that allowed the operator (remember him?) to preview the opening sound on the record off-air. As soon as the sound was heard, you would hold the spinning record on the felt cover of the turntable, then slowly reverse the record a few inches backward from the note.

For 78 RPM records, it was about a half a turn, otherwise the record would wow, or wobble, on playback because it hadn't reached full speed. For 45 RPM discs, just recently introduced with an eye to the younger generation, the back-turn was less, and for the long-playing 33 RPM LP's just coming into vogue and aimed at an older audience, the back-turn was even less.

To air the record, once it was properly cued, you turned on the power switch, while holding the record in place as the turntable spun beneath the disc. The technique was called slip-cueing. Once you got really confident, you could then open the volume control or pot input for the turntable to a pre-determined amount and just release your hands for an instant start. This production technique was called working a hot board, or Hot Potting.

Once this move was mastered, the next item of business was learning how to control the volume of each turntable, and the input from all the microphones. That's known as riding levels. In front of the control board were about eight input potentiometers or 'pots' that when twisted left or right would lower or raise the volume. The resulting level was monitored with a VU meter centered right in the middle of the board. It was important to keep a close eye on all inputs, because too loud a volume would cause distortion, while too soft an input would make it hard to hear. It was of utmost importance to keep the needle on the meter bouncing along in the centre black rather than pinning it against the right side of the device in the red overload area.

Within a couple weeks of intense after-school instruction and explanation, I was on the air a couple of nights a week, working my first shifts all by myself. I think recounting one of those shifts in detail is the best possible way I can illustrate the variety of styles of announcing they required, not to mention the skills required to read newscasts and sportscasts. It was a hectic few hours.

Let's go back to that studio where the green young kid is hard at work. I begin my shift at 6 pm, reading a package of news, sports and weather. From 6:10 to 6:30 it's Music for a Wednesday, or whatever day of the week is appropriate. Time now to flex my tonsils and do my budding DJ thing. At

6:30 I change gears again as we present a nightly remote broadcast of the Catholic Mass from a local monastery. I have heard it so often I can recite the Hail Mary like a regular Catholic.

At the 7 pm mark, it's time for In Memoriam, local funeral announcements that have to be delivered in a respectful manner to solemnize the passing of area residents. Stay tuned for more on that segment later.

At 7:03 pm, with the deceased carefully acknowledged, I launch into a program called The Music of Guy Lombardo. Back we go to the 78's and a torturous sixty minutes of shimmering saxophone syncopation. As each song plays I marvel at how much they all sound alike to me. The hour drags by, but I occasionally get to add a comment or two, apropos of something, or sometimes nothing.

"And now, here's Carmen Lombardo, asking the musical question, Boo Who?" Classic stuff, right?

At 8 pm, it's time for The German Hour. I slip back into the role of operator for a smooth-talking German entrepreneur who buys commercial time from the station and voices his own show, entirely in his mother tongue. I can't understand a word he says so he just points his finger at me to cue me when to spin the next record.

Auf Wiedersehn to my German friend at 9 pm and it's time for yet another quick change as Cousin Dickie spins a few country hits I introduce in my best good ole boy voice. Yeehaw. That cornfed interlude is followed by my favorite part of the shift, Jazz in the Night. At 10 pm, taking a leaf from Don Haney's book, I play a few jazz records, read some quick liner notes from the back of the LP's and try to sound as worldly and knowledgeable as Don, the master of jazz. It's a very laid-back and professional approach in theory, but delivered in my own unique sixteen-year old voice, it may not be quite as effective as I think.

Soon it's time for another fifteen-minute news, sports, and weather package at 11 pm, delivered in what is known as a rip and read style. That's an insider's term for the announcer pulling off about thirty feet of printed teletype copy from the news service, placing it on a counter, and ripping it into manageable segments long enough to fill the newscast.

I learned early on that it was a good idea to check the teletype machine frequently. One night another air staff guy came running into the control room during a shift I was working, yelling his head off.

"World War III has just been declared!"

I jumped out of my skin and ran to the closet where the loud, noisy machine was kept, only to find about one hundred feet of copy it had already printed had crumpled into the space behind it. I had neglected the printouts for most of my shift, and this was the result. Lesson learned.

I also found it was a very smart thing to read all the copy beforehand. Most of the announcers just read the Canadian Press wire service scripts verbatim for the first time when they actually aired the stories. That took a special combination of experience and nerves, and I opted to be safe rather than sorry. This was especially appropriate in my case because the Russian tennis greats at the time had unpronounceable (by me, anyway) names like Jaroslav Drobný and Anna Dmitrieva. What is it about Russian athletes' names, even way back then?

With the news, weather and sports safely passed along to my audience, from 11:15 till midnight the station featured a rotating schedule of shows like Charlie Chan, Boston Blackie, Mystery Is My Hobby, and my personal favorite, Suspense! Let me set the stage again.

I'm alone in a large building. It's late in the evening. I've just done a long and tiring shift. The studios are all dark. The transcription begins:

Now Playing: Audio Transcription of "Suspense" Radio Drama. (Establish theme music, Bernard Herrmann's Suspense Theme, then fade to background as the announcer intones…)

"The story told by this diary is tonight's tale of... suspense. If you've been with us on these nights, you will know that Suspense is compounded of mystery and suspicion and dangerous adventure. In this series are tales calculated to intrigue you, to stir your nerves, to offer you a precarious situation and then withhold the solution... until the last possible moment. And so it is! We again hope to keep you in...(Music Up, Dramatically)….*Suspense!"*

You can listen to some of these episodes at: The Internet Archive (https://archive.org/details/SUSPENSE)

Then follows an outstanding half-hour of acting by great stars, complete with music, sound effects, and superb writing. Stan Freberg, the satirist who sprang onto the scene around this time, called radio The Theatre of The Mind. How well he realized its power of imagination. No set designer could build the kind of ghastly crypt you can see in your own mind's eye. No makeup artist could come as close to imagining sheer horror as you can within your own head. No werewolf could be more threatening than the one you picture when you're listening to the radio with your eyes closed.

So now, I sit at the control board… alone, gazing nervously over my shoulder, then side to side into the darkened studios that surround me. I listen intently to the program, and start to tremble as it slowly unleashes its magic and terror. By the time the transcription rolls to a close, I am in a state of near-panic. My feet are actually quaking in my boots. Suspense be damned, that show was downright scary. Somehow, I do a station break, then fill the last fifteen minutes of the broadcast day with instrumental music before signing the station off the air with the immortal words of radio broadcasters everywhere.

"And now, we bid you a pleasant good evening".

I play the national anthem, shut down the transmitter, and all is silence.

I try to shake off the sense of foreboding from Suspense! because it's time for me to take the records and transcriptions I have played during the last six or more hours and carefully re-file them in the music library. Thousands of records are catalogued and stored there, for the use of the on-air personnel. I have a pretty good armful of stuff to re-file and I am still trembling. Suddenly, a strong gust of wind lashes the lone window, causing the glass panes to rattle and moan in protest. (They were obviously not Sash-less, Side-slide Windows.) In a blind panic, I scream out loud, throwing my hands into the air, and the records go with them! What goes up must come down, and they do, quite noisily. The transcription discs survive the adventure, as do the LP's and the 45's, but fate does not treat the fragile 78's so well. Most smash into shards all over the library floor, with a sound like breaking china.

I dash out of the radio station in a state of shock, not remembering or caring about locking the door behind me. Only after I get home and into bed do I completely calm down, and sleep is a long time coming. The next morning I wake up to a phone call from the station morning man, who wants to know what the hell went on in the library the night before. I decide my personal Theatre of the Mind needs to go out of business, at least while I'm working.

Cue the next record.

Track 11

The goal in radio pretty much all the time is to sound as confident and comfortable as possible, even when you are not. But learning on the job can make that harder still to master and I didn't find my indoctrination a relaxing way to learn the ropes. Nerves came into play from time to time in tense situations, and I made more than my share of beginner's bloopers, as they later became known. One of the more popular singers at the time was Rusty Draper, a star in both the Pop and Country and Western fields. His hit in 1955 was The Shifting, Whispering Sands and it reached #3 on the charts. Almost every time I introduced his song in my best hand-cupped-to-the-ear radio announcer voice, my mind would hiccup and I would make the same mistake.

"Now, here's Dusty Raper*!"* That's not an easy one to recover from.

In those days, one of the peak listening periods in radio was the noon hour, when people from every walk of life would tune in for the top-of-the-hour newscast. My job was to introduce it, then open the microphone to the news studio so the newscaster could begin his summary. On went the headphones. I opened my microphone switch, and with as much authority as I could muster, made my big announcement.

"Time for the twelve o'clock news, brought to you by Weston's bread...for the breast *in* bed*!"*

All I could hear from the newsman was the sound of strangled laughter. Which was, at least, better than coughing. In today's radio studios, there are so-called cough switches that can be depressed to briefly silence the microphone when the on-air person needs to clear his throat, swallow or sneeze. In those days only the larger radio stations were so equipped, so at our level it became the duty of the announcer to open and close the news studio's microphone if necessary. Paul Freeman was one of our newsmen and a heavy smoker who needed to cough frequently. That meant I had to stay in place for the entire five minute newscast, ready to kill his microphone whenever he signalled so his hacking would not be broadcast over the airwaves. I'm sure the need to cough while he spoke was as much a habit as a necessity but for him, it was very real and hard to ignore, no matter the circumstances.

One day, I had enjoyed a full thermos of coffee and needed to use the washroom. As soon as I introduced the newscast, I stood up and headed out of the control room. As I passed alongside the window to the studio I saw Paul look at me in panic. He gave me the slashing sign across the throat that meant he wanted the feed cut for a moment. Needing something pretty seriously myself, I just smiled and waved back at him as I ran to the men's room.

I was gone only a minute or two and as I was slipping back behind the controls the newsman, now in extremis from the perceived need to clear his throat, threw the broadcast over to me right away.

"And now, a word from Dick Williams!"

With nothing ready to read and nothing in particular I wanted to say, I declined the invitation and threw things right back to him.

"Now here's Paul Freeman!"

"Now back to Dick Williams!"

"Take it away, Paul."

"Over to you, Dick."

I have no idea what the audience thought about all this, but by this point he was well into hysterics, leaning backward in his chair as he squirmed with laughter. As I opened my mouth to toss it back to him again, I saw his chair tip over backwards, almost in slow motion, sending him crashing to the floor. His legs hit the desk and his script went flying everywhere.

Undaunted, and well away from the microphone now, he yelled from the studio floor.

"Back to Dick Williams."

Realizing this had to stop before someone got hurt, I grabbed the first piece of copy I could lay my hands on, and started to read a Public Service Announcement from the pile we kept for situations when we had a bit of time to kill. I don't remember it verbatim but I imagine it must have gone something like this.

"Canada Agriculture reminds you that the secret to cooking a delicious chicken is to remove the feathers first. This can be accomplished in a number of ways, including the use of a mechanical chicken plucker that will pluck your chickens more promptly than any human chicken plucker…… "

I tried my best but I could not keep it together. Some combinations of words just automatically make me smile, and chicken plucker is one of them. With Paul still on the floor and me doubled over as I tried to read the chicken plucker PSA, things were now in total chaos. We were both laughing, coughing, choking and gasping for air, and the only way out was to roll a record. I hit the switch to fire up the turntable, and the 78 on it slowly wobbled its way up to the right speed. And if it wasn't Guy Lombardo's 1949 version of the Chicken Reel, it certainly should have been.

Neither of us had any intention of breaking up like that when we started the newscast, things just went sideways and took on a life of their own. But there were also many times when such shenanigans were deliberately staged, at least by one participant. There are plenty of stories of people sneaking into a news booth during a live newscast and setting the script aflame as the poor newsman was trying to read it. Talk about a baptism of fire. Let me tell you, it's pretty hard to maintain your composure when you're live on the air and your script is being consumed by flames.

Another 'gotcha' was pouring a small stream of ice water down the back of my shirt. Sometimes, all it took was a tickle or poke in the ribs. And it was certainly distracting when he would push fast reverse on the tape machine sitting beside me, and the big twelve-inch, steel-rimmed reels would start to accelerate. If they weren't on tight, they would start to wobble as they loosened up at high speed. On several occasions a reel actually became an airborne circular saw blade, spinning wildly across the control board just inches from my head. But, what's good for the goose…

There were lots of other ways to introduce an element of insanity into an otherwise boring shift, like the daily recounting of the newly-deceased. As I noted earlier, every evening at 7 pm a local funeral home sponsored In Memoriam, a (supposedly) dignified acknowledgement of those who had passed away during the previous twenty-four hours. It was meant to be introduced with solemnity and respect, as befits this most serious of subjects. But as you can imagine, such a situation was ripe for radio mischief and this segment could be like catnip to a young kitten. It definitely brought out the worst in some of my co-workers when I began the introduction.

"This is In Memoriam, marking the milestones of our lives. Passed away yesterday, the late John Doe, surrounded by his family and friends at his home on Weber Street, after a long battle with cancer."

As the organ music swelled and I did my best to sound like a serious adult, my newsman friend would creep into the control room to wreak his revenge and try to crack me up. When he was (temporarily) out of new ideas to torment me, among the regular weapons in his arsenal was the studio fire extinguisher. He would pull the pin and let loose with a few second's noisy blast in my general direction. This was certainly an attention-getter and predictably would make me explode into laughter in the middle of a sentence. The problem for the victim in all these situations is that they are tethered to the control board with headphones and sitting between several turntables, so there is nowhere to run, and no way to escape the tormentor.

It became a nightly occurrence and finally got to the point where I had to lower my head, shade my eyes and grit my teeth to maintain the appropriate solemnity. Eventually, the only thing necessary to make me all but lose it was the sound of my tormentor jiggling the studio door-knob. All I can guess in retrospect is that the sponsors at the funeral home were too busy embalming their recent arrivals to pay attention to this segment of our broadcast day. Believe me, it was just as well.

Track 12

It was the last long weekend of the summer and as the new guy I must have automatically drawn the short straw to work on the holiday and provide on-air coverage of the annual Labor Day Parade. Our studios were on the main route of the parade, but in order to get to the broadcast location overlooking the street I had to haul a ladder out of storage and use it to climb through the library window. (Yes, the same window that had rattled and kept me in …*Suspense!*)

Once safely on the main roof of the building, I had to traverse about one hundred feet to reach the vantage point where I would cover the parade goings-on. I played out my long cable of microphone cord which connected me to the studio's control board and set myself up with all the equipment I thought I needed. In addition to the microphone, I had a clip board with all my talking points supplied by the parade organizers, detailing the many bands, floats and baton-twirlers who would be passing in review several stories below me. The only missing ingredient was a radio which would allow me to hear what was actually being broadcast to the listeners. This was before the days of transistor radios and I didn't have an extension cord long enough to let me plug a portable in, so I just had to get along without hearing what was being beamed out by our transmitter.

We had been told that the parade was due to start at 1 pm. Factoring in marching time, it was determined that I should hit the air with my comments beginning at 1:20, at which point the parade should be well into my view. As I organized myself, I was pleased that I was able to see back along the parade route well over a mile. At exactly 1:20 by my watch, I began to speak. It would likely have been easier had there actually been a parade. I began to slowly ad-lib from my information crib-sheet, and tried to fill time as best I could until the lead elements of the procession came into view.

"In a few minutes, we should be able to hear the passing parade from our vantage point high atop the Dunker Building, home of our CKCR Studios. Let me give you a brief preview of what we're going to see and hear as the parade passes in front of our broadcast position."

I padded and filled and adlibbed as best I could, trying desperately to will the parade into existence. I tried to build some excitement about the wonderful sights and sounds that were surely just around the corner by now. But the point far up the street where the parade would first come into view looked for all the world like a still-life photograph. No flags, no banging drums, no twirling batons or cheerleaders' skirts. No seventy-six trombones. No trombones, period.

"In case you're just joining us, welcome to the Annual Labor Day Parade. Here once again is what we're going to see and hear this afternoon."

Promise them anything to keep them tuned in. I stammered my way through my notes one more time and realized it was now 1:40 and still no parade. Not in front of our broadcast position, anyway, and nowhere the eye could see. It was pretty apparent I had to do something more than blather on, so I threw it back to the station.

"We now return you to our studios."

Confident the operator had closed the microphone and was playing something to fill the time, I trudged back across the roof, reeling in my many feet of microphone cable, and climbed back up the ladder into the library. As soon as I got inside, I was greeted by applause from an assembled audience of several fellow employees. Well, it's always nice to be hailed by your peers. I wish.

"Didn't you hear us yelling at you from the window? The parade was postponed for an hour. They called us just after you stepped outside. We've been playing music to fill the time 'til you decided to come back in."

"You mean I've been talking into a dead microphone all that time?"

"Well, the mic wasn't dead, exactly; we were listening to you on the cue circuit."

By now I had pretty much lost my patience and I let them know it.

"Why didn't you climb out and tell me?"

"We were having so much fun listening to you flap your gums out there we didn't want it to stop!"

I didn't know whether to laugh, cry, or punch someone in the eye.

An hour later I was back out on my perch, ready to describe a real parade this time, and I made it through with no stumbles at all. Why wouldn't I? I had already rehearsed it twice.

Track 13

At 6:30 pm every Sunday we presented a live broadcast from my family's church, St. Andrew's Presbyterian, located about three blocks from our studios. There was a permanent broadcast line installed between the church and the radio station and an amplifier/mixer that was pre-set at the source. Once the amp was turned on the microphones went live, and a tone was generated to match input and output levels in the studio.

The Reverend Findlay Stewart (Finn to his friends) conducted the radio broadcast, and the microphones also were positioned to pick up the organ and the entire choir for this thirty-minute broadcast. Normally, Finn would turn on the amps and feed tone to the studio shortly after 6:00, then begin his service. One memorable evening, when I switched on the circuit I noticed right away that there was no pre-broadcast tone. In a panic, I called the church and told Finn we weren't receiving his signal. He was a lot calmer than I was.

"I'll be in your studio before broadcast time and we'll do the show from there!"

OK. It sounded reasonable when he said it, but I was the only person on duty and I had absolutely no idea how to set up a multi-microphone live broadcast for both Reverend Finn and his dozen-voice choir. But when in doubt, tough it out, and I told him I would open the doors and await his arrival. At around 6:25 he showed up, slightly out of breath, with a stack of Electrical Transcriptions under his arm. He shoved them into my waiting hands.

"Put the top disc on turntable one, and cue it to track two. Then put the second disc on turntable two, and cue it to track five. I'll cue you as we go along. You announce the beginning of the program when I point to you, then just watch me for volume levels."

With that, he slid into one of the adjoining studios, put on his earphones and sat back like there wasn't a thing to worry about. Whether he said a prayer before beginning the broadcast, I don't recall. I'm pretty sure I did. Promptly at 6:30, I rolled turntable one at full volume, keeping my eye on Finn. He made a sweeping motion with his hand and then pointed at me. The organ music rumbling, I faded the volume, opened my microphone, and read the introduction.

"And now, from the Sanctuary of St. Andrew's Church, we present the Reverend Findlay Gordon Stewart and the St. Andrew's Choir."

I opened his microphone as he signalled me to fade the music behind his voice.

"Welcome to our Sunday Evening broadcast," he intoned, then pointed to me to roll the disc on the second turntable and keep the music behind him. This procedure was called a cross fade in broadcast terms, or sometimes a segue. Once again, the organ music swelled, and he signalled me to lower it behind him as he spoke over the musical introduction to the first song of the service.

"Our first offering from the choir this evening is O Wondrous Sight, O Vision Fair."

Incredibly, at that exact instant, the choir sang the opening words of the familiar hymn! My minister had hit the post! His intro had ended just as the song began, with no pause in between. That's the holy grail for a professional DJ.

He did the rest of the service perfectly, walking me through each break when he wanted to speak, and the contrived broadcast sounded so realistic the listeners at home couldn't possibly tell that he and the choir were anywhere but live in the Sanctuary of the Church. It was a masterful performance. Finally, the last organ notes faded away and Finn packed up his stuff. As he left the studio he leaned close to me.

"I don't know how often you pray when you're not in your regular pew for morning service, but you were for sure praying when I walked through that door tonight."

Amen to that.

Now Playing: Moments to Remember, by The Four Lads
"January to December
We'll have moments to remember
The drive in movie where we'd go
And somehow never watched the show
We will have these moments to remember"
"Moments to Remember" Robert Allen, Al Stillman ©
Columbia Records

Late one evening, alone in the studio, I picked up the phone
and heard a seductive voice on the other end of the line. It
was a listener who was quick to inform me, in a very
provocative way, that she was my biggest fan. After a few
minutes of conversation she suggested we should get
together sometime. It may seem hard to believe now, but at
the time I had never given much thought about girls being
attracted to DJs. It was a side benefit that had never really
occurred to me but once it did, I did what any other healthy
young high school male would do in response to such an
alluring suggestion. As coolly as I could in spite of my
nervousness, I suggested a date.

She obviously liked the way I sounded on the air- and on the
telephone. To many listeners, the imagination plays tricks
and they tend to imagine that the on-air person is somehow a
little larger than life. A deep male DJ's voice tends to make
people imagine an attractive, virile individual who's been
around and always knows just what to say. That can create a

definite interest on the part of the listener in seeing what they're like in person. And it works both ways.

A sweet, sexy voice on the phone suggests a sweet, sexy girl at the other end of the line. But as most any experienced young man or woman knows, it ain't necessarily so. Just because someone sounds great and sexy *on the phone* doesn't mean they're actually that way in person, but I was certainly game to find out. And if you ask pretty much anyone who's been on-air I'm sure they will tell you they've been in similar situations.

I didn't realize it at the time, but there was a great object lesson in life lining up in front of me. Within a few days, and after a few more steamy telephone conversations, the young lady and I set a time and place for me to pick her up. In my imagination I visualized someone who'd be a real looker, ideally with long, sexy hair and some serious va-voom. But reality can be a very stern teacher and I should never have tried to judge someone's appearance by hearing her voice on the phone. It could have been a hard lesson, but it didn't turn out too bad at all.

In person, she surpassed even what I had expected in my fevered teenage imagination. She was more than attractive, with long red hair and a figure that could only be described as voluptuous. And she was no teenager. I put her at around twenty-two or so, four or five years older than me. And she pretty much knew what she wanted. She suggested a drive-in movie, and who was I to refuse? Once we arrived and got settled in, it quickly became apparent we weren't going to be seeing much of the show.

Radio personality or not, I was still a young kid who had a lot more theory than practice on his sexual resume. But she was aggressive enough for both of us. I'm not one to kiss and tell, but I have to say she was one very uninhibited young lady. So much so that in my inexperience and callowness things spun out of control prematurely and we didn't get to complete what she had started. Prior to that night I had only been on dates with what were known at the time as Good Girls. Having a teen boy's dream date voluntarily steam up the interior of the little Austin Minor caused things to end much too soon. (But this is another teaser, so stay tuned. There's more to come!)

About this time, Dick Clark was a rising TV star in Philadelphia as the host of American Bandstand. But he was also making a lucrative side income from his Cavalcade of Stars touring troupes of new young artists that he had featured on his show. At any given time, several of these musical packages were criss-crossing North America doing concerts in local arenas. Naturally, when they passed through our town, Dick the DJ had the opportunity to interview the artists for later broadcasts. But there was a problem. Our little station couldn't afford a mobile tape recorder to conduct the interviews.

Where would we be without friends? A neighbor, Maurice Rosenberg came to the rescue and allowed me to borrow his own reel-to-reel tape recorder and microphone. Today, newsmen conduct interviews with tiny units that are hand-held. My loaner was the size of a suitcase, and even though it had a carrying strap, it must have weighed thirty pounds.

But I happily lugged this monster backstage, and interviewed some of the hottest stars of the day. Danny and the Juniors, who hit it big with At the Hop. Mickey and Sylvia, whose hit Love Is Strange burned up the charts. Jerry Lee Lewis came to town, courtesy of Great Balls of Fire, and the red-hot Platters sported their own steamy vocalist, Zola Taylor. I must say, even this many years later, that Sylvia and Zola were both zaftig, shapely and seductive ladies. No wonder they were stars.

I got all these acts on tape at the height of their popularity. They were used to being interviewed by big-city, mature DJs, and I must have been quite a sight by contrast, a tall skinny kid with a monstrous tape machine. Still, I did my best to be ever so Philly-hip cool, while sitting shoulder to shoulder and talking with some of the biggest names in the world of pop music.

As it turns out, I would meet The Platters again in the very near future, on another evening when things took a definite turn for the worse. (Attaboy, Dick, keep them flipping the pages with another tee-up!)

Track 16

When I wasn't on the air myself, I could often be found obsessively scanning the dial, listening to shows like The Breakfast Club with Don McNeill, which aired on the ABC Radio Network from *"The Tiptop Room of the Warwick Allerton Hotel on Chicago's Magnificent Mile"*. Quite a mouthful. It was really a talk and entertainment program and its songs, jokes, and interviews gave me ideas on how to perform on that kind of broadcast if and when I ever was offered the opportunity.

There was another informal place to hear examples of great timing and delivery for an enthralled would-be broadcaster. Bob Elliot and Ray Goulding, known professionally as Bob and Ray, were first-rate radio comedians and satirists, and extremely versatile actors to boot. Their deadpan style spoofed actual broadcasting at the time. Theirs was an act made for radio, and what classic radio it was! One of the zaniest characters they introduced was Bob's "Wally Ballou, winner of sixteen diction awards". Poor Wally would conduct man-on the street interviews, but he would always have started his on-air opening line just a half-second before the imaginary producers cut to him and opened his microphone. The first thing the radio audience would hear would be "-a*lly Ballou here"*. It was much funnier than if he had done the intro straight, and things would go downhill from there. You might hear his spiffy sportscaster, Biff Burns, who had devised the perfect radio signoff.

"This is Biff Burns saying this is Biff Burns saying goodnight!"

Another unforgettable character Bob Elliot created was Arthur Sturdley, a none-too-thinly-veiled parody of radio superstar Arthur Godfrey.

(This next paragraph is called a segue. In radio talk it means to roll from one record to a different one with no announcing in between.)

Arthur Godfrey, the ukulele-strumming radio and TV host of Arthur Godfrey Time was one of most popular entertainers of his day, and perhaps one of the best examples of what an announcer should be. I learned so much from listening to him *and* watching him! Arthur's shows were simultaneously broadcast on radio and television. The radio version ran an hour and a half; the TV version only an hour of that, though it was later expanded to the full hour and a half.

How lucky I was to have such a role model for my career. There he would sit, on television, no less, yet wearing his huge earphones like those used by fighter and bomber pilots in World War II, chatting with guests, interacting with the audience, and maintaining a personal connection to both listeners and viewers. Watching him was like having a first-class, front-row seat as a man at the top of his craft demonstrated show after show how to carry on a real conversation with his audience.

You had the sense his intimate, mellow voice was speaking to you and you alone, as he snuggled up to the radio microphone that was positioned *on camera,* not hidden out of sight dangling from an overhead boom microphone. And he had a strong visual appeal for his TV audience, too. His eyes would crinkle in a way that let you know he knew *you* were out there watching, never mind the other millions of viewers.

Godfrey was an absolute past master of ad-libbing, with an incredible ability to sound rehearsed and unscripted at the same time. He could use a folksy, throw-away "*Ah shucks*" delivery, or sell a product with such sincerity you would almost think he'd be personally disappointed in you if you didn't buy what he was selling! It was a master class teaching a lesson that can be invaluable in broadcasting. As the old saying goes, once you've learned to fake sincerity, you've got it made!

Track 17

One day, while spinning my way across the dial, I happened upon CFPL radio in London, Ontario, about an hour down the road from where I lived. It was one of the oldest stations in the country, but they were doing some fresh, new things. Something clicked as I listened to what sounded like the station of my dreams. Who would have guessed that in a few short years I would be working on their airwaves?

Their lineup of DJs included Lloyd Wright, the long-time morning man and a local country and western entertainer; the original nice guy, Dave Wilson; the multi-talented Al Mitchell; the solid Gene Kirby; the slightly off-the-wall Johnny Walters, and Johnny's brother Glen, who was known on air as Buddy Boy Hunter. Together, they were known as The Big Six and they made exciting radio for its day.

Tying it all together was something new on the contemporary radio scene: musical jingles. They had been a fixture on the old radio shows with live orchestras, but having them available in recorded form to identify individual stations was something else again. Sung by performers who mainly worked for a company in Dallas that serviced North America, they made the station sound ever so smooth and tightly knit.

Now Playing: CFPL Station Jingles
"Hear the news and weather
Hear the music and sports

They all sound better on
C-F-P-L, 980 in London!"

"Have a happy day
The 980 way
C-F-P-L, London"

I think the first CFPL DJ I heard on the air was Johnny Walters, a really slick, big-city-style performer. He went on to a later career in Toronto radio, then to WHK in Cleveland, then back to my home town of Kitchener, of all places, to host his own man-on-the-street TV show.

Another unique broadcaster, then working in the afternoon drive period, was an American named Al Mitchell. He had nice pipes, and was obviously a lover of the music he played. In addition, he did a pre-recorded show in the early evening called The Penthouse. What made this show so interesting is that he played a grand piano on the air, and chatted like a cocktail lounge entertainer along with and over the beautiful chords which would accompany his voice. Talk about sounding like the big leagues!

To someone who could barely walk and chew gum at the best of times, this was radio magic. The song would end, Al would reprise a few of the dying notes of the music on his studio piano, chat along, then segue (there's that word again) into the first few notes of his next song! The operator would then roll into the next recording and fade out Al's piano. A classic, and classy, delivery.

The biggest attraction to me as an up-and-comer in the business was a guy who billed himself as Old Dave, Dave Wilson. He didn't have a big, booming, or to use a radio term, ballsy voice. But working the mid-day shift, his soft-sell, sincere sound was perfect. He was very smooth in his on-air manner and he just plain sounded like a nice guy. I thought it would be great to visit with him and maybe learn more about my chosen field from a guy who obviously knew how to win the hearts of his listeners.

I wrote him a letter of self-introduction and he sent me a very nice reply, inviting me to visit with him whenever I could make it. A week or so later I was walking into the CFPL studios in downtown London. They were housed in a huge building that was home to the London Free Press as well. From the reception area, as you looked through large glass windows, you could see directly into a huge, three-storey former studio that had been converted into office space. What a sight! The working studios were nestled farther away on the third storey of the building.

Old Dave greeted me in the lobby, and once again, reminded me of the magic of radio. He wasn't *old* at all, probably at that point around twenty-five or so, yet he sounded so mature on the radio. Fooled another one, I guess. He led me to the announce booth, which looked down into the Master Control area. CFPL was one of the few stations of that time to have all programs under the control of an operator, who took care of all the physical chores, such as loading commercials onto the turntables, cueing the records, keeping an eye on the output levels, answering many of the phone calls, as well as being an audience and sometimes foil for the on-air DJ. This left the jock with much less to concern himself with, allowing him to concentrate on just his performance.

The next few hours flew by, and I soaked up the feel of being in such a professional environment, watching the smooth production of what went out over the airwaves. The Ops worked standing behind three massive turntables, each of which had its own sliding volume control. Wow! This was heady stuff, cutting-edge technology at play. Dave communicated with his operator on a separate talkback circuit only they could hear, and hit a buzzer when he wanted the next commercial or music to start. Dave and I got along well and I visited him several times over the next year or so.

A man named Ward Cornell was the General Manager of the station and on a couple of occasions he came into the booth and said hello to both of us. I'm not sure why, but I had a feeling I should keep in touch with this man who ran such a tight ship. Over the years, that turned out to be a good idea.

Track 19

While all this was going on in my radio life, my time as a high school student was drawing to a close and my Mother decided it was time to take my future into her hands. A nearby university in Waterloo was about to introduce the first co-op (work and study) program in Canada. They took their lead from an extremely liberal school in Yellow Springs, Ohio, known as Antioch College.

The dean of the college came to Waterloo to speak to their faculty and explain the benefits and advantages of this revolutionary system of education. Somehow, my Mom got an invitation. I'm sure you can guess that higher education was pretty low on my priority list at that point. My one and only love was radio, and all my ambitions centred around getting into the full-time radio workforce as soon as possible. My Mother, however, had other ideas, and insisted that I continue my formal education.

"At least by going to this school, you'll be able to get a job in radio or TV."

Sure enough, the school did offer an opportunity to intern as a page at NBC Radio and TV, so it wasn't beyond the realm of possibility that college might open some doors down the road. Left to my own devices I would likely have taken my chances, hustled for a full time job at CKCR and got on with my life, even if the pay was horrible and I might have had to live at the YMCA. At least it would have been a full-time start at what I wanted to be my life's work.

But I wasn't on my own, I was a dutiful son, and I wanted to make my Mother happy. And there were two things that gave me an advantage in seeking enrollment in Antioch College. One, the fact that I had three years' working experience in radio made me a prime candidate for the work-study program they were offering because it showed a proven performance history. My letters of recommendation from the Program Director of the radio station and Reverend Finn Stewart were both filled with praise for what I had accomplished.

The second and bigger thing that got me into the ivory tower set was the fact that I was technically a Foreign Student. Most colleges prided themselves on accepting people in that category because they thought it gave them an aura of international sophistication and accomplishment. Apparently the foreign student in question did not have to reflect the same to any great degree, which was very fortunate for me.

They certainly didn't take me because of my varsity sports career or outstanding grades, and that might be the biggest understatement of my whole career. As I have said, sports are not my thing. And thanks to my discovery of the opposite sex and my total involvement in all things radio, my grades were, to put it mildly, mediocre. All the same, before you could say stacks of wax I was enrolled as a freshman at Antioch College.

College-age boys living in America were subject to the draft in those days, but being signed up at Antioch got me a

Student Visa, which meant that I was eligible to work at any job I could get in the country, and was not in danger of becoming drafted as long as I was attending school.

Now Playing: School Days (Ring Ring Goes The Bell), by
Chuck Berry
*Up in the mornin' and out to school
The teacher is teachin' the Golden Rule
American history and practical math
You're studyin' hard and hopin' to pass!"*
Chuck Berry © Chess Records

That fall, I headed off to Antioch with my Dad and brother.
When I had told my classmates in Canada where I was
headed, most just looked at me blankly. Although the college
enjoyed a number four liberal arts ranking and accepted
students only from the top ten percent of applicants from the
best high schools in America, it just wasn't well known in
Canada. Or many other places. When we stopped for gas
about 20 miles away from Yellow Springs, where my future
Alma Mater was located, I told the gas attendant we were
going to Antioch College but all I got in response was the
same dull stare I had come to expect from my peers back in
Canada. In fairness, he didn't really look like the Antioch
College type.

There would be many things to remember about Yellow
Springs and the college, but one of the first was also the
biggest. It was the height of the Cold War, and Yellow
Springs was very close to the nearby Wright-Patterson Air
Force Base just outside Dayton. It was home to squadrons of
Boeing B-52 Stratofortress long-range nuclear bombers.

They were forever lumbering around the skies overhead, and I soon spotted one as we got closer to town. The B-52 is affectionately known as a BUFF, or Big Ugly Fat Fellow. (I'm told that within the USAF, the last 'F' is a little more colorful.) With a length of 159 feet and a take-off weight of 488,000 pounds, they certainly qualified as *big*.

Looking back, I can't help but wonder how many times they sailed overhead with nuclear ordnance in their bomb bays. In those days the alert aircraft flew fully combat loaded, and there were always some at the fail-safe point, ready to dash into Russian airspace in the event of World War III.

Seeing these incredibly-powerful monster planes overhead became an everyday event, and on more than one occasion a BUFF passed just over my car as I drove by the lip of the runway. When it roared above me, it created a huge patch of instant shade! Knowing what massive damage a nuclear-equipped B-52 could inflict, I'm glad that *shade* was all it created.

It wasn't long until I said goodbye to my Dad and brother, who left me in my new dorm in Stag Hall. I was excited to get on with this new stage in my life and as soon as I arrived I felt right at home on the beautiful campus. My dorm-mates were great guys, and we hit it off instantly. My bunkie, who shared a room with me, was a guy from Philadelphia named Jeff David. He was a handsome, confident and funny guy who had already enjoyed several professional roles on the stage. He went on to a career in acting and movies, and a pretty fair bit of income in the voice-over business in later life.

Since this book is by and large about radio, I won't dig too deeply into memories of campus life, except to say Antioch College was a phenomenal place to be. To say it was a *liberal* school was to put it mildly. All examinations were conducted under the honor system, which meant you didn't have to write them in a classroom setting. For those of a mind to cheat, it was a breeze to turn in a perfect score. The only mandated attendance days were opening and closing day.

There were no locks on any doors, and the dorms were open at all times, which meant no one was paying the slightest bit of attention as to whether or not there was a mingling of sexes in the building and common rooms, or even the student's rooms. (I promised not to kiss and tell, but I didn't say anything about a knowing wink. Wink.) There was no shortage of bright, witty, talented and young women of very liberal social views, raised in cosmopolitan cities like San Francisco, New York, Chicago, and Los Angeles, but learning about adult life in Yellow Springs. We all worked together in pioneering what would become the free love era. Enough said, and I'm sure you can imagine the rest.

I was particularly interested in one striking co-ed, and learned from my roommate that she was an aspiring actress named Mimi. She had already appeared in minor roles in a few off-Broadway plays. As luck would have it, there was an announcement on the main bulletin board in the Student Union building where we all gathered for meals and mail. It announced tryouts for several one-night, one-act plays for an upcoming fall event at the college theatre.

Jeff told me he was going to the auditions to give it a shot, and suggested Mimi might be there as well. That's all I needed to hear. Assuming she would want to audition because of her background in theatre, I made sure that I attended, too. I had no stage experience, but since I didn't think I would ever actually land a role anyway, I showed up for the auditions, plunked myself down in a back seat and waited.

Finally, there were only two un-auditioned people left, me - and Mimi. We introduced ourselves to each other and for our reading did a brief scene from Thorton Wilder's Our Town. It was over quickly, but I wasted no time in asking her for a date. Mission accomplished.

A couple of days later the lists of plays was posted, with the names of the successfully-cast actors. I was amazed that in spite of their previous stage experience neither Mimi nor Jeff landed a leading role. The cute Canadian kid did, however. Who would have guessed?

Now Playing: Everything's Coming Up Roses, by The Modernaires
"Curtain up! Light the lights!
We got nothing to hit but the heights!
I can tell, wait and see.
There's the bell! Follow me!
Everything's coming up roses for me and for you!"
Stephen Sondheim, Jule Styne

My excursion into the theatre was going better than I had expected. I had met the girl, and I was a leading man. But I was still bumbling around in something I knew very little about. When I picked up my script for The Old Man and the Mountain, I learned the plot line concerned a guy who was threatening to jump off a high precipice. I was shocked to see that I would be positioned at center stage for most of the play, with a ton of dialogue to memorize.

During the staging or blocking process, the director straightened me out as to what I would really be doing.

"Dick, you'll be off-stage for the entire play. You'll just read your lines from the wings!"

"But the staging directions on the script call for me to be front and center in full view."

"I know, but we really think it will make things much more believable if the actors throw their heads back when they interact with you completely offstage, so it looks like the mountain is really high. We picked you for the role because you really can project your voice, so it will work out just fine!"

As things turned out, my character in the play was never really in danger because he was firmly tied to a tree. The play ends with one of the other cast members talking him down from his perch. Because I was to be out of sight of the audience, it was the perfect role for a theatre novice, with lots of lines, some good laughs, but no memorization required. A dream role, in my opinion.

And then, suddenly, it was opening (and closing) night. I read my lines well, got lots of laughs in the right places, and felt quite satisfied when the curtain finally came down. I had read my parts assisted by a little flashlight, so I simply turned it off and waited for the curtain call from the blackened backstage. The cast bowed to stage right, then stage center, then all of them turned stage left, at which point I had clambered up onto a large box, and jumped, as if from a height, from the *mountain* onto the stage.

We hadn't really bothered to rehearse the curtain call. How hard could it be? But I was blinded by the stage lights, my jump was bad (remember, I was no athlete) and I tripped as my feet hit the stage. My ass-over-teakettle dive into the orchestra pit got a bigger laugh than any of my lines in the play because the audience thought it was all part of the act. It sure wasn't, but by some miracle I wasn't hurt and it actually turned out better than if we had staged it.

Even so, I figured I had come close enough to realizing the old theatre good luck wish "break a leg", and that night marked the beginning and the end of my stage career.

Track 23

"I found joy in almost every record." Gary Owens on his days in radio.

"The important thing was that I was still on the radio." Dick Biondi, when asked why he took a job at a lesser-known South Carolina station after being a big-time Chicago DJ.

WYSO FM Yellow Springs, Ohio, 1958 Playlist:
"Fugue in G Minor" Bach
"Rondeau" Mouret
"Fanfare for the Common Man" Copeland
"Hungarian Dance No.5" Brahms

It didn't take me long after arriving on campus to find myself inside the studios of the campus radio station, WYSO 91.3-FM. It had just signed on the air seven months before I arrived, and broadcast with a mighty ten watts of power as a student-run station on the Antioch College campus. On the air a full four hours a day back then, it featured local public affairs and music programming. It couldn't be heard much farther than the edge of our tiny campus, but it was still the place I had to be. I was able to wangle a shift one evening a week, playing classical music, and trying to sound like I knew what I was doing. I had no previous knowledge of this type of music, and frankly, very little interest in gaining any.

One evening as I read the news, there was an article about Theodore Bikel, an Austrian-American actor, folk singer, musician, and composer. Having no idea who he was, I pronounced his last name to rhyme with pickle. How very continental, I thought, but I took quite a ribbing about it from my new buddies when I got back to the dorm.

One of the most noteworthy things I did at the station was to interview each of the original Mercury astronauts, in depth, prior to all of them becoming legends in the American space program. At the time, they were at Wright Patterson Air Force Base preparing for their upcoming space missions.

These were the men who piloted the manned spaceflights of the Mercury program from May 1961 to May 1963. The seven original American astronauts were Alan Shepard, Gus Grissom, John Glenn, Scott Carpenter, Wally Schirra, Gordon Cooper, and Deke Slayton. How I wish I had managed to hold onto the tape recordings of those interviews. They were really a slice of history.

The most charismatic of the group was John Glenn, who really had a sunny personality compared to the others who were, after all, not performers but hard-working military pilots, the type not often known for their conversational skills. Most of the astronauts-to-be responded to my questions with one- or two-word answers. But John Glenn was different from the other six. He was a born leader, and had the requisite personality to go with it.

Years later, after he became a world-wide hero, he acknowledged that the question he heard most often after the fact was what he was thinking as he sat alone in the capsule listening to the count-down. His answer was classic John Glenn.

"I felt exactly how *you* would feel if you were getting ready to launch and knew you were sitting on top of two million parts all built by the lowest bidder on a government contract!"

Mercury 7 Astronauts Autographed (l-r front) Wally Schirra, Donald (Deke) Slayton, John Glenn, Scott Carpenter; (back) Alan Shepard, Virgil Grissom, and Gordon Cooper.

Track 24

I continued to work my shift at WYSO, but my heart lay elsewhere and I was growing restless for a fix of a real radio station! I didn't want time and opportunity to pass me by. I had also been looking at the job postings available for my upcoming work period, and quickly realized that the NBC Page job was the only radio- or TV-based position the college had available to me. I didn't want to work in New York City herding tourists around NBC, so I decided my best and most immediate option was to apply for a job back in Canada at CKCR. Lucky for me, they were happy to have me back.

Track 25

"Radio was where I belonged. I could feel it." Jack Gale in his outstanding book, *"Same Time, Same Station"*

CKCR REVISITED, 1958-59 Playlist:
"Volare" (Nel Blu Dipinto Di Blu) Domenico Modugno
"All I Have to Do Is Dream / Claudette" Everly Brothers
"Don't / I Beg of You" Elvis Presley
"Witch Doctor" David Seville
"Patricia" Perez Prado
"Sail Along Silvery Moon / Raunchy" Billy Vaughn
"Catch a Falling Star / Magic Moments" Perry Como
"Tequila" Champs
"It's All in the Game" Tommy Edwards
"Return to Me" Dean Martin

Now Playing: Get a Job by the Silhouettes
"Sha na na na, sha na na na na,
Yip yip yip yip yip yip yip yip
Mum mum mum mum mum mum
Get a job Sha na na na, sha na na na na!"
Beal, Raymond, Edwards, Lewis, Horton © Ember Records

I arrived back home just in time for the Christmas Holidays, and looked forward to the prospect of working in familiar surroundings to polish my craft some more.

Remember the seductive lady with long red hair? And how I told you she would pop up again? Well, she had written me several letters while I was away, and in each letter she had drawn a well-rendered picture of an animal or a bird. She also included a few poems she had written. She was quite a talented young woman, it appeared, and I admit I was more than a little excited to finish what we had begun a few short months earlier.

It was not to be. A few quiet chats with the guys around the station revealed my drive-in damsel had not restricted her fascination with broadcasters to just me, but had in fact been spreading her charms far and wide. Several of my colleagues had needed massive doses of penicillin to counter what was known in those days in polite society (but mentioned as little as possible) as a Social Disease.

And I had missed all the commotion because I'd been south of the border. Cue the theme music for Mr. Lucky!

Track 26

Now Playing: Tossin' and Turnin', by Bobby Lewis
"I couldn't sleep at all last night
Got to thinkin' of you
Baby things weren't right
Well I was tossin' and turnin'
Turnin' and tossin'
a-tossin' and turnin' all night"
Ritchie Adams, Malou Rene © Beltone Records

As far as the on-air work was concerned, little had changed since I left for school in the fall, and I quickly fell into the rhythm of a full-time employee, particularly enjoying the novelty of actually receiving a weekly paycheck. Perhaps, given its modest amount, I might better say *weakly*. But living once again under my parents' roof, I was able to sock away pretty much all the money I made, though it was precious little in retrospect.

If it was nice to be back among my old friends from high school, what was even nicer was the extra interest some of my high school girl friends were showing in going on a date with a college boy who was a DJ, too. I've never quite figured that one out, frankly. More of the mystery of radio, I guess.

The most memorable aspect of my work at that time was a fund-raising radiothon during a week I'll never forget. At the time, several DJs in America had been going on-air without a break for hours or days at a time, raising funds and awareness for whatever charitable cause they were championing. As the days increased, so did public interest, and lots of good press coverage ensued for everybody.

I suggested to our Program Director that CKCR should do something similar and he bought into the idea. How hard could it be?

I began my stint of non-stop broadcasting (with no sleep allowed) on the following Monday at 6 am. I was provided meals and coffee or soft drinks as I required them, round the clock, but Job One was basically just staying awake. I would do a live show in what was called Announce/Operate mode, meaning I was in charge of regular programming and had to operate my own controls for several hours. I would then hand things over to one of the other announcers and they would carry on while I popped in from time to time to read a live commercial or do the weather forecast and plug the fact that our listeners were invited to contribute to our fundraising efforts for charity.

We made arrangements to allow visitors to come into our studios at any time of day or night to drop off their donations, say hello to the sleepless wonder, or simply check that I was still alive and breathing. All went well until about 3am on Tuesday morning, as I was nearing twenty-one hours without sleep. I had eaten an apple a couple of hours earlier, and was seized with an attack of stomach cramps. I managed to weather it and stay awake, however, and we ventured into Day Two of the big event. By the morning of Day Three I had been sleepless for forty-eight hours and was becoming delusional thanks to sleep deprivation. They had to take me off the air at times, because my language was becoming way too salty as I drifted in and out of rational thought. As spaced out as I may have been, though, I was still able to operate the controls and broadcast for several hours at a time without many problems - that I remember. One thing I am pretty sure of, some 78 RPM records were likely played at 45, and vice versa.

On Thursday, I was given the sad news that my Grandfather had passed away, but there was so much riding on this broadcast that my family insisted I keep going. In the old tradition of show business, no matter what happens the show must go on. Which it did. By now we were getting calls from radio stations across the country as word spread of the length of time I had been awake. The press was also spreading the news because by that time I had beaten every other radiothon duration record to date.

By Friday morning, Day Five of purgatory, I was becoming less and less coherent. I struggled my way past the noon hour, which was pretty much a blur. Noon, or hour one-oh-eight was pretty hazy, too, and by around suppertime I passed out for a few moments right in the middle of reading a live commercial. I was pretty sure I'd had a micro-nap because there was drool all over the copy page!

The big finale saw me introduced at a hockey game at the Kitchener-Waterloo Auditorium at 8 pm, by which time I had been without sleep for one hundred and sixteen hours. There were brainwashing victims in the Gulag who'd gotten more sleep than I had over the past week.

My parents piled me into the family car, and I immediately fell sound asleep in the back seat as we drove to Tavistock for my Grandfather's funeral on Saturday morning. I slept like the proverbial log until we pulled into a motel where I passed out again until around nine the next morning. After a quick breakfast and a shower and shave, I headed to the funeral home with the family.

During the service, the minister bowed his head at one point and invited us all to pray. Our family was seated close to the open coffin, in full view of the entire funeral home, and the moment I closed my eyes I fell fast asleep and slid onto the floor from the folding chair on which I was sitting. Oblivious to everything around me, I continued to sleep soundly until the service ended. I can't imagine what our small-town neighbors and friends thought, unless they knew about the Radiothon. Falling asleep in public is not something normally associated with grief at the loss of a relative.

Now Playing: The Day the Music Died, by Don McLean
"I was a lonely teenage broncin' buck
With a pink carnation and a pickup truck
But I knew I was out of luck
The day the music died."
Don Mclean © United Artists

Don McLean's landmark hit was written to commemorate
February 3, 1959. I was on the air that day when we received
a teletype bulletin that musicians Buddy Holly, Ritchie
Valens, and J. P. "The Big Bopper" Richardson had died in a
plane crash near Clear Lake, Iowa. The story was driven
home even harder for me by the fact that Richardson was a
fellow Disc Jockey.

Due to a quirk of fate, Dion DiMucci, who was the lead
singer of Dion and the Belmonts, didn't board the plane
because the flight would have cost thirty-six dollars,
reportedly the monthly rent for the apartment in which he
grew up, and more than he was willing to pay for
convenience. In today's currency, that's about three hundred
dollars. Future country superstar Waylon Jennings, Holly's
bass player, gave up his seat to the sick J.P. Richardson in an
act of kindness that had unimaginable consequences for his
life and career. It was the first fatal plane crash involving big
rock and roll stars, though it would not be the last. Among
others, Otis Redding, Jim Croce, Rick Nelson, John Denver

and Stevie Ray Vaughan all perished when their aircraft went down.

Some people, like Don Mclean, believe the deaths of Holly, Richardson and Valens marked the end of whatever innocence rock and roll might have had. For them, it really was the day the music died.

My job period was over all too soon and it was time to return to the academic world waiting for me in Ohio. But stay tuned...big things were coming up right around the corner!

"Let people you admire show you the way, then use your own creativity to build on that base." Don Berns on how to develop your own radio persona.

"Top 40 remains unique ... in its ability to be the most democratic, the most eclectic, and the most lively of all formats." Ben Fong-Torres' closing words in his book The Hits Just Keep on Comin'.

WSAI CINCINNATTI 1959 Playlist:
"The Battle of New Orleans" Johnny Horton
"Mack the Knife" Bobby Darin
"Venus" Frankie Avalon
"Lonely Boy" Paul Anka
"Dream Lover" Bobby Darin
"The Three Bells" The Browns
"Come Softly to Me" The Fleetwoods
"Kansas City" Wilbert Harrison
"Mr. Blue" The Fleetwoods
"Sleep Walk" Santo & Johnny
"Smoke Gets in Your Eyes" The Platters

Now Playing: Personality, by Lloyd Price
"Cause you got personality
Walk, personality
Talk, Personality
Smile, Personality

Charm, personality
Love, personality"
Lloyd Price, Harold Logan © Universal Music Publishing
Group

Our dorm rooms were filled with music from the local
stations in nearby Dayton, WING and WONE, that were
locked in a battle for the emerging Top Forty teen audience.
WING had street-level studios, superb engineering, and a
crisp on-air sound. WONE strived to be similarly
professional. The difference between stations was The
Singing Clock that had its home on WING. It was just like
you might imagine from the name. Each minute of each hour
had its own jingle, and several times during the hour, at the
end of a commercial, a group of jingle singers would burst
into song.

"It's 11:47 from the Singing Clock!"

It was just noteworthy enough to set the station apart from
the competition.

One night I was rambling up and down the dial and hit upon
a station that really had it happening. WSAI was located in
Cincinnati, about an hour's drive away, and it jumped out of
my radio's speaker. The DJ was a man named Herb Knight,
and his on-air jingle sent chills down my spine.

"Knight time's the right time for radio listening
Knight time's the right time to hear the latest news!
Listen to WSAI..."

I was instantly hooked! This was the real deal. *Personality* Top 40 radio! An audience built by broadcasters who could put their own stamp on the music of the day, and create that invaluable one-to-one relationship with every listener that marks the best in the business. I needed to know more, so I called the station, got through to Herb and asked him if I could come down to visit him in the studios the next night. When he said sure, I was over the moon. One of the biggest players in one of the top twenty radio markets in America, and I was going to meet him!

I borrowed a car from one of my dorm buddies and after about an hour's drive found myself in the heart of Cincinnati. I located the station and around 9 pm found myself in a studio that just took my breath away. Standing in front of me was the ultra-smooth guy who had captured my imagination on the radio, and he was doing a radio show *standing up*, surrounded by six turntables. He had a lavalier microphone that he wore like a necklace. It and his headphones were both connected to long cords that allowed him to walk around the various turntables and activate them from wherever he stood. It was like nothing I had seen before, and a very slick setup. I sat in the studio for a couple of hours while he did his show, soaking up the sights and sounds. I knew I was being a little forward for a kid still in college, but I screwed up enough courage to ask him if the station had any openings.

"Funny you would ask, but we do have an opening right now!"

When I told him I actually had three years' radio experience under my belt, he suggested I should certainly talk to their

General Manager the next day. I probably don't have to tell you that I followed up with a phone call first thing the next morning. Herb had already put in a word for me and left a note telling the GM I would be calling. I expected to be interviewed and hoped I was ready. I never imagined what I would actually hear.

"Here's the deal. We're looking for a guy to do overnights starting right away, and then do the evening show for the summer while we have guys off on vacation. Come on down tonight at midnight and do our overnight show till six in the morning. If you sound OK, you've got the job!"

The big time (almost), just like that.

Thanks to borrowed wheels again, the following evening at midnight I was all hooked up and I rolled into the overnight show. Herb stuck around for a few minutes to make sure I had the technical aspects working properly, then wished me luck and left me all alone in the studio to give it my best shot. I couldn't believe how much fun it was. I was having a great time working with the superb equipment, and the station was tuned like a watch. It was one of the first to have a 'level devil' device that kept the volume constant even if the music input was a little low or a bit too high. Also, the signal was compressed electronically to tighten the broadcast sound and give it some real punch as it sailed into the ether.

Think of it like this. If you stand with a garden hose and turn the water on partway, it will normally just dribble out of the end of the hose. But if you stick your thumb over the end of the hose, the pressure builds and the water is forced out, shooting a strong stream of liquid farther away from you.

There is the same amount of water going in and coming out, but it has a lot more oomph behind it. Compression is essentially why some stations seem to almost jump out of the speaker, and are perceived to be louder than others. And in radio, that perception makes a big difference. Before it left the transmitter the signal was also passed through an audio processor that accented the mid-range and bass end of the audible scale, which made the DJ's voice sound bigger, richer and smoother.

Also, for the first time in my life I was working with just a stack of 45's. No speeds to change, just a pile of forty records. That was the basis of Top Forty radio and it was pretty simple, really. You played a record and when it was finished you took it off the turntable and turned it upside down in a growing pile. When you had played your allotted songs, you flipped the pile and started over again. It took a little more than three hours to complete the process and I loved the challenge of weaving my chatter through the records and jingles.

A couple of hours later the private phone line in the control room lit up. It was the GM.

"Sounds good to me, Dick. You got the job. Come in tomorrow and we'll get you all signed up."

Talk about dreams coming true!

Now Playing: Teach Me Tonight, by the DeCastro Sisters
"Did you say I've got a lot to learn?
Well don't think I'm trying not to learn
Since this is the perfect spot to learn,
Teach me tonight!"
Gene De Paul, Sammy Cahn © Abott Records

Be careful what you wish for, the old saying goes… I had rubbed the lamp, and now there was no way to get the genie back inside. The good news was that I was exactly where I wanted to be, but my situation was not without its challenges, the most pressing of which was the need for a set of wheels. I had to get back and forth between school and the radio station on a six-day-a-week basis, on what was then an old-fashioned two-lane highway. I managed to find an old clunker with a few miles left in her and my transportation problems were solved.

Another problem was maintaining my attendance at school on a regular basis. For the next month until the upcoming formal job period started, I would have to commute back and forth to Cincinnati, do a six-hour overnight air shift, attend a full day's classes beginning at 8am, participate in frequent afternoon workshops, do my homework to keep on top of my studies, do my laundry and eat three meals a day. Oh yes, and somehow find time to sleep somewhere along the way. What could possibly go wrong?

Today, part of my old commute would be on Interstate 75, one of the busiest highways in North America. In those days, it was a whole different story with a lot of traffic squeezing into only two lanes. Early mornings on the way back from my overnight shift I frequently fell asleep at the wheel and was blasted awake by the horns of truckers as we hurtled towards head-on collisions. Though I had many close calls thanks to my dazed drives in the mornings, by the grace of God I never caused or participated in any traffic accidents.

It was a grueling schedule and I had to repeat it daily. I would make my way through early rush hour traffic as soon as my shift ended at 6am, arrive back in the sleepy village of Yellow Springs at around 7:30, grab a quick breakfast, then head off to class. I would have a two-hour nap, do some studying, grab some dinner and another quick snooze, (which was no easy thing to do in a men's dormitory) and be rolling down the highway by 10 pm to get back to work. Mercifully, after a few weeks the term came to an end and I moved to a rooming house in Cincinnati.

Track 30

"All deejays are crazy." Andy Travis to Venus Flytrap in a final-season episode of WKRP in Cincinnati.

The story of most radio stations is the story of its people. So here's a quick rundown of the cast of characters I was working with on-air. The morning man was Will Lenay, who had worked in the area since 1943, bouncing between several local stations. He was a very amusing old-style radio announcer, and tried his best to make the transition to the fast-paced tempo of this new Top 40 format. He used many pre-recorded bits by a female actress who was skilled at impersonating sexy characters. In one of these skits, he would interact with her as though she was there with him. Listeners would hear someone knocking on the control room door.

"Oh mister announcer man, you've got to hide me in here! My boyfriend just found out I've been seeing another guy, and he's chasing me everywhere!"

As the sketch evolved, Will would hide her under the broadcast console, and in between the next several records, she would pester him for updates about her boyfriend.

"Can you see him coming? Do you think he will find me?"

It was very imaginative broadcasting in those days. Our mid-day guy was another transitional figure who was well-known in the market. Ron Allen was a very urbane guy, smart as a whip and completely at ease behind the controls. His real love was jazz, but a job is a job and he was trying to adapt to a style of radio that was very alien to him. To illustrate where he was coming from, for his intro break on each show he would quote a well-known line from Walt Whitman, of all people.

"I hear America singing! The varied carols I hear."

Not exactly typical Top Forty DJ lingo.

Ron incorporated little musical stingers or stabs into his performance quick quips designed to raise a smile, things like the following.

"That's Dave 'Baby' Cortez and The Happy Organ. Hope **your** *organs are happy too!"*

(Insert musical stinger, the well-known last six notes of Count Basie's April in Paris.)

He was a well-read, intellectual guy who drove around town in a Jaguar XK140 Drophead Coupé, with the steering wheel on the right-hand side. A genuinely classy man. I admired his smooth delivery and fell in love with the smooth lines of his car, too. I vowed that someday I would have the money to buy one! (Stay tuned, dear reader.)

Our evening man when I began was known as Doc Holiday. He was no wild West gunslinger, but he was a Texan who had come out of the West after learning his craft at stations back home. And it was a neat radio name. He was replaced just weeks after I joined the staff by another guy who used the moniker Jim Dandy, taken from an early rock and roll hit called Jim Dandy To The Rescue by Laverne Baker, His show began with her singing,

"Jim Dandy to the rescue
Jim Dandy to the rescue
Jim Dandy to the rescue
Go, Jim Dandy "
Lincoln Chase © Atlantic Records

Jim (his real first name) was another up-and-comer, but from Arizona, not Ontario. We were the same age and he had an up-tempo delivery that was his very own style. But what really set him apart was an imaginary young friend named Suzie Q.

That name, too, was the title of a hit song from 1957, recorded by Dale Hawkins on Checker Records. Jim had previously recorded hundreds of snappy lines with a twelve-year old girl back at his prior job in Phoenix. He would use her lines as drop-ins or gimmicks, as they were known.

Jim Dandy: *"Hey it's a great night here at WSAI in Cincinnati and I'm Jim Dandy!"*

Suzie Q: *"Why don't you shut up and play a record!"*

It sounds corny today, but it was cutting-edge radio entertainment in those days.

Track 31

As Ben Fong-Torres points out in his book, *The History of Top 40 Radio*, "*No matter how close we got to a station or a disc jockey ... they could disappear into the ether without so much as a wave goodbye or a farewell song.*"

These aspiring jocks moved quickly through the station, either to local competitors or onwards and upwards to larger markets. There were always people on the move, creating a never-ending stream of opportunities. When a Program Director changed stations, he frequently wanted to build his own team and would recruit from people he had worked with in the past. That created more opportunities for movement within the business. The turnover rate was so rapid that after a year or so at WSAI, I was the senior guy on staff in terms of job tenure.

Jim Dandy moved on to a competing radio station 'across the street', the industry term for another station in the same market. He was offered not only an air shift on the station, but the promise of his very own TV Dance Party show. Hard to turn that offer down. His replacement was another Westerner, Dave Steer, known on air as The Wild Child. His theme song was taken from the song written and performed by Johnny O'Keefe.

"Oh yeah, I'm a wild one
Gonna break it loose
Gonna keep 'em movin' wild

Gonna keep a swingin' baby
I'm a real wild child"
Greenan, O'Keefe, Owens, Leedon © Festival Records

Dave's on air patter was delivered at a mile-a-minute pace as he machine-gunned his chatter, break after break, in between the hits.

"Hey, we're rockin' and reelin', winnin' and spinnin, movin' and groovin' with stacks of shellac and dynamite vinylite! This is the Wild Child on WSAI, rollin' and a-strollin', reelin' with the feelin' and swingin' and a-singin."

This was really Personality Radio. While our format and tempo were fairly standardized, each jock had his own style, and we cross-pollinated each other's development into cutting-edge communicators.

Taking a page from all these guys, I started to collect my own repertoire of gimmicks, drop-ins, stingers and stabs culled from our record library and movie commercials promoting new films.

*"Hi there kids, I'm here in the Night-Nik Nook with wax to watch! You're on WSAI with the Dick Williams Show, (*insert gimmick with a movie announcer's excited voice*) starring Richard Burton and Elizabeth Taylor!"* Another variant might mention Doris Day and Rock Hudson or Martin and Lewis.

I also spent hours culling one-liners from old radio plays that were lining the walls of the station's library. Performed by professional character actors, these voice snippets became my personal stock in trade. For instance, I had the voice of old-time Wild West prospector to help move the show into the next record.

"Hand me down my guitar, son...I feel a ditty coming on!" A perfect segue into my next record. I also used tough, gangster-sounding snippets.

"So you got it all figured out, huh, punk? How'd you like a knuckle sandwich?" Lines like that would provide perfect punctuation at the end of my between-the-record breaks.

I always made sure to stay in contact with Ward Cornell, the GM back at CFPL in London, writing him about some of the contests and promotions we were doing, and enclosing an audition tape or air check of my recent on-air performances so he could hear how I was progressing.

Track 33

"The old people said it wouldn't last six months. That's because they didn't understand it." WKBW DJ George "Hound Dog" Lorenz on rock 'n' roll.

"Number one, one, one on wonderful WINO." George Carlin routine from the album FM & AM, © Little David Records

The jocks came and went, sometimes literally overnight, as did Program Directors. I was just about to do a break one night at around 1:30am when the studio door opened, and there filling the entire door frame was a huge man dressed in pajamas, a bathrobe and slippers! Since we were broadcasting from a hotel, I figured he must be a drunk or a sleepwalker, but I had to get on the air that second. I quickly cleared my throat, said the call letters and rolled into the next record.

As soon as I closed the microphone switch, he pointed his finger at me and spoke.

"I'm your new boss, Frank Ward. Don't clear your throat when you go on-air, you'll ruin your pipes. Just swallow instead. I want you back here tomorrow in the studio when I do my show and I'll teach you everything you need to know. Be there!"

He turned and walked back upstairs to his room in the hotel, where it turned out he was living as one of the perks of his new position.

"I started to realize that, hey you can talk over intros."
WIBG legend Joe Niagara on Top 40 radio's early days

In later years, I came to realize what a legend Frank Ward really was in the radio business. He is credited in the book, This Business of Radio as being the *first* DJ to actually talk over a record. Prior to that, the announcer would formally introduce a song, along with the artist, and *then* spin the record. Frank was already a seasoned radio performer, one of many disc jockeys to use the name Guy King on WWOL in Buffalo. That was not uncommon in some markets where the name was more important than the person who used it. Another legendary radio performer, Tom Clay, used the same name and was once arrested for disturbing the peace after he crawled out on a billboard in Buffalo, instructing his engineer to play Rock Around the Clock over and over, and encouraging people to drive by his downtown Buffalo perch and honk!

Frank had worked for years in the Buffalo area, at several radio stations including one in Niagara Falls, Ontario. He hosted the Spotlight Serenade show on WKBW Buffalo as well. I had never heard him on the air and was absolutely mesmerized as I watched him sail through his program. His voice was smooth as glass, rich, powerful and assured. He sounded like the Voice of God, if such a thing was possible. I suspected he was putting on a bit of a show for me, but I didn't care.

"Good afternoon ladies and gentlemen! From the entertainment capital of the world, you're in The Ward Room with Frank Ward, the Woman's Home Companion. Smoke 'em if you got em! We chug along and sing our song; you, me, and our flat bald-headed friends the records making three. We set the style on Cincinnati's radio dial, and we do it all here on WSAI!"

The several hours I spent with him each day gave me increasing confidence as a performer. Frank showed me that if you were going to talk over the music, you should talk to the exact millisecond before the vocal. As I have noted before, that is called hitting the post. If you committed the cardinal sin of clobbering, or talking over the beginning vocals, you were in for a personal dressing down that might land you on the street looking for work. Pretty much every nuance of presentation and microphone technique was covered in his informal tutorials. And every evening I could expect a phone call or two from him as I worked away on my show. I was proud it was usually a positive one.

As much as anything, it proved to me that he was absolutely serious about making sure I was living up to his broadcasting standards. His call would frequently come in over the two-way circuit from our Mobile Unit as he cruised the streets of the city. Frank's calls were usually pretty much the only ones I received in the control room. The only other telephone call I might expect would be from the station's transmitter engineer out on Cincinnati's Transmitter Row in Mason, Ohio, where WLW's towers were located.

The mobile units themselves did double duty. It was Frank's idea to show the flag by driving them around as much as possible to present our call letters to as many sets of eyes as we could. To do this, one side of the station wagon was painted with our station logo, and the words Mobile Unit 3, but the *other* side of the wagon said Mobile Unit 5, making it look as if we had a fleet of these rolling billboards. Pretty clever, I'd say!

Frank, with his dazzling mouthful of capped teeth, was also a fancy dresser. He always wore expensive suits, high-end footwear and pricey ties. Frequently he would treat me like a butler, peel off a wad of bills from his wallet, (more on that later) and send me off on a shopping expedition.

"Nip out and get me two pounds of underwear and three pounds of socks, would you?"

He was very generous, too and more than once pulled off a big-ticket watch and just gave it to me.

"Lots more where that came from," he would say.

Speaking of clothing, back then everyone arrived at work in either a suit or sport jacket with a dress shirt and tie. Even the lowly overnight guy was required to be dressed in business clothes. Times have certainly changed!

Every rock station had a news staff, and just like their DJ counterparts, the newsies came and went with great regularity. Most had worked in the Texas stations, KLIF, KBOX and KILT, and like true Texans many of them carried guns, either in their briefcases or their cars. Many of them had interesting on-air names, too, just like their partners in the DJ booth. I recall two specifically, Bill Gill and Ray Carnay. The early seventies found Bill at ABC-TV in Washington, where he was their White House correspondent.

The newscasts were delivered in rapid-fire style, and ours were billed as Bannerline News. Each dateline, such as Moscow, was preceded with an electronic Morse code sounder, generated by a tiny device designed by our engineering staff, while a pre-recorded teletype machine clattered away in the background to emphasise the urgency of the delivery. Then, wrapping up each newscast, was WSAI Electrovac Weather. I'm pretty sure whoever coined that term was alluding to the *Univac* Computer developed by Remington Rand, which was used by CBS Radio and TV to predict the results of the 1952 Presidential election. Whatever its background, Electrovac sounded pretty damn impressive to our listeners.

Track 36

Now Playing: Come Fly with Me, by Frank Sinatra
"Come fly with me, let's fly, let's fly
Pack up, let's fly away!! "
Sammy Cahn, James van Heusen © Imagem Music LLC
O.B.O. Cahn Music, Cahn Music Co.

One afternoon I was hanging around the station when a
newsman asked an unexpected question.

"Do you want to go flying with me?"

I've always loved airplanes and it must run in the family. My
Father was a doctor, but served as a Squadron Leader in the
Royal Canadian Air Force in Britain back in WWII. My
brother, John, (call sign *Jock*) was a fighter pilot as well.
More on that later.

For all my fascination with flight, at that point I had never
been off the ground in anything but an elevator. We made
the short drive to the Greater Cincinnati Airport (which is
actually located in Hebron, Kentucky- go figure) and for the
first time I slipped the surly bonds of earth. What a great
thrill to be airborne for the first time, and looking down on
the entire region. The newsman levelled the nose, trimmed
the two-seat aircraft and leaned over to speak to me as he
gently put his hand on my knee.

"I could fly like this for hours and not touch a thing!"

I quickly removed his hand and replied.

"Good! That works for me."

The rest of the flight was a quiet one, and there was no more touching.

One of my favorite songs, and I suspect of most every other on-air jock at that time, was El Paso by Marty Robbins. Not that I admired it for the musical content. It was the *length* of the song that made it a standout. At 4:40, this song was exceptionally long by pop standards, a full minute or so longer than any other #1 song that year. Most records of the time ran only about 2:40 or so, which made El Paso the perfect bathroom break for a solo DJ with no one else available to run the controls in the wee small hours of the morning. It wasn't physically possible to race to the public washroom on the mezzanine level and get back in any less than 3 minutes, so old Marty was a godsend. Next time you hear that record, imagine the smile of relief on my face!

Track 37

Billboard, the premier music trade magazine, was founded in Cincinnati in 1894, and with the coming of the jukebox in the 1930s, began to publish Pop Record Sales Charts. As a result, it became very important to receive as much airplay as possible, especially in the local marketplace. Independent record companies as well as the established labels were eager to pay DJs or Program Directors (or both) to play their labels' songs. The practice came to be known as Payola, and it worked two ways. Some bands would be forced to play at station-sponsored record hops for free, in order to stay in a station's good graces. The bands got exposure, and the station got revenue they would otherwise not have generated. Labels and popular bands could also be dinged for money for stations to hold meet the band contests, in exchange for air time for one of the label's newer, lesser-known groups.

Every week, the record representatives would arrive at stations in the area, carrying with them envelopes of money to distribute to the DJs. Payola also took the form of gifts. I recall attending a function sponsored by a major record company that had just introduced a line of AM/FM/TV Home Entertainment Centers. After I mentioned to the rep that I thought the unit was pretty cool, an identical unit was delivered to my boarding house the next day. In today's money, it was probably a several-thousand-dollar Home Entertainment Center!

The whole thing was actually funny to most of us. We were being paid *extra* money to play songs we had to play anyway, dictated by the Program Director. It seemed harmless enough and went on with nothing more than a nudge and a wink until it suddenly became a scandal. Congressional panels were formed, and several well-known DJs went to jail. Even the career of legendary DJ Dick Clark of American Bandstand was in jeopardy until he quickly changed his ways.

As I have noted, the station-sponsored record hops were great revenue-boosters. Every weekend, we would go out to a venue somewhere, play a few records over the PA system, schmooze with the station's listeners, and take our share of the profits from the gate. Usually the site was a commercial banquet hall that benefitted from the on-air promotions mentioning their name, and gave us the room for nothing. The bands were in the same category as mentioned previously, and touring artists such as any of the big name performers in the area would appear gratis in exchange for the promotion. The admission was a dollar or two, and you could always tell who the DJ was. He was the guy with a wallet thickened an inch or two by a wad of singles.

I always used to enjoy being at the hops and would often sing with the band. My vocal skills are such that I needed a really easy tune, and my staple was a 1959 hit.

Now Playing: Long Tall Texan, by Jerry Woodard
"Well I'm a long tall Texan
I wear a ten-gallon hat
(He rides from Texas wearing a ten-gallon hat)
Yes I'm a long tall Texan

I wear a ten-gallon hat."
Henry Strzelecki © Epic Records

One day, after hearing me sing my song at an afternoon function, one of the label's record reps sat me down and asked a question I had never expected to hear.

"Have you ever thought about being a singer? You're the right age, you know how to work a microphone and a crowd, you're not bad looking, and we could make you a lot of money!"

It wasn't something I had ever thought about until that moment, but I had to be honest.

"Hey, I can't really carry a tune, I'm just fooling around!"

"Look, you've talked to Fabian, and he sold millions with that song of his called Tiger. He made $250,000 last year. We can fix things up if you go flat by speeding up or slowing down the tape when we master the record!"

Actually, during the payola scandal, Fabian testified before Congress that his vocals had been tweaked electronically to "significantly improve my voice."

In his dual role as an A & R representative, which stands for Artists and Repertoire, my friend was talking as a talent scout, and as such his job was to find and sign new talent. We were pretty good pals and he did warn me of the potential down side of a record deal.

"You know, though, you'll be dealing with some pretty big Mob connections. Down the road, if somebody big in the biz is having a birthday blowout in Vegas and our boys want you to perform in a tribute show, you'll be there *or else*."

Even though I was pretty green, I got the message loud and clear. The same record rep was sitting in the diner in the Hotel Sinton one day, where our station was based. He was having lunch with my PD Frank when I dropped in and joined them. Fresh from a record hop the afternoon before and with a pocket full of small bills, I scooped up the check.

"So long," I said, then paid the bill and went upstairs to the radio station. I was listening to some new songs in the station library when Frank yanked the door open, and yelled.

"My office. Now!"

When I walked into the cramped space I learned another important lesson of broadcasting in those days.

"You jerk! You don't ever pay for a rep's meal. THEY pay for everything. You want to ruin this for everybody?"

No, I did not. From then on I always left the check for the rep to pay.

Now Playing: Dick Williams Show Intro Donut Jingle
"Clap hands and shout for joy
Here comes that Music Boy
With Big Sounds, Big Sounds
The Dick Williams Show!
We're WSAI
Big Sounds That Satisfy
Music News and Weather too
On the Dick Williams Show!" Commercial Recording
Company Dallas Texas ©

Wow! There it was. My first and very own custom-made jingle! It was part of a new jingle package that Frank bought for the station. Now, each of the guys had their very own show intro! It ran almost a minute in length, long and wordy by today's standards, but big and bright-sounding.

But it wasn't without its complications. Later on it would almost cost me my job, and later still put me out of the running for a big job at a major 50,000-watt radio station. (There it is- yet another tee-up. As veteran DJ Bobby Ocean once said, "*I'm always bill-boarding. Coming up, something's always coming up. The curtain's always rising.*")

During the research for this book, I discovered a couple of largely meaningless but fascinating facts for those of an historical inclination.

WSAI first signed on the air in Cincinnati back in 1922, and was owned by the U.S. Playing Card Company, operating as Standard Amusement Incorporated. Hence the SAI in the call letters.

Also operating from Cincinnati is WLW, one of the nation's most respected stations. Its call letters identify its early history as the World's Largest Wireless, hearkening back to the days in the 1930s when it broadcast at a mind-numbing 500,000 watts. (The largest AM stations in North America are today capped at 50,000 watts, still a formidable number.)

One of my later radio homes in London was CFPL, which stood for Canada Free Press London and identified its connection to the local newspaper, the London Free Press.

The TV sitcom WKRP in Cincinnati was produced by Mary Tyler Moore's company, MTM. In 1979 a new radio station in Dallas, Georgia applied to the FCC for those call letters. The producers objected but it was ruled that MTM did not have the legal right to trademark the call letters because it was not a licensee. The real WKRP lasted ten years until it asked for new call letters.

Track 39

Now Playing: Smoke Gets In Your Eyes The Platters
"They asked me how I knew
My true love was true
I of course replied
Something here inside
Cannot be denied
When your heart's on fire
You must realize
Smoke gets in your eyes"
Jerome Kern, Otto Harbach © Universal Music Publishing
Group

I wasn't the only performer to have improved my standing.
The Beverly Hills Supper Club was a classy nightclub in
Southgate, Kentucky, just across the river from Cincinnati. I
was enjoying the music of The Platters on stage, not to
mention a few cocktails without having to show any ID. The
entertainment lineup was big-time, from places like Las
Vegas, Nashville and Hollywood, and there was no question
the club was mobbed up. The Beverly Hills had started as an
illegal gambling house as far back as the Dirty Thirties and
Dean Martin was a blackjack dealer there at one point. In
May of 1977 it was the site of the third deadliest fire in
American history. One hundred and sixty-five people were
killed, and a further two hundred injured in the horrific
blaze.

But that was well into the future. On this evening The Platters were riding the charts at #1 position with Smoke Gets in Your Eyes. I was very pleased to discover they remembered I had interviewed them in Canada a couple of years before. They asked a few of our jocks to ride back in taxis to Cincinnati after the show for a little party. It sounded like a lot of fun, but I had to jump out of the cab downtown because I was scheduled to work the mid-day shift the next day.

Somebody must have been looking out after my best interests, because later that night four of the male singers in the group were arrested on drug charges and accused of having sexual relations with four female minors, including three white girls. At that time, these were *very* serious crimes. The men were eventually acquitted, but the scandal pretty much scuttled their career as a vocal group. That's one party I'm very glad I missed!

Track 40

Soon enough the summer was over, and I returned to Antioch College to resume my formal education. I continued at WSAI as a Weekend Warrior, doing shows on Saturday and Sunday during the school term. Years later, one of my dorm mates commented on my work schedule.

"You really had it made, Dick! The rest of us were doing pissant menial jobs on our work periods to qualify for credits, and you were getting paid big money and working at a *real* job in radio. We were all pretty jealous of you."

I couldn't argue with him because things had been pretty good for me in those days.

As luck would have it, just as I was set to return full-time chores at WSAI after my four months in the classroom I got a call from Jim Dandy (remember him?) He told me he'd been offered a job at a San Diego radio station, and had turned it down, because he had such a sweet deal with his local radio and TV shows. In a very thoughtful gesture, he had taped my show and scoped it (cut out most of the music, leaving only the actual telescoped spoken word sections of the show to make it faster for a Program Director to listen to an audition). On top of that, he had strongly recommended they give me a shot at the job he had declined. I was going to need employment one way or another within the week, and with the warm California breezes calling I was ready to go!

I then got a call from the new station's Program Director, gulped hard when I heard what they were willing to pay me, and that was that. I asked my dorm friends to ship some of my winter clothes back to my family in Canada. They did, and helpfully included someone else's unused prophylactics, which my Father forwarded to me in San Diego along with a brief note.

"Here are the *rest* of your personal belongings. Make sure you use them!"

Track 41

"New voices spoke to the young in a language that baffled those too old to listen." Life Magazine on the emerging radio phenomenon.

"I fell in love with radio. And when you love something, you always had a lot of fun, and I've always had fun." Veteran deejay Charlie Tuna.

KDEO AM San Diego 1960 Playlist:
"Theme from a Summer Place" Percy Faith
"He'll Have to Go" Jim Reeves
"Cathy's Clown" The Everly Brothers
"Running Bear" Johnny Preston
"Teen Angel" Mark Dinning
 "I'm Sorry" Brenda Lee
"It's Now or Never" Elvis Presley
"Handy Man" Jimmy Jones

Now Playing: Itsy Bitsy Teenie Weenie Yellow Polka Dot Bikini by Brian Hyland
"Two three four
Tell the people what she wore
It was an Itsy Bitsy Teenie Weenie Yellow Polka Dot Bikini
That she wore for the first time today!"
Lee Pockriss, Paul Vance Kapp Records © Emily Music Corp, Music Sales Corp.

These were the days when airliners had propellers, not jet engines, so the cross-country trip from Cincinnati to San Diego was a series of puddle-jumping hops. I still remember seeing my first palm tree in Phoenix, Arizona, one of our refueling stops. Landing at Lindbergh Field in San Diego was another eye-opening first. I had never flown on a commercial airliner before, and I can't say I wasn't pretty terrified on final approach. Instead of an easy glide down an unobstructed flight path and onto the runway, the eastern approach to the field is steeper than most because the terrain drops from two hundred and sixty-six feet to sea level in less than one nautical mile. The only runway began west of a hill with several distractions below, including Interstate 5 and the lush stands of trees in Balboa Park.

If by some freak chance the seat I was in is still around somewhere, those indentations in the arm rests are from my fingers squeezing them as I waited for the plane to crash, er, touch down.

This was a true red-eye overnight flight, and I arrived in San Diego in the early afternoon with what would now be called jet lag. Coming into the terminal, I was dazzled by the brilliant sunshine streaming down from crystal-clear skies. There to meet me, dressed in a slick-looking Canary Yellow sports jacket and huge sunglasses, was Mel Hall, the man who for more than the next forty years would shape my life in broadcasting.

A Hollywood smile beamed at me, and a warm handshake sealed the deal. He drove me to a nearby motel, where the station had reserved a room in my name for the next week. Mel told me to get some rest, and said he would be back around eleven that evening to take me to the station to do my first show. I enjoyed a dream-free, refreshing sleep, cleaned up a bit and went out to dinner at the steak house next door. As promised, Mel arrived to take me to work, although I've always considered it play. Real work is digging a ditch or building a house.

The station itself was perched on a hillside extremely close to the runway I had landed on just that afternoon. The studios overlooked Pacific Highway, and the freeways were busy, even at that hour of the night. The premises were wrapped around an inner courtyard of a two-storey office complex. Since San Diego enjoys such a marvellous climate, with summer temperatures floating between 67 and 77°F, no air conditioning was required. The control rooms did have full-length louvered (not Sash-less Side slide) windows, which could be opened to enjoy the temperate breezes. There's more to come about the sameness of the weather, by the way.

As I sat down at the controls, with four turntables surrounding me, I got my first surprise of the evening, from Mel.

"By the way, your on-air name is going to be Shadow Johnson. You're going to be replacing a guy who just left us to move down the street to KCBQ, and he was called Shadow *Jackson*."

Maybe I was still over-tired, but even though this looked like a dream job, I rebelled.

"My name is Dick Williams. You *hired* Dick Williams. I have my own singing jingle, and that's the name that's on it. I'm sorry, but if you don't like it, I'm gone!"

It was actually a pretty idle threat, given how much I wanted the job, but it worked. I was to remain Dick Williams for the rest of my career. I pulled out all my heavy discs filled with drop-ins and the other production aids I had recently made at WSAI, plopped the theme on the turntable, cued it up, and started the show. *Dick Williams* was on the air in San Diego, California.

I hit the airwaves of Southern California at the crack of dawn. Amazing how full of caffeine (or helium) I sounded! Listen in:

AUDIO/VIDEO: Dick Williams 1960 KDEO San Diego

KDEO was actually licensed to El Cajon, a suburban community just outside San Diego, but as the studios were in San Diego we sounded like part of the dusty little city it was in those post-war years. The call letters were K-D-E-O, and it was known as (what else?) Radio Kaydeo. I have always thought that's the greatest set of radio call letters ever!

For the first few breaks in my first show I couldn't get it right, though. I kept saying Kaydeo Radio. But I quickly got the hang of it, things smoothed out, and by the end of a couple of hours I was set to wrap up my premier performance on the airwaves at the new station. That's when I got the second shock of the evening, something similar to the old Double Whammy, a phrase taken from the Al Capp comic strip Little Abner and spoken by Evil-Eye Fleegle. (Come to think of it, that's a pretty great on-air name for a DJ!)

Mel took me aside as we walked along the balcony to the stairwell.

"I know we hired you as the evening jock, but the more I heard you tonight, I think we're going to make you our morning man. You start tomorrow at 5:30! Don't be late."

Morning DJs are usually the key to a station's success or failure, setting the tone for the station during its most-listened-to period. They are generally paid a premium, too, if only due to the fact they have to rise and shine at such an early hour. As I recall, the increase in my paycheck didn't really make much difference. But the new position put me in the prime-time hot seat right away and I was up against the legendary San Diego morning man Harry Martin at KCBQ, who was known as Happy Hare. I can't imagine Harry lost any sleep over his new competitor, and I'll bet he didn't lose many listeners, either.

My newsman was another young guy like myself, who had actually been in the control room during my first shift, and who had been moved with me to mornings. He offered to give me a quick night-time tour of San Diego and that sounded like a fine idea. As he drove me around the beautiful city, he looked over at me with a raised eyebrow.

"Have you ever heard of the Coronado Ferry?"

"Yeah, I have." It was a famous boat ride across San Diego Bay. At least, that was one definition.

"Well that's me!" he suddenly lisped. "*I'm* the Coronado Fairy!"

I passed it off as a joke, but later learned he wasn't kidding. At least this time I wasn't two thousand feet off the ground.

KDEO was a 1,000 watt station, flailing away against the newly powerful 50,000 watt KCBQ, so in terms of pure signal strength we had our work cut out for us. Radio 91-derful or Colorful 91 were our positioning statements. Ironically, when KCBQ upped their power they actually *lost* signal strength in the city itself, due to tightly controlled directional patterns required by the FCC for such a full-strength signal. We used to joke that while they were losing *local* listeners, they were picking up new ones in Hawaii.

All we could do to increase *our* signal strength was to make sure that we watered the transmitter. No kidding. A technician at the transmitter site was tasked each morning with hosing down the ground all around our transmission towers in the belief it would somehow enhance the radiated strength of the signal. Whether it actually made a difference is a matter for the technical types. I do know that many radio stations have put their towers near or actually *in* the water, as a lot of stations in the San Francisco area did back then. Other stations have planted theirs near garbage dumps because the liquefaction process of the rotting garbage would supposedly cause the soil to be more moist. So who knows? The entire idea that you can increase your coverage area by applying H2O could be a lot of garbage! (Rim shot!)

Wet transmitter or not, we sure had fun. I was getting the time to fine tune my on-air approach, and Mel gave me a new opportunity to learn even more about being a real performer. He had a very glib, hip, tongue-in-cheek manner, both on- and off-air. His timing and comedic talents were superb, especially in support of our sponsors.

"Chevy! What a car! Why not rush out and buy a few today!"

Then to punctuate the punch line he would slam directly into a fast-paced KDEO jingle. He had other memorable lines, too.

"You're on Radio Kaydeo, where the wife we're entertaining might be your own, and the one you're entertaining had better be!" (Run jingle.)

He even brought his own six-year-old daughter, Jeffery, into the studio in the first few days I was there, and had her record some drop-in lines for me. In her little girl voice, she would say the cutest things, but with a twist.

"It's the Dick Williams Show...*how do you like it, big boy?*" The last part of that drop-in was delivered in a Mae West style. There were other lines that cracked me up, too.

*"My mommy listens to the Dick Williams show...my **daddy** listens to my mommy!"*

Now, back to the weather in San Diego that I teed up a few pages back. Since we were required by order of the FCC to mention our Station of Origin (or transmitter location) once per hour, we were actively encouraged to mumble or cough our way through the statement as to where the heck our towers were. We weren't about to admit that we were anywhere but San Diego, let alone a scrappy suburb like *El Cajon*. As a result, the weather would generally be introduced with a little sleight of hand.

"Here's the Radio Kaydeo Weather Watch from (mumble, cough or cover your mouth with your hand,) *El Cajon's* 91, KDEO."

Temperatures and sky conditions were almost like a broken record, so we took the liberty of recording our weather reports from time to time and just playing them back from a 33 RPM transcription disc. They would invariably say the same thing.

"Early morning and late evening coastal low cloud and fog, otherwise, clear skies, with a high today of 77° and low of 67°."

Even that got tedious after a while and we started to play back the forecast at 45 RPM, so it sounded like weather-wise chipmunks had invaded the studios!

A daily problem for me was the Morning Fishing Report we aired at around 7:30, right in the heart of my show. The report listed the poundage of all the fish caught by commercial fishermen in the area the day before. When I think back on it, I have to wonder if anybody really cared. Certainly not private fishermen, to whom fishing wasn't a hobby measured by the boatload. But the feature was sponsored, which was all the justification we needed. Although it generally ran only about sixty seconds or so, I dreaded it with a passion. It's hard to think of yourself as a big-city DJ when you're mixing your records with reports on fishing hauls, and dealing with incoming overhead intruders.

The microphones in the studios picked up a lot of background noise, including the planes in the landing pattern as they descended on final approach right over our studios and the Pacific Highway. Morning was a busy time of day at the airport, and was further heightened by the frequent commuter traffic from other cities such as Las Vegas and San Francisco, plus connecting flights to and from Los Angeles.

The lumbering prop planes would first make their presence known as a very low rumble, but as they passed directly overhead it sounded for all the world like they were going to land on top of our studios. I had to continue reading as if nothing was happening, even though the noise would drown me out as they flew over at what seemed like only feet above my head. I would find myself hunching down even closer to the controls every day, as though that would have protected me if one of the planes had gone through the building instead of over it.

As had become my habit, I kept sending air checks from The Left Coast to Ward Cornell at CFPL back in Canada to keep him posted on my progress. I may have been living in the balmy south, but a big part of me was still connected to the cool blue north.

Track 45

Now, a story that spans almost 50 years. One evening I had to MC one of the hundreds of beauty pageants that seem to be epidemic in Sunny Southern California, where every possible avenue is explored and exploited in the search for instant fame for yet another fresh-faced pretty girl. I was one of two judges, the other a jock from KCBQ. We were, of course, introduced to the contestants and their mothers backstage just prior to the event. I was approached by an extremely beautiful young mother, and her equally breathtaking daughter, who was just my age at the time. The mother brushed up close to me, put her hand on the back of my neck, and gushed.

"We'd *both* be so happy, we would both do *anything* for my daughter to be named Miss San Diego Sunshine."

Always the master of the perfect bon mot, I smiled back at her as sincerely as I could.

"Well, good luck and all the best!"

It was only decades later that I suddenly woke up out of a deep sleep one night with the realization, after all those years, of exactly what those two California cuties had actually been offering. Talk about slow on the uptake!

California is car country, and I needed one to drive from my apartment in nearby Mission Beach to the studios downtown.

I had the good fortune to stumble across a beautiful vehicle for sale at a decent price. It was a Messerschmitt KR200, or Kabinenroller (Cabin Scooter), a three-wheeled bubble car that caught my eye. It was made by the same folks that brought you the legendary Messerschmitt Bf109 fighter plane in WWII. It actually looked like a fighter plane without wings, just a cockpit on wheels. It was a fascinating piece of machinery and I really liked it. For a link to this beauty, click http://www.microcarmuseum.com/tour/messerschmitt-kr200-1955-2.html

But I had spent a couple of hours driving in multi-lane traffic on the busy Pacific Coast Highway and I knew the Messerschmitt's fifty-six-mile-per-hour top speed was a trifle slow for the competition. Not only that, but it was small (the passenger sat *behind* the driver under the glass bubble roof) and I was pretty sure its chances of surviving a high-speed accident would be Zero, pardon the aviation pun. Instead of my own personal fighter plane, I bought a 1956 Nash Metropolitan. It was a British-built, three-seater economy car that today might be called a sub-compact. It wasn't much faster than the Messerschmitt but there was a lot more tin between me and the rest of the traffic, and that did the trick for me.
http://www.allpar.com/cars/adopted/nash-metropolitan.html

Track 46

Life was good. I had to be at the studios by 5:20 AM, having driven from the shores of the Pacific through the coastal low cloud and fog we announced every day. But once my shift was over at 9am, I was back at the beach for the day. I took full advantage of every available moment to bask in the sunshine, though I had a few initial problems with even that simple task. I hadn't given any thought to the intensity of the sun in those parts, where the rays were far more direct because of the southern latitude. I did quite a few of my earliest shows sitting extremely upright, with my back well away from the backrest on the on-air-chair.

With that much time on beautiful Mission Beach every day, I quickly made a lot of new friends to spend it with. Well before the movie Beach Blanket Bingo with Annette and Frankie, our group of beach buddies and bunnies had played a few games of our own in the sand. And speaking of beach moves: (Segue to next segment)

Track 47

Now Playing: The Hukilau Song, by Jack Owens
"We throw our nets out into the sea
And all the amaama (Little fishes) come a-swimming to me
Oh, we're going to a hukilau
A huki huki huki hukilau"
Traditional Hawaiian Folk Song © Owens-Kemp Music Co

When my newsman Bill told me one morning that he wanted to show me the Grunion Run on the beach that night, I thought he was pulling my leg. It sounded like the hazing that goes on at universities called a Snipe Hunt, where innocents are duped into believing they can catch the elusive snipe by running around in the woods at night carrying a bag in which to snag them. It's the equivalent of a wild goose chase. But what the heck, I didn't have anything better to do at the moment.

The experience turned out to be nothing like a Snipe Hunt. We wandered out onto the beach at the designated time, just after highest tide of the month under a full moon. That's when the forces of gravity exert their strongest pull on the waves, and the grunion take full advantage of it. These little guys look a lot like smelt and are very tasty. They are also famous for their remarkable spawning behavior, which often evokes the same response from people seeing or hearing about it for the first time.

"I don't believe it!"

As waves break on the beach, the grunion swim as far up the slope as possible. The California Department of Fish and Wildlife publishes the details of what happens next.

"The female arches her body and digs into sand with her tail to create a nest." (Trust me, the rest of the spawning process you don't really need to know about.) "As many as eight males may fertilize the eggs in a single nest. After spawning, the males immediately retreat toward the water while the female twists free and returns with the next wave. While spawning may only take thirty seconds, some fish remain stranded on the beach for several minutes."

That doesn't really capture the drama of the event. What a sight to behold! The beach was filled with thousands of these flopping fish, while fishermen scooped them up with their bare hands and dumped them into pails. There were fires burning up and down the beach as some people cooked their catch al fresco. The grunion run seemed to be as much about partying as catching fish. Kind of like ice fishing back home.

Now Playing: Transistor Sister, by Freddie Cannon
"It's Presley, Darin, and US Bonds
And it's Fats and Connie and Orbison
She's my transistor sister
Playing her radio"
Steven J.Rubenstein Electric Spectric Music © Swan Records

One of the neatest things I did in those days was record a Saturday afternoon program of hits, which was played back on air by an operator while I lay on the beach listening to myself on my first transistor radio. This little gizmo would revolutionize the way people, particularly teenagers, listened to radio. They would no longer be tied to home or automobile, they could listen on the go wherever they were, and particularly without adult oversight. The transistor radio became a major factor not only in delivering music and advertising, but in creating a cohesive youth culture that led to society-changing cultural, political and sexual revolutions.

It didn't take me long at the station to realize that Mel was a production master, capable of creating extremely-polished commercials, an art that's highly thought of in the radio business. He would splice bits of music and sound effects into his work to create a seamless finished product. A sixty-second commercial might contain eight or ten individual snippets that he would edit into a finished sequence by slowly rocking his rough compilation audiotape over the exposed playback heads of the studio recorders and determining what he wanted to remove. He would establish the points where the actual splices were to be made by marking them with a grease pencil on the back side of the tape. He would then mark both his entry and exit points, make his cuts, remove the strips of tape he didn't want, and splice the two new ends together. The danger was that if he didn't mark and cut accurately enough, he could destroy that part of the commercial and wreck the whole thing, leaving him to start all over again.

He made his work a little easier by recording all production at a speed of fifteen inches per second, rather than the half-speed seven-and-a-half inches per second normally used for playback and recording. This left more space on the tape for each note or sound, and allowed a more accurate cut. The entire splicing process is very similar to that used by film editors, who put various scenes together to create the finished motion picture. It's a very delicate procedure, and requires a well-developed sense of timing to make it all happen correctly. I learned a lot of tricks from Mel's production style that continue to serve me well even today.

Mel Hall, my life-long mentor and Program Director of KDEO, WJJD
Chicago, KQV Pittsburgh, and KRLA Los Angeles. A master of
production, and one of the most skilled performers I have had the
pleasure of knowing.

Another perk of working at KDEO was a value exchange deal the station had with Bonanza Airlines. We would give them free commercials and they would give us airline passes for the station's management and DJs, a process that is known in the business as contra. Based in Las Vegas, Bonanza flew Douglas DC-9s, dubbed *Fun Jets,* and served as a local carrier between San Diego, Las Vegas and several other cities in the west. It became a common practice of all of us to call them *Banana* Airlines when we introduced their commercials. I would occasionally run a sound effect of an out-of-control plane in a power dive in the background of their spots. I'm still not sure why they never seemed to complain. Many's the time we would arrive back in San Diego in the wee small hours of the morning, after an afternoon and evening spent in the lounges and slots of Las Vegas.

Typical of the mind set of that era, our jocks were known as The Men of Music. But the name was wrong in this case. There was one woman, and she was an *exceptional* announcer, as well as the first female DJ with whom I had the privilege of working. She was not only a colleague but a friend, and she was the one who found me an apartment right next to her on Mission Beach.

Her radio name was Sie (pronounced sigh) Holliday, though her real name was Shirley Schneider. She could do the sultry, late-night, close-to-the microphone trick that many women DJs were stuck with, and do it as well as anyone, but she preferred to talk naturally in a normal tone of voice. That really set her apart as something special and she later spent sixteen years at KRLA in Los Angeles.

Announcer: *"Our story continues when we come back, right after these words!"*

Track 50

"If it weren't for Philo T. Farnsworth, the inventor of television, we'd still be eating frozen radio dinners." Johnny Carson, host of the Tonight Show.

Radio in the mid to late fifties was in a quandary. TV sets were proliferating everywhere, and many observers were predicting that would mean the death of radio. Profits that had once flowed to radio networks and local radio stations were plummeting. Even people at the Radio Sales Bureau were feeling the pressure, and called upon Stan Freberg, the well-known satirist who had recorded a few singles that skewered many topics, including a famous single called St. George and the Dragonet. This disc took aim at the delivery style of TV's Dragnet. With Daws Butler and June Foray, two well-known character voices, he had a #1 hit for four weeks in October, 1953, on Capitol records.

Earlier, in 1951, Stan Freberg had produced a parody of the then-popular soap operas. The disc was titled John and Marsha. Stan played both roles. The back and forth dialogue was simple as could be.

"John." (pregnant pause)

"Marsha." (pause)

"John, John, John!" (spoken in passion)

"Marsha, Marsha, Marsha!" (equally passionate)

I'm sure you get it by now. Much ado about nothing, which essentially was the content of the radio soap operas of the day.

For the Radio Sales Bureau, a nationwide sales aid provider for radio stations, Stan created a memorable Public Service announcement that praised the power of radio over television. The core concept of the commercial was to tell would-be advertisers about The Power of Radio. Here's the transcript of the script. Daws Butler, or perhaps Freberg's sidekick Paul Frees, plays the role of a skeptical merchant who thinks a radio buy would be a waste of time. Stan is the spokesperson for the entire radio sales industry. Pretty big shoes to fill.

Here's the transcript of the spot:

Sponsor: (Skeptical delivery) "Radio? Why should I advertise on radio? There's nothing to look at, no pictures…"

Stan Freberg: "Listen, you can do things on radio you couldn't possibly do on TV!"

Sponsor: "That'll be the day."

Stan: "All right, watch this." (Clears throat, then announces loudly,) "OK people, now when I give you the cue, I want the 700 foot mountain of whipped cream to roll into Lake Michigan, which has been drained and filled with hot chocolate. Then the Royal Canadian Air Force will fly overhead, towing a ten-ton Maraschino cherry, which will be dropped into the whipped cream, to the cheering of twenty-five thousand extras! All right, cue the mountain!"

Huge groaning sound effects would be followed by a monster splash.

"Cue the Air Force!" (sound effects of several propeller-driven bombers)

"Cue the Maraschino cherry!" (sound effects of falling object, mixed into a gigantic *splat*)

"OK, twenty-five thousand cheering extras!" (insert sound effects of monster crowd cheering at the top of their lungs, then cut all effects for a millisecond of dead silence)

Stan: "Now, you want to try that on Television?"

Sponsor: (Perhaps seeing the potential of what he's just heard) "Well…."

Stan: "You see, radio is a very special medium, because it stretches the imagination."

Sponsor: (Still questioning) "Doesn't Television stretch the imagination?"

Stan: "Up to twenty-seven inches, yeah." That was the size of the biggest TV screen available at the time.

Now *that* is a sales pitch!
You can listen to this glorious promotion at this link:

VIDEO: <u>Stan Freberg Radio Promo</u>
<u>"Stretching the Imagination"</u>

Track 51

Announcer: *"We're back! On with the program!"*

One morning after my morning shift at KDEO, I got a call from the Program Director of KOMA in Oklahoma City, the clear-channel radio powerhouse I had once listened to late at night back in Canada. It was owned by the Storz Broadcasting Company, who also owned KLIF in Dallas and KILT in Houston, Texas. The Program Director had heard my show, and asked if I wanted to come and work in Oklahoma. With their monstrous 50,000-watt signal, they really covered a lot of ground.

He was specifically interested in me doing their evening show. Hmm. From where I sat on the sunny beaches of California, the Sooner State didn't sound all that attractive, though I was aware this might be a good career opportunity. I asked him a bit more about the plans for the show, and he told me it was going to be called Staying up Late in the Great 48.

The significance of the *"48"* came from the fact that with the reflective power of night-time radio caused by the Kennelly-Heaviside layer (ionized gasses that could reflect and bounce medium-wave AM radio transmissions) the station would be heard in the 48 continental states.

It really was a tempting offer, beach life notwithstanding, and I agonized over taking him up on it. But I would shortly have to return to Antioch College again for another classroom term, and I couldn't do both. Reluctantly, I turned him down, but not without a lot of second-guessing. Did I do the right thing? There's really no way to know. Well-known jocks Charlie Tuna, J. Michael Wilson and Machine Gun Kelly graced KOMA microphones, and my career might have taken off in a completely different direction. But you can't spend your life wondering what might have happened down the road not taken. I packed my bags and went back to the halls of academia to resume life in a dormitory. Not exactly the big time, yet.

While I was back in school in Ohio, I got a call from Bill, my KDEO newsman. He had moved to Las Vegas, and was working at a station called KENO. For the non-gamblers in the crowd, Keno is a popular lottery game, so for Vegas it was the perfect set of call letters. Bill was curious to know if I wanted to join him on the air in Sin City. I had spent quite a few nights there, as I mentioned earlier, but I'm not much of a gambler. The allure of the bright lights and night life wasn't as strong for me as Bill thought it might be.

"But Dick, school gets out at three here!"

"So what," I replied, "School gets out at three everywhere!"

"Yeah but here it's *three am!*"

I finished out my next school term, then headed back to a bachelor's life in California. The sacrifices we make for our careers!

Track 52

"The deejays were hired based on their ability to be entertainers." KFWB Program Director Chuck Blore

KROY Sacramento Playlist:
"Only the Lonely" Roy Orbison
"Where or When" Dion & Belmonts
"Puppy Love" Paul Anka
"Walk, Don't Run" Ventures
"Save the Last Dance for Me" Drifters

Now Playing: Good Timin', by Jimmy Jones
"Oh, you need timin'
A tick, a tick, a tick, good timin'
A tock, a tock, a tock, a tock
A timin' is the thing
It's true, good timin' brought me to you"
Fred Tobias, Clint Ballard Jr. © Cub Records

My timing has always been pretty good, in comedy and life in general. Following up on another tip from Mel Hall, my mentor in San Diego, I was able to get my first (and second) job title. It was time for a change and I was hired as Program Director and Production Manager for KROY in Sacramento, a 1,000-watt station competing in the same market as KXOA, another of those big 50,000-watt stations. What made it even *better* timing was that my girlfriend from Antioch College was at her home town of Palo Alto, a San Francisco suburb about a two-hour drive away.

KROY had recently switched to a Top Forty format, and wanted to up their game. That was the first station where I worked with a new invention in radio, the tape cartridge, a sister of the once-ground-breaking 8-track stereo music cartridges. The ones we used came in various lengths; for commercials they could be forty seconds or seventy seconds, to hold either a thirty-second spot or a sixty-second spot. Roughly ten seconds after the spot ended, the cartridge stopped back at the beginning and you just pulled it out and replaced it with another one. All of our jingles, commercials, and production aids were recorded to cartridge. Later, all the music was put on carts as well.

The mechanics of the thing were simple. It was really just a spooled loop of tape in a plastic shell. It would start instantly when you hit the start button, play its content, then stop at the beginning again. It was the original plug-and-play system and did away with cueing up records and commercials. Eventually, records became a thing of the past in most radio control rooms. Carts were much easier for the DJ to use, and there were no more surface-noise scratches on our music, commercials and jingles. Plus, it finally put an end to DJs playing records on-air at the wrong speed!

I did the afternoon drive shift for KROY, from 2 pm to 6 pm, and met a lot of very interesting people. I've mentioned tee-ups before, and I came up with one of our station's more memorable promotional lines.

"It happens <u>tomorrow</u> on KROY!"

A lot of bars use that teaser now, as in *free beer tomorrow*! When you come in the next day to collect, the bartender quickly sets you straight.

"Read the sign buddy! The beer is free *tomorrow*!"

Another drop-in gimmick I used a lot was a quick, two-word phrase made popular at the time by Dayton Allen, a comedian who had achieved success on the Steve Allen TV show. His signature catchphrase was "WHY NOT?" so I recorded these words on a cart, and the station ID would come out with a twist.

"K-R-O (hit cart) *"Y NOT?"* That was the kind of craziness that prevailed at the station.

KROY was where I was introduced to Ted Randal, who worked on air at nearby KEWB Color Radio Channel 91, just up the road in San Francisco. Ted was also one of the first radio consultants and was hired by our station to critique our on-air sound. Unlike broadcasting consultants I ran into later in life, Ted was an experienced on-air DJ and his comments and criticisms were pretty much on the money. That wasn't always the case. Too often a consultant is someone who saves his client almost enough to pay his fee, in my books anyway. But Ted was definitely the exception to the rule.

For about a year I did personalized production pieces for his fifteen or so subscribing stations across America and Canada, things like News Introductions, The Pick Hit of the Week, The Number 1 Song and so on.

After a long career, Ted moved to British Columbia when he retired. At one point, Ted asked me to critique a client radio station of his when I was back in Canada. I walked into CKOC in Hamilton to talk to their Program Director, and gave him my summary of what they were doing wrong. He was an old pro and I am surprised he gave this twenty-year-old whippersnapper the time of day. Maybe he just had a good sense of humor!

Through Ted's good graces, I even managed to do a couple of overnight shows on KEWB in San Francisco. (The station was actually based across the bay in Oakland.) It was the thrill of a lifetime but I knew I wasn't by any means up to the challenge of performing in that kind of major market radio. At least, not yet. But these were last-minute fill-ins when they were desperate just to have a warm body in the studio with an eye on either side of his nose, and I grabbed the opportunity for some more experience.

I spent a lot of time in the KROY production room, too, slaving over a hot tape recorder. I was trying to produce material that would be comparable to what I had watched Mel put together in San Diego, and the more I tried, the better the results. Slowly but surely, I was getting a good background in radio beyond being just a jock.

Track 53

One weekend when I was in San Francisco driving around, I heard a familiar voice on KYA. It was a guy I knew from WING in Dayton, Hap Hopkins. I had listened to and met him in Dayton, and now here he was on one of the legendary Bay Area stations doing a show! I called his studio line, renewed our acquaintance and sat in with him for his shift to get caught up on what had brought him out to California. He had a wonderfully-mellifluous voice both on and off the air.

"I just got bored with Ohio in general. Walked into the office and quit right there and then! Then I packed up my stuff, including my vibraphone, headed out here, and got the mid-day show right off the street!"

Talk about a lucky break! *His* timing was pretty good, too.

"Hap, I didn't know you played the vibraphone! That's a heck of a thing to lug cross-country."

"I don't! I figured I might have some time on my hands and I could maybe pick it up when I was twiddling my thumbs."

After his show was over we had some dinner, and I told him I was going to be back in San Francisco the next weekend, and I would give him a call so we could talk some more. I called as promised only to discover that Hap no longer worked at KYA. I had his home phone number and I called him right away.

"Dick, I got fired this week. I slept in on Tuesday and was late to work and got reamed out by our Program Director."

I knew Hap's shift started at 10am, not exactly the crack of dawn.

"And they fired you for that?"

"Not exactly."

"So what happened?"

"I slept in again the *next* day, too."

As luck would have it, we had an opening at KROY and I had enough authority to pull some strings. Within a day or two Hap and his vibraphone went from the cool bay breezes of San Francisco to the oppressive heat of Sacramento. He proved to a big asset to us, and to his credit was never late. Hap Hopkins finished his career at 77 WABC in New York City, the genuine big time, so he certainly could deliver the goods.

KROY was making inroads into the market and the ratings were beginning to show improvement when I was called into the Manager's office one afternoon. We'd had a good, professional relationship, and I thought I might be in for a raise. Not exactly!

"Dick I hate to do this, but by law we have to take transmitter readings every hour, and the FCC mandates that the person doing the readings has to be an American. I'm afraid I'm going to have to let you go."

I was stunned! I walked out of the studios in a daze and was sitting in the coffee shop below the station when I had a stroke of inspiration. I rushed back into the Manager's office and explained my idea.

"Hey! Listen, since I work in the daytime, any one of the secretaries here can take the readings! They are all Americans, right?" They were.

"Take the rest of the day off, Dick. See you tomorrow!"

I wish every problem could be solved that easily.

Soon enough, my six-month work period was up, and it was time to head back east for another crack at the books.

Track 55

Now Playing: Graduation Day, by Four Freshmen
"When the ivy walls
Are far behind
No matter where our paths may wind
We'll remember always
Graduation day"
Joe Sherman, Noel Sherman © Capitol Records

I didn't know it yet, but my days in America were running short. My last months at Antioch College were filled as usual with exams, reports and lots of studying. That I could handle. But towards the end of the session I got a call from the friendly folks at Selective Service, wondering about my plans when my student visa expired at the end of the term. Oddly, I hadn't really thought a lot about the draft before then, but I became more than a little concerned when the person on the other end of the line said that since I had enjoyed immunity thanks to my student visa, I would soon have to register. He also candidly admitted that since I had enjoyed the hospitality of this great country as a student, barring any major medical problem, I would be classified as 1-A, or, in more direct terms, I would go to the head of the line.

As I was stewing about how little I wanted to have my picture taken in a uniform, I was called to the phone in the dorm. On the other end of the line was Ward Cornell from CFPL back in London, Ontario. He was in the process of revamping the lineup of their staff, and asked me if I would be interested in coming back to Canada. He told me that he wanted me to consider doing a morning talk show on the station. *Morning talk show?* Talk shows were always afternoon material in those days. The conventional wisdom was that no listener would have time to sit and listen to chatter before noon, and I agreed with it.

I felt certain that any attempt to change the listeners' habits with a project like that would be doomed to failure. I was soon to find out differently. Ward and I had a couple of discussions about it, and I finally told him that what I really wanted to do was an evening Top Forty show. And, so I wouldn't get pegged as just a teen jock, a late night adult-oriented music show for an hour or so.

Ward agreed after some discussion and we also agreed on a very nice financial arrangement for me. It was the first time I ever really had an opportunity to do any bargaining for what I would be paid, and Ward was more than generous. With both things settled, it was just a matter of packing my bags, saying goodbye to my friends at Antioch and heading back to Canada.

Announcer: *"Let's take a quick break for these words!"*

My brother and I both enjoyed plinking away at targets with the .22 caliber rifle our dad had bought us when we were kids and John wanted to upgrade his arsenal. He asked me to buy an M-1 .30 caliber semi-automatic carbine and bring it back to Canada. I didn't have the money to buy both the rifle, *and* a scabbard to carry it around, so I just wrapped it in tinfoil and carried it right onto the plane, stowing it in the overhead storage bin! Can you imagine what would happen if you tried that today?

Announcer: *"We're back again, so here's more!"*

"I feel I have done a day's work after only three hours on the air." High-energy deejay The Real Don Steele

"It was a wondrous time of learning and adventure without restriction, a time of total and complete freedom on the air." LA radio legend Jim Ladd on his early days in the medium

"These guys would leave like they finished their shifts in a coal mine." Norman Davis describing KYA San Francisco in 1959, where in those pre-cart days operators sometimes juggled ten or eleven discs on three turntables for each break. (From Ben Fong-Torres bookThe Hits Just Keep on Comin')

CFPL London, Ontario, 1961 Playlist:
"I Fall to Pieces" Patsy Cline
"Michael Row the Boat Ashore" Highwaymen
"Cryin'" Roy Orbison
"Runaway" Del Shannon
"Pony Time" Chubby Checker
"Wheels" String-a-longs

Now Playing: Travelin' Man, by Ricky Nelson
"I'm a travelin' man
I've made a lot of stops all over the world
And in every port I own the heart
Of at least one lovely girl"
Jerry Fuller © Imperial Records

Coming back to Canada I was in a dream! I had just arrived at a station that really had everything going for it. CFPL was only one arm of the Blackburn media empire. They had a firm grip on all communications media in the city, AM, FM, TV and the London Free Press. This meant that cross-promotions were not only common, but expected. Plus, at that moment back in 1961, there were only two other stations in the market, unlike America, where in a competitive Top 10 market you would expect fifteen or so. (Today, there would be triple that number.)

I had about a week to get ready, because there had never been any high-energy Rock and Roll on CFPL, and I had to hit the ground running. I produced a lot of material to go along with the travelling production aids I had now used for several years back in the States. Since none of the operators who would be doing all the work in the control room had any experience in this field, we spent a few days trying out some of the younger operators. I finally found myself teamed with a very funny guy named…well, I'm going to call him Yogi for now, like Yogi the Bear, the popular cartoon character at the time.

Over the next several years, he was a fabulous audience of one for my performances. When we did something funny, either intentionally or otherwise, he would just crack up. I could see him doing it through the thick double-glass windows between my announcer's booth and the master control room. We got so used to working together that it got to the point where I would ask him over the intercom to cue up a particular gimmick insert and he would already have it on the turntable, ready and waiting. Although CFPL had a lot of technically advanced equipment, none of their music or production aids were on tape cartridges yet, so there was a lot of work for an operator to do. Yogi earned his money, believe me!

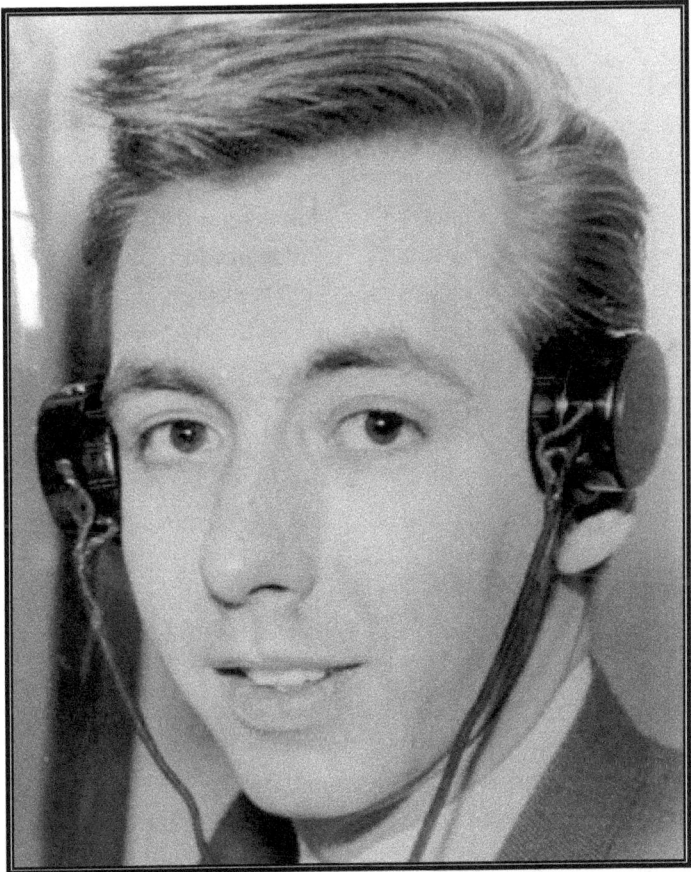

An early CFPL in-studio portrait of a young "Tall One."

Track 58

Canadian broadcasting legend Max Ferguson has detailed some of the zany backstage goings on at CFPL in his fabulous book, And Now Here's Max. His first radio job in his home town of London earned him twenty-five dollars per week, and that was due in large part to the fact he had a university degree. He moved on to CBC Radio in Halifax, and quickly became a well-known character on their airwaves and eventually across the country as a crusty old character named Rawhide. Fortunately, by the time I arrived at CFPL I was making a lot more money than he had, even adjusting for inflation in the years between our first paychecks. Thank goodness for Rock and Roll.

Several legendary stories were associated with CFPL prior to my arrival. One involved Pat Murray, who was a deep-voiced rascal if ever there was one. Dr. Lotta Hitschmanova, who headed up the Unitarian Service Committee of Canada, would set out across the country once a year, conducting radio interviews to raise money for her humanitarian efforts in poverty-stricken parts of the world. She had been born in Prague, and had a very thick Czech accent.

She would arrive for her annual interview with Pat, dressed in her habitual army nurse's uniform and military-style hat, and be shown to Pat's studio. Prior to her arrival, Pat would reach under his seat and pull small pieces of foam padding from the cushioned seat cover of his studio chair. He would then insert them into his nose, ears, shirt and pants. The unsuspecting Dr. Hitschmanova came well prepared herself and would hand Pat a script for him to read, covering the various interview points. She also would bend her head down close to the table to read her portions of the script through thick glasses.

Pat would ask each question, then as Dr. Hitschmanova began to read her prepared remarks, he would remove his earphones and begin to explore his ears, extracting one, then another and another of the pieces of foam from each of his ear canals, examining it critically before throwing it into the studio wastebasket. This delighted the small crowd watching his antics from the master control room through the studio window. As his guest pored over her script and read off her responses, Pat would explore both his nostrils, his shirt and his pants, discover more hidden treasures, and toss them into the trash basket, too. His guest, focused on her reading, had no idea any of this was going on, which made it even funnier. A sold-out crowd lapped it up every year.

Another bit of craziness that went on shortly before I arrived involved an altercation between one of the radio operators and the Managing Editor of the Free Press, Ivor Williams, who had his offices just below the control room. Like pretty much all of the newsroom folks on the floor below the radio station, Mr. Williams had a fairly dismissive attitude about the bunch of people upstairs who God knew weren't any kind of serious news organization.

This little sidebar story begins with one of the operators tapping his feet to the music coming out of his large control room monitors, which had been turned up quite loud.

Annoyed, Ivor came storming out of the tiny elevator that served the building and rampaging into the control room.

"Turn that damn music down, and stop stomping on my ceiling!"

Having given his orders, he strode angrily back to the waiting elevator.

The operator, unimpressed and unintimidated by all the bluster, climbed up and stood on the elevated chair the operators used to lean on during their stand-up shifts. From a height of about three feet, he jumped off his perch onto the studio's linoleum floor with as much force as he could muster. That would show those snotty newspaper types downstairs.

It did, too. Sort of. Instead of thumping down *on* the floor, he went right *through* it up to his waist and ended up with the rest of him dangling from the ceiling of the Managing Editor's private office! As a public relations move, it didn't do much to ease the inevitable tensions between the print and broadcast media in the building.

The previous all-night announcer, Buddy Boy Hunter, was a real prankster, too. The overnight show didn't have an operator, so a special Announce/Operate studio in the back of the CFPL studio complex was set up for this sort of shift. It was equipped with turntables, tape machines and a full-blown console and was generally used to pre-record weekend or late evening shows by the regular announcers.

One of his favorite stunts occurred late at night. Our building was separated by an alley at street level from the London Club, a very prestigious and exclusive men's club. It was frequented by the local movers and shakers of the day. Buddy Boy would put on an LP album to give him some time, then fill up a small washtub with water and carry it to the Emergency Exit fire escape from yet another studio adjoining his overnight booth. As the LP spun through several cuts he would sit at the top of the fire escape, lying in wait for members of the club to come out of their side entrance.

It wasn't long before two inebriated gentlemen made their exit, and Bud sprang into action, dumping the water from the tub onto them, then quickly closing the exit door and re-filling the washtub. As he poked his head out the Fire Exit for the second time, he caught sight of a police car pulling into the alley. Carrying the full tub of water, careful to avoid splashing any of it on the studio floors, he rushed to his isolated studio and placed the bucket, still full of water, into the area between the turntables and beneath the mixing console.

A buzzing at the night entrance door led to a policeman being admitted to the building, and he was soon standing in Bud's studio. The record came to an end, Bud waved to the officer to be quiet, opened the microphone and did a quick break, and then, (*with his feet sitting in the full washtub*) asked what the policeman wanted. When he was told about the recent shower and its apparent launching pad on the fire escape, Bud was indignant.

"Look, I'm on-air here, I can't leave the microphone, and I sure have better things to do than dump water over those rich farts next door!"

His fake bluster must have sounded convincing, because the policeman left the building, according to legend to be soaked just like the earlier victims. To hark back to the old radio soap opera days, *The Lone All-Nighter rides again!*"

CFPL didn't let a lot of grass grow under my feet after I arrived. The station was in the heart of the city and during my first week I broadcast from street level just outside the radio station. We had a Volkswagen Van known as the CFPL Mobile Studio and being out in public allowed for great instant feedback. I would ask on-air for people to honk as they drove by, to let me know they were listening. Word spread that something was happening at CFPL, and people came by to have a look at the new kid in town.

The specially-designed VW bus had been modified by a local body shop. They had cut out most of the roof and replaced it with a cockpit of Plexiglas, so the announcer could stand up inside. It was a high-enough dome that even at around six foot, two inches, I could stand up inside it. The control board in the van had a talkback switch so Yogi and I could talk to each other just as if we were in the studio together, and it was equipped with a mini control board, volume meter, microphone and radio monitor to let me hear the station's on-air program feed through my headphones.

Many stations by that time were beginning to do remote broadcasts, and some favoured incorporating turntables and other studio gear into their mobile units. All this did was drastically increase the size required for any remote broadcasts. All *we* had to have was a parking space in a sponsor's lot to be in business. A high-end broadcast pair of telephone lines would be plugged into the van from the remote site, and then we were ready to broadcast. If a sponsor wanted to do an in-store broadcast remote, the console in the van could be wheeled directly onto the sales floor. Our van had external speakers that would play the program to anyone nearby, which added to the feeling of excitement when people began to gather.

In those days a remote was a really big deal, and generally, believe it or not, drew crowds when a show was done from anywhere. Keep in mind that there were just two radio stations in London at the time, and seeing an on-air personality in person was still a novelty. CFPL had a sister FM station, but few people were drawn to it, mostly because there were very few sets built in those days incorporating FM receivers. It's ironic, given the ultimate power of FM, but in those early days the most successful FM station was the one that lost the *least* money!

I mentioned my height earlier, six foot two or so, and around this time I started to call myself The Tall One. It was just another handle designed as a unique signature, and also acted as a positioning statement. I thought of my days back at WSAI when I would sing Long Tall Texan, and it all seemed to fit. Even today I regularly run into listeners who think my full name is 'Dick Williams, The Tall One'.

My arrival was part of a major rollout of the station's new programming and for the first couple of weeks I spent a lot of time shaking hands in Wellington Square. This massive new enclosed building was claimed to be the first downtown shopping centre in North America, and it was instantly successful. The station set up a daily meet and greet session for me there, and people were urged to drop by and say hello as we shook hands. I was issued the kind of clicker commonly used in venues to record how many people have come through the doors, and I kept track of every handshake. Listeners filled out a coupon with their guess as to the exact number of hands I would shake over a five-day period, and the winner would receive a substantial prize.

I don't recall how many hands I shook, but it was a lot. And it's hard on the hand, too. But the promotion really let me press the flesh with thousands of people. It was extremely effective in getting my name and face known in the city in a hurry. Since CFPL was a part of the empire which included the city's only daily newspaper, we had free access to cross-promotion, with almost daily ads putting our names and faces in front of potential listeners.

The original classic Volkswagen Mobile Studio on one of hundreds of remotes. The Plexiglas dome made the unit a real spa in summertime beach broadcasts! +++

I mentioned earlier that I didn't have much confidence in Ward Cornell's morning telephone/talk show idea. How wrong I was. He had created an audience-building monster. Dubbed The Open Line, and hosted by John Dickens, it was…wait for it… The Talk of the Town. Ratings were soaring, and John was quickly able to command a lot more money in his contract, due to his almost overnight rating success. Like a lot of broadcasting professionals, I wondered how I could have been *so* wrong about the appeal of a phone-in show in the morning.

On traditional phone-in shows, every call was taken in sequence, live on the air, good, bad or indifferent. (Of course there was a seven-second electronic delay to avoid any profanity). John (or Ward) had a different idea. Every call that came in was recorded on tape, and John then selected the ones he wanted to be played back to his listeners. I'm pretty sure I wouldn't have done it that way, but it worked for him.

Another John Dickens trademark as host was his refusal to take sides, one way or another, on *any* issue. I heard some outrageous opinions expressed by his callers, and John would always end each call the same way.

"Thank you for calling."

I believe that by staying impartial and not arguing or agreeing with the caller, he avoided offending anyone, which added to the program's longevity. I imagine his guidepost was to be unbiased and act as a sounding board. By taking this high road, he left it to the listeners to call in and chastise previous callers who had said something out of line. Whatever John's rationale, the format generated lots of calls, pretty much the whole idea of a call-in show, after all! The end result was a smashing success for both John and the station.

In those days the station was doing well enough to able to sell annual contracts with leading stores all around the city. This meant that from 10 am on any given weekday, till my show wrapped up at 9 pm, we would be either in front of or inside these businesses doing our live remotes. Monday, for instance, was dedicated to a big furniture and appliance store, Tuesday to a department store, Wednesday to a clothing store, Thursday to an automotive outlet, and Friday to the large new Sayvette shopping center located in the suburbs, which drew people from all over the region to sample their many bargains.

The station encouraged the owners to interact with the DJs on the air for the commercial time they were allotted. Since these folks were salesmen, they often talked much longer than they should have, thereby getting more free air time than they paid for. Some were grateful, others not so much. I will never forget the manager of the automotive store giving us a cheap wallet for Christmas after really abusing his commercials' time allotment. Apparently, he felt that was sufficient acknowledgement of all the extra promo we had given him on-air. "Ho, Ho, Ho," indeed.

Come the weekends, we hauled our mobile units to the crowded nearby beaches at Port Stanley and Grand Bend, and broadcast from the water's edge in both resorts. It wasn't southern California, maybe, but it was still a lot of fun.

In terms of the format, I was living a dream. I had complete freedom to create my own playlist. I could decide how many songs I would play, in what order, and how often. This may not sound like much, but it was my ability to manipulate the records, patter, drop-ins and gimmicks to create my own on-air sound that allowed me to make a pretty good living. Believe me, it was great to have total authority about what happened on-air during my shift.

Dick and some listeners, during one of the many street-side remotes in the new and improved "Mach 2" Mobile Studio. Larger, more spacious and better equipped, this model even had a functioning air-conditioner for long on-air shifts.

My boss Ward Cornell, a former school teacher and long-time sportscaster, also worked as an in-between-periods interviewer on the wildly popular CBC TV Hockey Night in Canada telecasts. This kept him travelling all over North America for the broadcasts and left him little time to keep a close eye on the people he had hired to entertain the listeners. Once Ward made the decision to give the job and time slot to a specific on-air personality, he then left the execution totally up to them. Later in this book I'll share a conversation we had about that late one night. (Once again, I'm bill-boarding - stay tuned, there's more to come.)

Always trying to improve my show, I decided there were several things I could do to encourage what is known as Time Spent Listening. First, I found a very space-age sound effect that was really attention-getting. I called it the Pandemonium sound, and it might be played over, under, and between any elements at any time during my evening show. I hired a few school kids to handle the studio phone lines, and once the sound played on-air, the first listener to get through won a prize. It may not have amounted to much, but they got their name on the air and in those days (and these, for that matter) that was a thrill! It was never really about the prizes. As Detroit DJ Clark Reid said about contests, *"I remember one contest that was like a spelling bee. The winner got 15 dimes!"* (Quote from David Carson's Rockin' Down the Dial)

Several of these young kids who worked the phones for me went on to careers in radio in later years. I don't know if they hate me or love me for infecting them with the radio bug.

Yet another arrow in my quiver was The Tall One's Club. To join, all the young listener had to do was send an S.A.S.E. (Self-Addressed Stamped Envelope) to the station, or drop by to pick up a membership card. For a minimum cost to the station's promotion budget, we were creating what is now known as Loyalty Reward Points. You couldn't win without signing up and giving us information for our primitive (by today's standards) data base, which was verifiable when the winner presented their card for a 45 RPM record such as the Pick Hit of the Week, or as I called it, Dick's *Disc*-overy of the Week. (The records, of course were supplied by the record companies in exchange for airplay.) To this day, I continue to have white-haired men and women come up to me and with a certain amount of pride pull out a dog-eared, fluorescent-orange Club Card! Not much of a legacy, perhaps, but I'll take it, and the memories that come with it.

We also encouraged the young listeners to call our Teen line, to vote for their favorite songs for the Instant Survey. Voting began as I signed on at 6:30 in the evening, and we tabulated the votes and played back the top three most-requested songs each night at 8:45, which took us almost to the end of my show. This would enable us to end our show playing the most popular music of the day, and leave the audience wanting more.

The first Christmas we aired this feature on the show, the General Electric Company produced a beautiful Christmas jingle about their Christmas lights package. Just for the heck of it, I said, "That's a super song! Let's hear it again!" We were actually drawing extra attention to a musical commercial, something that happened very seldom (the general idea is to sell advertising, not give it away). But it was really pretty, and captured the mood of the season. I guess the listeners agreed with my assessment because the Christmas spot came in that night as the third most-requested song!

"Half statistics and half helium." 'Mad Daddy' Pete Meyers on Top 40 lists.

The record companies were not shy about spending money to promote their product, and even paid money towards the compiling and printing of the weekly CFPL Fabulous Forty survey, that we produced in-house at the Free Press and then distributed to record stores across the region. This printed, pocket-sized record rating chart also served as a vehicle to get pictures of all our DJs in front of the younger set of listeners we were attracting.

We used a lot of ways to present ourselves in print, including large newspaper ads showcasing our pictures. Add that to the high visibility we had because of our remotes and it is safe to say we were well-recognized in our community.

When I arrived at CFPL, our Chief Engineer had installed an intricate system to give us an unattended, cost-free overnight show. This was years before any station I'm aware of went to any form of automated playback. We called the overnight show, "Night Watch." About ten tape machines were linked together to supply elements over the midnight to 6 AM time slot. It is way too complicated to explain, but music was on two or three machines, which ran at a very low playback rate of speed, so each machine could play back at least three hours of music. Other machines each had their own playback role; one dedicated to commercials only, the other to weather, and yet another one that played six pre-recorded newscasts, one at the top of each hour.

Surprisingly, it worked extremely well, but every so often, things went spectacularly wrong! I recall listening on several occasions when there would be music, newscasts, commercials, and weather forecasts all playing *at the same time*!

Early three-head portrait of Dick which was featured on the CFPL Fabulous Forty Survey. No, Dick didn't have three heads!

An early Ting Cartoon of "The Tall One." This artwork frequently served as the front cover of the CFPL Fabulous Forty Survey.

A few months after I arrived on the London radio scene, Ward managed to bring back to London one of the most talented radio announcers I've ever worked with. His name is Bill Brady, and I've never met a faster wit in my life. He could have carved out a career in many other fields, such as stand-up comedy or writing, but his first career was as a mere mortal Disc Jockey. I often say "I knew him before he became a legend."

With the passage of time, he became Program Director, Operations Manager, and then General Manager at CFPL, and eventually became a VP of the far-flung Blackburn Group. He was also very active in the community, and was awarded the Order of Canada. Bill had left London radio for a while to take a job at CKEY in Toronto, and while he did well there, I think in his heart he much preferred the quality of life that London offered. Ward lured him back with the mid-day show, and Bill did extremely well. He was also given a TV show on our sister station CFPL TV. (More on that show later). He really added a lot of sparkle to our sound, and was an instant ratings hit for us.

Bill invited me over to his house one night when his wife was away. Another of his talents, I might mention, is his skill in the kitchen. He was so good at it that he rightfully earned a cooking feature in the London Free Press. Again, cross-promotion didn't do anyone any harm. The meal was great and so was the wine. Bill graciously (and wisely) suggested I should sleep at his place.

Here's where the plot begins to thicken. In his travels, Bill had acquired an air-raid siren from the foundry at Dofasco Steel in Hamilton, Ontario. Its original purpose had been to signal shift changes and be heard over the ungodly din that exists in that hellish surrounding. Little did I know that as I slept like a child he was in the basement, setting up my trap. He unplugged the light bulb from inside the freezer in the basement of his home, and plugged in the siren. When the lid to the freezer was lifted, the siren would begin to wail.

The next morning when I awoke, Bill asked me to go downstairs and grab some OJ from the freezer, since he was busy frying up a hearty breakfast. Unsuspecting, I opened the lid and the siren began to howl! Remember, this was the morning after the night before. I was literally paralyzed with shock. I froze in place, not knowing, in my delicate hung-over state, what was happening, why, or how to make it stop. It was sensory overload taken to the extreme. If I'd had some presence of mind, I could have just closed the lid, but I just stood there propping it up for what seemed a very long and confusing time. Finally, Bill dashed down the stairs and closed it for me.

A few years later, Bill, another colleague and I went to the wilds of Northern Ontario on what was billed as a Fishing Trip. This time, he smuggled the siren into the cottage and placed it under my bed on a timer. The results were predictable, including Bill's laughter.

I am pleased to report that years later the tables were turned one night, and Bill found himself on the receiving end of the siren's wrath for a change. His tormentors were avenging themselves for years of such tricks played on them. I wish I had been there, but many enjoyable pictures were taken of Mr. Brady trying to stop the howling.

The CFPL Radio "Tiger Cruiser" and General Manager Ward Cornell, the driving force behind CFPL's dominance. +++

Cover art for the CFPL Fabulous 40 Survey.

There used to be an old TV show called Bowling for Dollars. One of the standing techniques that the operators used to break up the newsmen I referred to as Bowling for Newsies. Frequently, some of the large discs or LP's would become a bit warped, and to make sure the needle wouldn't drop off the flawed surface the operators had heavy iron pucks they placed on the center on top of the discs on the turntables to flatten them down. These weights were about half again as large as a regulation hockey puck, and weighed about four pounds each.

The area behind the stand-up turntables and the back wall of the control room formed a perfect bowling alley, and it was just a matter of time before the sport began. Once the newscast was started, the operator would stand at the farthest end of the room and roll the heavy weight the length of the room, where it would crash resoundingly against the wall of the News booth. You could hear it rumble, rolling along on its collision course with the wall. Of course, so could the newsman. Usually it would take about two of these crashes to break up the unfortunate victim, trying as best as he could to not laugh in the middle of the newscast. Some of the operators could well have qualified as Olympic medalists at their chosen sport.

Perhaps it was for the best that my show was on remote so often, because I had an inspired way of tormenting my news guy. His nerves were shattered to begin with, and frequently he arrived for his evening shift having already downed a few shots.

One of my favourite gags involved carefully emptying the wastebasket in the news booth before he arrived. As he started to read I would go to the water cooler and fill up a milk bottle (remember this was a *long* time ago). I would then open the door into his booth, slip past him, and quietly move the metal wastebasket to the corner of the booth. I stayed facing away from him, so he could not see the bottle of water. I would take a broad stance, then loudly unzip my zipper and assume the position.

Moving carefully so as not to give myself away, I would begin to pour a stream of water into the empty tin basket. The booth was a tiny room, so I would be only a couple of feet or so away from my tormented friend. Usually about ten seconds of this would have him at the edge of his cliff, and if he hadn't broken up yet, I simply maintained my pose, waited a few more seconds then dribbled a few more times into the wastebasket. That would generally do it. Mission accomplished!

We employed a part-time operator at the time for occasional fill-in work. He was a young student beginning his first year in Pre-Med at the University of Western Ontario. It is worth pointing out that today he's a renowned surgeon at University Hospital in London, a world-class teaching hospital. Even so, he showed up for his first shifts with the required frosh beanie perched on his head. The headgear was part of the hazing that went on in those days. It looked a little on the nerdy side to me, and I figured a little initiation ceremony of our own was called for.

I prepared well in advance for my stealthy attack by emptying the control room trash bin. I also rolled down the window blind of the door. Next, I went to the area where the acetate discs were created. When commercials had been taped, our practise was to make a record of them for playback. As the turntable lathe created the "soft cut" of the Electrical Transcription, (or audio disc) the shavings were stored in a bin until they needed to be thrown out. These shavings, when lit with a match, produced thick quantities of smoke, but very little flame.

I filled up a tin cup with the shavings and fired it up. Then, shortly after 5 O'clock one Friday afternoon, when I thought everyone had deserted the building, I watched and waited until the unsuspecting freshman looked the other way, then quickly dumped the cup into the wastebasket. It began to smoulder, and smoke started to fill the control room. I quickly closed the door to the room and held it tight, so he was trapped inside. He was pounding on the door but couldn't budge it, due to my resistance on the other side. He also couldn't see out of the room, since the blind was rolled down. I'm sure he didn't know what was going on, but with that much smoke, there had to be fire somewhere in the studio!

Braced, holding the door shut, I happened to glance down the hall towards the executive offices that adjoined our studios. Coming down the hall towards me were Ward Cornell and Murray Brown, then second-in-command of the Blackburn Group. These were my two most powerful bosses and things could have gotten tense. But they had lots of experience in the broadcast business, and knew boys would be boys, and neither missed much that went on in the station. With my heart almost stopping, I must have looked like a deer in the headlights, but I kept just enough cool.

"Nothing to see here, just move along," I said.

To my shock and relief, they both walked past literally looking the other way, and punched the elevator button. For once, the tiny elevator was parked at our floor. Praise be! The door opened, and they were gone.

Having dodged what could have been a pretty big bullet, I quickly released the surgeon-to-be from the Smoking Section. After all, as doctors are quick to note, smoking can be dangerous to your health.

"The CFPL Lively Guys" Artwork by Cliff Kearns

Track 65

In those days, most big radio stations had a librarian, not for books, but to look after the records and keep them properly organized. The stunningly-attractive Hilda was ours. Shortly after I arrived at the station she left to get married. She had a younger sister named Rosemary who was also a knockout and quite witty, and we had a number of fun dates. But like all the other males on the staff, I couldn't help but be especially attracted to Hilda's replacement, Debbie Dennis. She quickly learned the ropes, and was soon picking the songs to be played by the other "Lively Guys." Actually, the only songs she didn't select were the hits I played during my show.

Debbie and I were married several years later. When our son was born we named him, of all things, *DJ*. Now stop it! Even I am not that radio-crazy! DJ stood for Dennis, (her last name) and Jason, another CFPL announcer. After growing up in a radio family, our son is now enjoying a career in radio sales in Denver, Colorado. He realized long ago that performing wasn't his strength, and sales were where his heart lay. Like father like son, though. DJ eats, sleeps, and breathes the radio business.

That first year in London, the station presented a timely display at the Western Fair, a large fall event that attracts attendees from all over the region for about a ten-day run. This was the time that the U.S. Space Program was really in high gear. Allan Shepard and Gus Grissom had completed sub-orbital missions before John Glenn successfully completed several orbits and found himself on front pages everywhere. Their successes always reminded me of the interviews I had done with them in Yellow Springs at WYSO years before.

Through Ward's contacts in the business community, we got our hands on a construction elevator that would normally be used to lift bricks several stories into the air. We used that as our broadcast "launch pad." Our remote console was installed on the floor of the open-air elevator, which rode on rails to a height of about four stories or more. The other DJs broadcast their shows either from terra firma, or perhaps a few feet in the air.

I found an early G-suit worn by jet pilots, and a pilot's helmet, both of which I had spray-painted metallic silver to match the silver suits worn by the Mercury astronauts. Talk about looking sharp! To tie into all the excitement about space, I did my show dressed as an astronaut. Several times during the day and evening, we raised the elevator to the top of the tower and released handfuls of balloons, which would drift over the crowd. A small percentage of the balloons had bills of several denominations inside them. It caused quite a scene during their release and became a real focal point of the Fair, as we had a prime outdoor broadcast position plus that massive tower!

The G-suit had an umbilical cord attached to it, which would inflate bladders inside the suit to counteract the forces of gravity to keep the blood in the upper body of the pilot when inflated during high-speed turns. Another of our smart-aleck operators on site thought he would be funny and inflate my suit by blowing into the umbilical. It didn't seem to do anything, so I ignored him and carried on.

But when I was finished my air shift and walking to my car, I felt the need to visit the men's room, *and right that minute!* Knowing how tight the suit was, I unzipped two vertical zippers on the back of the suit just to give me some flexibility to manoeuver when I approached the urinal. When I did that, and unzipped the full-length front zipper of the G-suit, the inflated suit bladders ceased to give *my* bladder any support.

It went completely out of control. To paraphrase Rod Serling, who taught at Antioch College and hosted The Twilight Zone on TV:

"For your consideration, we present the following tale: Tall, skinny DJ, dressed in a flight suit, walks uncomfortably to his car after voiding himself in a tragic mishap in the Men's Room. Note, if you will, his awkward stance, and how curiously he waddles with legs wide apart, leaving a trail of droplets wherever he passes."

A more down-to-earth way to put it was, I peed my pants!

For several years CFPL also arranged to contract the services of Chatter the Chimp for our annual Western Fair displays. He was a great crowd-pleaser for passers-by. I loved interacting with him, and being that close to such an amazing creature. Chimps must either have a wonderful sense of humor or a great memory, because when I first met him, he reached down and quickly took off my socks. Every time he got near me he would do this, much to my embarrassment, year after year.

Chatter didn't interact this way with anybody else and when a primate with nimble hands and feet wants to do something, he *will* do it. One evening when I was doing my show a couple of years later, I wandered away from my broadcast console. Chatter hopped up into my on-air chair, put on my bulky headphones, leaned into the microphone and then started screeching loudly.

Funny thing is, he was more entertaining than some jocks I've heard. Who knows, maybe he'd wanted to be a DJ all his life, and just seized the opportunity. As I was admiring his almost-human impersonation, he ripped the wind-sock covering off my microphone and started to eat it! But he probably wasn't the first overwrought DJ to do that.

"Hello Earthlings!" Ground level shot of the CFPL Western Fair Display looking skyward with Dick waving from his perch during an evening broadcast! +++

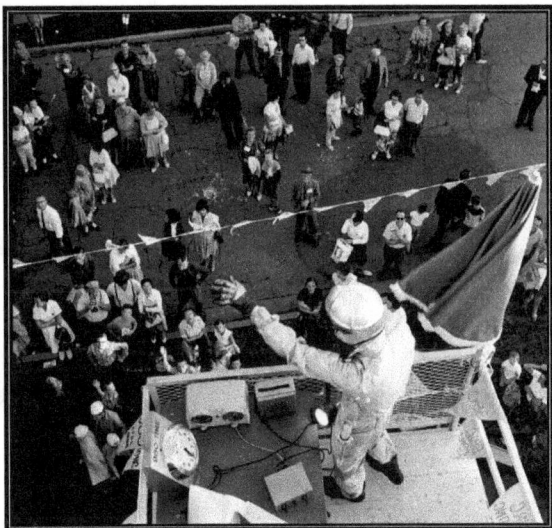

*Looking down at earth from "The High Perch" dressed in Astronaut garb.
Note the umbilical cord on the left side of the flight suit that caused
problems a few hours later! +++*

Dick and "Chatter the Chimp!" (Dick is the one wearing headphones.)
Once again, Darwin was proven right!

Track 67

A week after the Western Fair, the nearby hamlet of Ilderton held a much more rural and decidedly smaller Fall Fair. It was quite a let-down after the major crowds the Western Fair attracted in London... I arrived at our mobile studio site just a few minutes before the start of my shift, and found that a guy I'll just call Bob, another of our operators, had set everything up with the entrance doors to the studio accessible right alongside a racetrack used normally for horses.

While I sat down inside the van with my back to the track, arranging my commercial scripts and station logs and getting myself plugged into the console, Bob suggested that if he could borrow my car he could hit the local liquor store and pick up a couple of snorts to help pass away the long, hot, dusty afternoon. I just threw him the keys and rolled into the show. Soon, he was back, with a brown paper bag firmly in his grip. While I continued the remote broadcast, he surreptitiously made us a couple of refreshing drinks. The air-conditioner in the domed Plexiglas van wasn't working well that day, and it was quite uncomfortable in our cramped booth. I guess we both needed something to cool us down.

You can probably guess where this story is heading. At four in the afternoon I was teeing up the Livestock Parade, which was coming up shortly and touted as the highlight of the day. Feeling a little smug and with some big-city sass, I prepared the audience.

"Folks, we're just seconds away from the big parade, and since we're track-side, we're going to give you live coverage from our location!"

I don't think there's much question that the contents of the brown bag had rendered us both a little tipsy when I suddenly heard a loud bellow from a bull. Out of the corner of my eye, I saw Bob collapsing with laughter on the seat of the van beside me. The microphone was on a removable peg on the console, and as I mentioned, I had my back to the track. The mic had a coiled cable attached to it for extension purposes if we had to move away from the console.

From my cramped sitting position, I was attempting to turn around to better see the track and the parade. As I turned, I could see the bull in question mounting a small cow. This city boy had no experience with farm animals, let alone a bull in such an obviously excited state. Let me say only that is was something you had to see to believe! It was as if the bull had grown another leg! I leaned backward in my chair, totally out of control with laughter. As I did so, the doors of the van swung open behind me from the weight of my body, and I fell onto the dusty track right on my back.

And that wasn't the worst thing that happened. I had trained my new young operator back at the studio to refrain from doing *anything* technical until I buzzed him on the console to roll the next event. I was flat on my back for the count, Bob was doubled up in the van laughing himself sick, and the operator wouldn't do anything until he was told to. I think I eventually put us out of our misery by rolling over to the connecting telephone link at the side of the van and yanking the cables out of the sockets. Better dead air than two idiots giggling while the cattle were prepping for Penthouse Letters.

To our surprise, neither Bob nor I ever heard anything from management about this embarrassing event, in spite of the fact we had gone off the air without authorization. There must have been angels on our shoulders, though I hope mine avoided the horse manure on my shirt.

Track 68

Still on the topic of the great outdoors, one spring day while driving around I stumbled on an idea for another contest that would involve our listeners. I saw lawn after lawn turned almost yellow with dandelions, and thought, "Why not have the audience bring us their favorite dandelion?" Simple idea, right? Doesn't cost anything to qualify. I didn't really record any production for the contest, and candidly I hadn't even arranged for a prize of any sort, large or small. I just started to talk it up on air, and encourage folks to bring in their favorite weed. There wasn't a lot of response at first, but that was OK. I was only trying to get some on-air buzz going.

Things took a different turn, however, when one day when a farmer hauled about six bushel baskets of dandelions from his field into our reception area and left them there. Goop was dripping out of the bottom, and very quickly the station was filled with a load of creepy-crawlies. That prompted another early morning phone call from Ward Cornell, who was somewhat annoyed I hadn't clued anybody in about any dandelions being delivered to our station. Let alone bushels and bushels of them and plenty of passengers. In the end, I had to pay to have the area fumigated. The whole adventure did kind of give new meaning to the concept of getting the bugs out of a station promotion!

An infrequent visitor to my studio in those days was a young singer and songwriter named Gord. It was very early in his career, and he would implore me to play his music.

"Gord, it's a nice song, but it's *Canadian!* None of the American stations are playing it, or charting it, so it would be a waste of time for me to put you on the air with a non-hit that nobody else is airing!"

Not a very patriotic thing to say, perhaps, but this was before the days when being Canadian had any credence in the radio industry. It would be a while yet before our beloved Canadian Radio and Television Commission, also known as the CRTC, decided Canadian radio should reflect at least some Canadian content. They called the concept Can Con, and mandated thirty per cent of the records played on any given station had to have significant participation by Canadians.

But that was in the future and in the meantime there wasn't much I could do for my friend Gordon Lightfoot. Later on, I think I more than made up for it, though. And what a career he carved out for himself. Trust me, you'll hear more about Gord later in this story.

Another performer who I had fun working with on many occasions was the rockabilly legend Ronnie Hawkins, a transplant to Canada from Arkansas (at the suggestion of his pal Harold Jenkins, later known as Conway Twitty). He was one of the few ground-breaking rock entertainers to enjoy a career of more than 50 years, with more than twenty-five albums to his credit.

They called him Rompin' Ronnie and he lived up to and often surpassed his billing! He was a singer, a dancer (one of the first to do what Michael Jackson later called the moonwalk), a boxer, a homespun philosopher and a friend to people like John Lennon, Kris Kristofferson, Bob Dylan, Neil Young, and even President Bill Clinton.

He later became famous for the musicians he hired to play in various incarnations of his backup band The Hawks. Some were just great players, others went on to various levels of stardom. The latter list includes all five members of rock legends The Band, mega-producer David Foster, and actress Beverly D'Angelo.
Ronnie and his gang appeared at various spots around town, but if he had a home away from home it had to be The Brass Rail in London, a smoky basement bar under a steak house east of the downtown. I was sitting at my remote broadcast console in a store just across the street one frosty night, when I saw Ronnie and the band walking by. I waved, and they all piled into the store to say hello. Ronnie was wearing a full-length leather greatcoat and I mentioned how much I admired it.

"Hell, Slippery Richard, it's yours!" Ronnie was a great guy to hand out nicknames, and that was mine.

He pulled the coat off his shoulders and handed it to me. Just like that. A spur of the moment thing, for sure, but a truly spontaneous act of friendship, too.

One summer a few years later, Ronnie and his band and I were hired for a weekly record hop by a local promoter. It was held at the historic Stork Club, an old-time dancehall that overlooked Lake Erie in Port Stanley, Ontario. Coincidentally, that's the lovely village where I now live six months of the year.

Sadly, the Stork Club has burned down like so many other dancehalls, but in its day it was a top venue with a large and lovely dance floor. During the Big Band Era it had hosted all of the big-name touring groups, and London's Guy Lombardo was a regular feature there. In the final years before it burned down it attracted such name performers as Chubby Checker and Johnny Rivers.

Our deal for the summer engagements was that Ronnie and the band would entertain for sets of about 40 minutes, then they would take a break while I played records for about a quarter hour.

I remember one night, having finished my radio show and driving to nearby Port Stanley, I mentioned to Ronnie that I was really tired. I had been very busy that particular week, and I asked him if he had anything that might perk me up. Bad mistake to ask that kind of question to a road musician. Ronnie opened up a little pillbox and handed me a tiny black pill.

"That should fix you up, Slippery," he said in his southern drawl.

Sure enough, my energy quickly spooled up and after the dance I returned to London wide awake. Unfortunately, I stayed that way until Sunday afternoon, when I was finally able to fall asleep!

Next Friday we were once again in Port Stanley, and I had to ask The Hawk a question.

"What the heck was that pill you gave me last Friday?"

I had the sense he'd been expecting the question.
"Hell, man, that was a Black Maria. A triple Dexedrine!" he said in his Arkansas accent, with a big punch in the shoulder and a belly laugh to go with it!

Later in this long train of events, I'll return to both the Stork Club *and* the Big Bands!
To listen to my show, circa 1964, during the British Invasion, go to:
AUDIO/VIDEO: CFPL 1964, London

Our News Director at CFPL was a true gentleman named Hugh Bremner. He was a consummate professional, and could have written his own ticket anywhere in the country. He also did the evening news package on our Blackburn TV station. He was a very handsome man with a wicked sense of humor, and wrote a daily well-informed commentary which aired several times. He had travelled the world and reported back to the station from such far-away places as Moscow, or London, England. This, of course, helped cement his reputation as a serious broadcaster. Hugh and I hit it off from our first meeting, and he allowed me to do one afternoon shift a week as a newsman. I sure wasn't qualified, but appreciated the sincerity of his offer. I don't believe I was paid for the shift, but I enjoyed getting experience in another area of broadcasting.

One afternoon I was shuffling my stories, putting them in sequence for the next newscast, when I looked up and saw a silver-haired gentleman with a well-clipped mustache standing near the elevator. I approached him and did my duty as an employee.

"Sir, you're not allowed in this area without an escort. I'll have to ask you to go back to our reception area."

I walked him back to the front desk, and left him with the Receptionist. When I came back, the operator on duty was almost beside himself.

"Do you know who you just kicked out of here? That's Walter Blackburn! He owns this whole joint!"

Talk about a career-limiting move!

At the Christmas party later that year, Mr. Blackburn approached me again, and gave me friendly poke in the arm.

"Merry Christmas, young man. Under the circumstances, you did the right thing when we met each other last time. I should have introduced myself!"

Maybe I'd have a career after all.

Track 71

Speaking of Christmas, now's as good a time as any to tell you about one memorable Christmas Eve I spent, (or misspent) at the CFPL studios. I had received a few bottles of rye and gin from various record companies, and had stashed them away to give to my operator Yogi. I thought it would be the kind of present he would appreciate, and he certainly deserved something for all his help as my operator. Earlier I had been on a remote broadcast, and hadn't had time to pre-record my late evening show called Journey into Melody.

Between my sign off at 9 pm and my later show, in which I morphed into a laidback beautiful-music announcer, there was an hour of network programing. As an affiliate of the Canadian Broadcasting Corporation, CFPL was required to insert an hour of CBC content into each evening's schedule. I arrived back at the studio from the remote shortly after 9 pm, and gave Yogi his Christmas bottles. He was a happy recipient but it turned out to be a bad idea! He was one of those individuals whose pictures could be posted in the dictionary under Can't Hold His Booze. In little more than half an hour, he was weaving and staggering around the place and it was pretty obvious he was not going to be able to produce my show in that condition. I hadn't had a drop, since I knew I had to be back behind the microphone, so I took my albums and commercial recordings and headed to the Announce/Op studio, where I got ready to go live on the air by myself.

I didn't see him leave, but the story goes that Yogi then walked through the Editorial Room of the London Free Press, with my gift bottle of Seagram's Crown Royal, still in its velvet display sack, tied around his waist. He was on his way to the company cafeteria for some mix and his progress didn't go un-noticed.

I rolled into the beautiful-music segment, and then spotted Yogi through the glass in our big studio below my booth. The station had just delivered a lot of gifts for needy children with a Toys for Tots promotion we had completed, but we were left with several broken Barbie and Ken dolls that had been collected and stored in the studio. Yogi was by now really in the bag, and was trying to break me up by arranging the dolls in some bizarre sexual poses.

It was worth a chuckle but I had to block him from my thoughts and concentrate on what I was doing. A few minutes later, I looked over and noticed that Yogi had taken the mover's throw rug from the studio grand piano, and thrown it on the floor. He then propped open the lid, leaned over the exposed innards of the instrument as though he was inspecting the strings, then vomited all over the mechanism! It would be several days before his little indiscretion was discovered, which made his adventure even less "grand."

Sure enough, early in the morning of my first day back at work I got a call from Ward Cornell.

"What the Hell were you guys doing on Christmas Eve? I've had calls from the Managing Editor about your Op running around with a Crown Royal bag on his belt, and now the cleaner tells me the studio is a total pig pen."

I saw no point in denying that I had given Yogi the bottle in question, but denied that I knew any more than that. Nobody lost their job over this foolishness, but judging by Ward's demeanour it was a close call. I'm pretty sure it resulted in at least one more paper reprimand added to Yogi's personnel file, which was already quite thick.

Later in my stay at CFPL I latched onto a new operator named Len Marucci, who also doubled as an overnight jazz-oriented DJ later in his career there. His on-air name was Len Michaels. Len, an Italian to the core, was capable of whipping up great Italian meals, and a past master of the art of making 'gravy', the delicious tomato sauce with which he would cover his fabulous hand-rolled meatballs. Many a starving announcer can remember how filling his feasts were, and he loved to share them with others. Sadly, Len passed away as I was writing this book. He will be missed by many, including me.

Len loved to laugh, and had a pretty well-developed sense of humor. He was a great foil for my antics, and proved a steady partner to work with. We developed a particular rhythm for what we had to do. Usually I would call for a specific cut for the first and second gimmick insert, so we would have a structured, pre-prepared piece ready to roll as soon as we came out of the end of a hit song. I would back-announce the song, saying something like, *"That's 'Born Free!' Hey I was born free too! My daddy's a doctor! (Rim Shot.) That's Roger Williams and his piano on Channel 98 and I'm Dick Williams, The Tall One!"* Then the second pre-arranged drop-in would hit me with *"Everybody knows your name, lunk-head, and stay out of the icebox!"* (Roll Commercial.)

One of the many memorable things about Len was his glass eye. Once, he showed me a dress-up version he would wear to parties. If you got right up close and looked deeply into his eye, you could see a tiny naked woman where the pupil would normally be. On the few occasions when we worked in-studio together, he would frequently sit behind the glass looking directly at me, tapping himself in the eye with the sharpened end of the pencil. That was more than a little upsetting to watch, but at least he never confused his real eye with the glass one.

*Lively Guys (Front-Rear): John Dickens, Al Mitchell, Bill Brady, Dick Williams ***

*Lively Guys (L-R) John Dickens, Al Mitchell, Bill Brady, Dick Williams ****

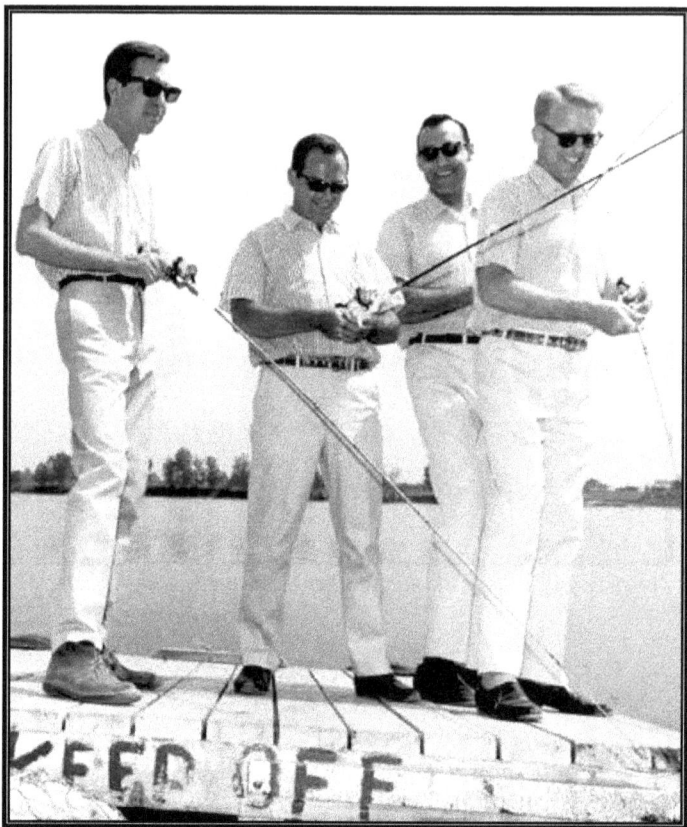

Lively Guys (L-R) Dick Williams, John Dickens, Bill Brady, Al Mitchell ***

Lively Guys Clockwise: (Back Row L) John Dickens, Al Mitchell (Front Row) Bill Brady, Dick Williams ***

Now Playing: Little Honda, by The Shondells
"It's not a big motorcycle,
Just a groovy little motorbike.
It's more fun than a barrel of monkeys,
That two-wheeled bike.
We'll ride on out of the town
To anyplace I know you like."
Brian Wilson, Mike Love © Universal Music Publishing
Group

One of our salesmen arranged for the temporary use of a
Honda scooter and came to us to figure out how we could
promote this new little motor-bike. The solution was to find
out how many miles it would go on a full tank of gas. The
listeners would send us their guesses, and the winner would
receive a prize. Even though this promotion took place in the
winter, it certainly worked well, and we covered the entire
endurance test with our mobile unit following on the heels
(or wheels) of the little two-wheeler. We did live cut-ins
from the station's two-way telephone mounted in the van.
All the Lively Guys, as we were now known as a group, took
their turn driving around a course in the heart of the town.

I don't know who started it, either Bill Brady or me, but soon
both of us were going off-roading- in the city. Bill once
opened the front door of one of our weekly remote sites (I
believe it was the auto supply store I mentioned before) and
drove the Honda right through the store's sales area and out

their back door! When it was my turn at the controls, I drove through the indoor customer service area of a downtown A & W location, making it truly a Drive-In! (Or to be more precise, a Drive-Through.) I'm a little fuzzy as to how many miles we put on that little two-wheeler, but I'm pretty sure we drove it continuously for about 4 hours before it sputtered out of gas. Fortunately, that was not enough time for any of us to get into any serious difficulties as we buzzed about.

"From the first time I heard the 'Tall One' as he was cast by the station, I knew this guy was something special. He was the best at disc jockeying I had ever worked with. He ruled the London airwaves for many years." Bill Brady, London Free Press column, 2005

I hate to put words in Bill's voice, but I recall him speaking to a group at one of many occasions he was asked to deliver a few impromptu remarks. Bill once told a story about Demosthenes, the greatest orator of ancient Greece, who had worked very hard to improve his speaking skills. He practiced speaking with pebbles, or marbles, in his mouth in an attempt to improve his articulation. Each day, he would reduce the number of marbles he stuffed into his mouth by one, and once again recite his speech. In Bill's version of the story, he put it this way.

"Demosthenes' idea was to fill his mouth with marbles and try and make himself understood in spite of the impediments. Each day, he would remove one marble from the jar he kept them in, and once again recite his speech. Finally when he had lost all his marbles, he was ready to start a career in radio!"

That was vintage Brady, delivered as always with impeccable timing. Bill was always the prankster amongst us, and he put his wit to good advantage one night at the beginning of our all-night live show, hosted by a DJ we called Stud off-air. He was a young, inexperienced guy, still learning the radio ropes. Where better to learn than the overnight show, traditionally the spot reserved for novices to get a little experience?

Each of our DJs had our own pre-recorded top-hour jingle, which began with "*He's A Lively Guy*," followed by about a fifteen-second musical 'pad' where the jock would say something like, *"I'm Pete Moss, and welcome into our overnight show. Coming up, we'll hear from Frank Sinatra and Petula Clark."* Then, the music would swell to full volume and the group would sing, *"CFPL in London!"* This would be followed by the first song of the hour.

Bill recorded on top of that jingle and added his own spin to it. When the unsuspecting young Stud played his DJ intro at midnight, what he heard on-air went way beyond a surprise.

"*He's A Lively Guy*," sounded fine, until Brady launched into his intro.

"He's repetitive. He's redundant! He repeats everything twice! Here he is, Pete Moss!" That's as good a moniker as any to hide his real name.

This was followed by the "CFPL in London" sing-out of the jingle. Naturally, we taped the entire segment off-air to hear his response. At the end of the show's customized Bill Brady introduction, there was a second or so of silence before Stud spoke.

"Bill Brady, I'll get you! I'll get you, Bill Brady!" Talk about redundant, it sounded like he was in an echo chamber.

It got lots of laughs at that year's Christmas Party, where the year's goofs and bloopers were replayed for the entire staff. Out-takes were fun, even back in those days!

'Pete Moss' was involved in a car crash one winter, and wound up with a broken leg. Complications set in and he lost a couple of toes to gangrene. He only came back to reasonable mobility after he was fitted with a corrective boot.

One Wednesday, while we talked in the station's library, he told me a story about how he and a group of his friends had been on a Smelt Run in Port Stanley, on nearby Lake Erie. In the sixties, this was a common rite of spring, when thousands of smelt would swarm the harbor and beaches of this scenic lakeside tourist town. It was a little reminiscent of the grunion runs back in California. Using beach fires or even just flashlights, and nothing but scoop nets, amateur fishermen would often be able to catch pails full of the tiny, finger-sized fish. It was considered a manly thing to bite the heads off the wiggling creatures prior to frying them in a pan.

It seems that Pete and his friends had indulged in a few beers before they toddled home to bed. He arrived home, took off his boots, and was met in the kitchen by his mother as he plopped down his bucket of fish on the table. With her Irish up, she proceeded to berate him for his disheveled appearance and for showing up in the family home under the influence. Expressing her motherly displeasure, she threw the small fish at him, scattering his catch all over the kitchen floor.

Thursday, Pete started to complain about his foot, and confided his problem to me. He often called me 'One', a contraction of my on-air nickname, The Tall One.

"One, I think I've got some gangrene coming back. My foot is really starting to smell bad!"

By Friday, when I next saw him, he told me he was convinced he might have to go under the knife again because the smell was even worse!

On Monday, when I ran into him again, he was in much better spirits. With a big smile, he told me the source of his 'gangrene'.

"One, I'm not going to lose any more toes! I guess when my mom started throwing the smelt around the kitchen, one of them fell into my boot, and I've been walking around for the past four days *with a dead fish in there!"*

It made perfect sense to me. That smelt *smelt*!

Track 75

Around this time I heard from my old mentor Mel Hall, who had just moved to Los Angeles and was now Program Director of KRLA. He had hired legends like Dick Biondi from WLS in Chicago, and Sie Holiday from KDEO, whom you've met before in these pages, and he wanted me to join him out there as well. Wow! That was some pretty serious talent he had there. Most Program Directors like to surround themselves with people they know and trust, and his asking for me was pretty much the biggest compliment he could have given me. But I was newly married, with a young child, my wife Debbie was very close to her family, and I had to turn him down.

On top of those problems, I envisioned months, if not years of delay waiting to get the U.S. visa needed to work in America since at that time I wasn't an American citizen. In radio, when you need or want something, it is usually something you need resolved *right that moment,* and waiting for the mills of the bureaucrats to grind through my application wasn't really an option, either.

If only I had known then what I know now (as a somewhat newly-minted U.S. citizen) my life might literally have taken a different direction, wife and baby issues notwithstanding. It turns out that since my Mother had been born in America, I was automatically an American citizen! All I would have had to do was present the paperwork documenting her background, her birth certificate, marriage licence, and so on. It was just a matter of shuffling papers. It is sometimes very ironic how things work out.

DICK WILLIAMS

Cliff Kearns Portrait

In 1963 I read with interest about an upcoming celestial event, a total solar eclipse on July 20. I won't bore you with the details, but I produced a dramatic ad, like a movie trailer, with ominous background music and an announcer trumpeting the cosmic event.

"Daylight turns to darkness as CFPL Radio presents an event truly massive in scope! We have arranged for a total eclipse of the sun, in appreciation for your making us Number One in London! For almost twenty minutes, the world as we know it will be plunged into blackness!"

We played this up big-time for several days before the event was scheduled to occur. I thought it was a great bit of fun, and we handled it pretty much tongue in cheek. After all, we didn't really book the eclipse. That sort of thing pretty much happens on its own.

I was on a remote that Saturday, and about an hour or so before the event was scheduled to happen the clouds rolled over our entire coverage area. You couldn't see the sun even if you were foolish enough to look up at it. Back at the station, our skeleton weekend staff consisted of my operator and one newsman. The phones started to ring off the walls, and my op told me over the intercom that people were asking the strangest questions.

"Are you going to *delay* the eclipse and have it when the clouds move away?"

"What happened to your eclipse? I can't see it!"

"Will the eclipse be rescheduled to another day?"

Apparently, some of our listeners were a little weak on their cosmology, and this event provided another glimpse into the power of radio. It was not unlike the silly question that all radio stations get on days when a fireworks display is to be held.

"What time will the fireworks start?"

Oh, for goodness' sake.

"When it gets dark!"

I can give you another example of how radio can create another reality for the listener. I had been asked by Ward to dump the Journey into Melody segment I aired every weeknight, and replace it with something to be called Countdown to Midnight. It would substitute the mellow music we had been running between eleven and midnight with Top Forty hits, and replayed the Top Three Songs requested by our audience in the early-evening segment.

I would pre-record most of the segments of the show, and every time I was on-air, I ran background sound effects of people laughing, talking, diving and splashing in what sounded like an Olympic-sized swimming pool. I would announce that I was broadcasting from the rooftop pool in our new headquarters in another part of the city. Several times a week young listeners would show up at the entrance to the London Free Press building on York Street anyway, geographically confused but looking to join in the pool-side fun!

Announcer: *"Straight ahead, fast times with fast cars! Stick around for pedal to the metal excitement!"*

Cover art for the CFPL Fabulous 40 Survey.

Now Playing: Dead Man's Curve, by Jan & Dean
"I was cruisin' in my Sting Ray late one night
When an XKE pulled up on the right
And rolled down the window of his shiny new Jag
And challenged me then and there to a drag"
Brian Wilson, Artie Kornfeld, Roger Christian Jan Berry ©
Liberty Records

I mentioned earlier how much I had lusted after the beautiful Jaguar that one of my fellow DJs drove at WSAI in Cincinnati. You may remember I told you I had more to say about Jaguars and me. Because of my public profile (and gift of the gab, no doubt), I was able to cut a deal with a local import car dealer, who gave me a fabulous price on a brand-new XKE convertible. Often called the E-Type, it was an almost unbelievable machine, a stunning piece of performance art (pardon the pun). I'm not a serious car fan, but this baby was awesome, not to mention gorgeous! It had a six-cylinder in-line engine which produced around two hundred and forty horsepower, and would go from a standing stop to sixty miles per hour mph in seven seconds. That was fast, baby.

But it did have a few little peculiarities. It didn't like Thursdays, for one thing. Rain or shine, with only a day to the weekend it just wouldn't start. On rainy days it always leaked where the canvas convertible top locked into the window frame. From time to time when I closed the door the trim fell off. To make matters worse, there was no synchromesh shifting down into first gear, so if the revs weren't perfectly matched when you did it there would be horrible grinding noises. This usually happened just as I would be driving around town, and someone would point at the car and say, "Wow, look at that Jag!" Very humiliating.

One Friday evening, I did my usual remote from Sayvette, and this night we had put the mobile control board right inside the store. As it was a lovely evening, I left the top down on the convertible. Throughout the evening, we had beach traffic reports, broadcast live by one of the other DJs at the Station, Jack Nixon. He was a pilot and did the traffic reports on the weekends from a single-engine Cessna. I thought that his reports that night were a little dramatic, as he was talking about big thunderstorms developing in the area but the weather had been nice when I went on the air. Much to my dismay, when I went outside after my show the rains had begun in London, and my car was really soaked. Water had pooled into the wells of the floorboard to about a depth of an inch or more.

Another time, Jack and I decided to look into the prospect of earning a few extra bucks to augment our salaries, and Jack said he had found a great franchise for a car wash. He said I should go to a downtown location and try out an existing franchised outlet. Most carwashes featured the standard configuration of a chain pulling the car along through the various wash, rinse and dry cycles. In our would-be business, the car would drive onto a stationary pad, and then would remain sitting there while a large, U-shaped rig passed over the car a few times from back to front, spraying and washing it, then blowing it dry.

The idea sounded pretty good to me, so off I went for a look-see. I was scheduled to do a remote broadcast in a little while but I had a few extra minutes to do a test of the new system we were going to plunk our bucks into. Dressed in a spiffy new suit, I pulled up on the wash pad, made sure the windows were rolled up tight, and waited for the test to begin.

The rig had just begun to move from the rear of the car when I suddenly realized that when the bar passed over the driver's cabin, it was then going to be blasting high-pressure jets of water directly at the windshield. There was no question what would happen next: there would be water all over the interior. I rolled the window down to yell at the attendant to stop the process, but my timing was bad and a torrent of water came pouring into the car through the window, drenching me completely. As the mechanism moved forward, sure enough, water started to spray through the gap above the windshield just as I had feared.

I had to get out from under Niagara Falls, and thought my best move would be to start the engine and make my escape from the infernal device once the bar had passed over the car on its way back. The attendant obviously hadn't heard my shouts for help, so I was on my own. No sooner had I popped the clutch for what I hoped would be a speedy getaway than I stalled the motor!

Now the bar was behind me, and beginning a *second* pass with what I knew would be even more disastrous results. Once again, I rolled the window down in a blind panic to get the attendant's attention. They say one of the signs of stupidity is doing the same thing over again and expecting different results. I guess I was some kind of stupid that night. Like an instant replay I received yet another dousing, and the foot wells of the car where the clutch, brake and accelerator were housed were ankle-deep in soapy water.

I did my show from inside the Mobile Studio that night, cursing both Jack's misguided business sense, and my own stupidity. The only dry area on my body ran from my knees to my ankles. I probably don't need to tell you that we never did invest in that franchise.

I used to wonder if the car hadn't come with a jinx instead of a warranty, because of all the misfortunes it heaped on me. My brother John had by now become a jet pilot in the Canadian Armed forces, and asked me one day if he could take the Jag out for a spin with his girlfriend. I really didn't want to let anyone but me drive it because in spite of all its peculiarities it was still my pride and joy. But he was pretty persuasive.

"Look, the government has just invested hundreds of thousands of dollars training me to be a pilot and control an airplane that costs well over several million dollars. And you think I can't drive your car?"

I handed over the keys, and watched him roar away, every inch the fighter jock on a spree. About 45 minutes later I got a phone call from him. He got right to the point.

"Dick, I've just totalled the Jag."

Yeah, right. Very funny, John. As it turned out, though, not funny at all.

A year or two later, at the bachelor's party on the eve of my wedding to Debbie, he finally admitted that it wasn't the jet pilot that couldn't handle my little rocket. Turns out he had let his girlfriend drive the car. They had apparently come off a paved road and onto a gravel, and the young lady had lost control. The heavy engine and lack of power steering proved too much for her and the car left the road, hit a telephone pole, crunched up the front end, then spun and hit a farmer's fence. Backward, still at a pretty high rate of speed.

Well, there's always the collision repair shop. But Jaguar in England was on strike, and one of the hinges that allowed the front hood (or bonnet, as the Brits say) to be raised or lowered wasn't available in Canada until the strike ended and parts began to flow again. There wasn't a spare hinge to be had anywhere in Canada, so I had to wait for almost six months to sit behind the wheel again.

Of course, my new wife Debbie wanted to have a spin in the big beast as well. She's a good driver, but wasn't really used to driving a stick-shift, high-performance car. Our garage had a little raised lip at the entrance, and I was concerned about her parking the car too deep into the garage. Visibility over the long hood was tricky and the driver had to really pay attention or else he (or she) would prang the car's nose against the far end of the garage.

I took my position in front of the back wall, intending to show Debbie where she should stop. But her foot somehow slipped off the clutch as she was trying to slowly accelerate into the right position. The car leaped forward, and I barely managed to jump out of the way as the car crashed through the garage wall. Once again, it was back to the repair shop.

I eventually decided to sell the car because of the ongoing expense of keeping the motor in tune, coupled with the fact we were now parents and needed a much more practical method of transportation. The trunk (or boot) couldn't even hold a case of beer! How practical is that? I found a buyer for the car and agreed to sell it to him as is.

My prospective new buyer was at the door ready for a test drive. He didn't look like a Jaguar type, but he was an earnest, hard-working guy who loved cars, I guess. I let him take it out for a spin and he was back shortly, elated with the car's performance. We agreed on the price, and I was quick to remind him that our deal was for the purchase of the car in as is condition, and that I hadn't had a mechanical inspection done on it.

I also told him up front that I had noticed a little rumble in the long pair of exhaust pipes under the car over the past few days. We completed the financial arrangements and he drove off very happily in that long, sleek machine. A few minutes later, (and I mean a *few* minutes) he was back at the door to ask if he could call for a tow-truck. Turns out that less than two blocks away from our home both exhaust pipes had fallen off the car and onto the ground. I guess there was something behind that rumble I warned him about.

I felt bad for the new owner, but I had no way of knowing the car would start acting up before he even got it home. But with an as is car deal, all you get is an Oklahoma warranty: if it breaks you get to keep both pieces.

Announcer: *"We're back on the air with the Beatles, and how the Fab Four were heard first on North American radio!"*

Dick behind the wheel of the powerful Jaguar XK-E. Although it was an eye-catching set of wheels, it had its own set of adventures! Even all these years later, it still was a beautiful vehicle.

"I wanted to grow my hair long and be the disc jockey who played the Beatles." Legendary deejay Terry Young

Now Playing: From Me to You, by The Beatles
"If there's anything that you want
If there's anything I can do
Just call on me and I'll send it along
With love, from me to you!"
Lennon, McCartney © Sony/ATV Music Publishing LLC,
Universal Music Publishing Group

Well, it turns out I had what everyone wanted. First rights on the airplay to the Beatles music in North America! But first, the back-story.

As far back as 1961, the Beatles had auditioned for Decca Records in England. Surprisingly, considering their later success, they were not well received.

"Guitar groups are on the way out." Right. Imagine being that executive years later, watching millions of dollars float by and knowing you were the one who turned down The Fab Four!

Shortly afterwards, they were signed by EMI's Parlophone label. Apparently their people were a little more astute judges of talent and potential. As word started to leak out of the U.K. about this pop phenomenon called the Beatles, a local woman named Rita Wood was receiving original studio pressings of their early recordings from a friend of a friend inside Parlophone. She was kind enough to pass these gems on to me for instant airplay. More than a year before the Beatles became overnight sensations after their Ed Sullivan Show appearance on February 9 of 1964, some of their first singles, She Loves You, Please Please Me and From Me to You were in my hands and I was all over them on the airwaves of Channel 98.

I would generally receive the music from Rita within a couple weeks of the recording's release in the U.K., and I was very glad to have them. I had been closely following the International section of Billboard Magazine, and realized this band was going to be huge. Sooner or later the world would be clamouring to hear them, and I had them on my radio station! Rita was a godsend to me as she continued to supply new Beatles albums and singles well in advance of any material becoming available for sale in North America. This allowed for some amazing tee-ups.

"We've got a world premier song you can't hear anywhere else in Canada or the United States! And I'll have it for you here, next hour! You hear all the Beatles hits here first, on CFPL!"

It doesn't get any better than that in the DJ business, believe me. When any of the Beatles songs would air, I would play a whispered *"CFPL Exclusive"* right over the middle of the songs to keep anyone else from recording it off the air and playing it on their station!

Not that this made me a penny more in income, but it sure helped the ratings, and I that's what drives the radio business. It also illustrated how the deep pockets and fat promotion budget of CFPL could make a difference. The Beatles were scheduled to play Maple Leaf Gardens, so we chartered a bus and took a load of hormone-fueled teenage girls to Toronto for the live performance. Were the chosen contest winners in heaven? Silly question.

Toronto was in crisis mode. The date was September 7th, 1964, and four thousand police officers were on duty, with some assistance from the RCMP. A five-block area around Maple Leaf Gardens had been cordoned off for almost half a day before their stage appearance and the show was delayed for more than an hour due to the utter chaos in the arena.

The show itself? A total farce. The crowd noise was so intense nobody could hear a thing. Flashbulbs popped by the thousands, creating a strobe-like effect that made it almost impossible to see the four tiny figures far away on the stage. I know now the Beatles were used to this situation but frustrated by it, too, since nobody could actually hear what they were playing. But our bus-load of listeners had no complaints.

Debbie Dennis, who was engaged to Dick at the time, pictured above with 50 thrilled Beatles Fans on their way to see The Fab Four in Toronto.

Now Playing: Bits and Pieces, by The Dave Clark Five
"(I'm in pieces, bits and pieces)
Since you left me and you said goodbye
(I'm in pieces, bits and pieces)
All I do is sit and cry
(I'm in pieces, bits and pieces)"
Mike Smith, Dave Clark Lyrics © EMI Music Publishing

Fast forward almost two months, to November 3rd, 1964. A man named Pat Quinn (no relation to the legendary hockey coach) was the manager of the Sayvette department store where CFPL had done hundreds of remote broadcasts. But he was a lot more than that. He was a showman, a promoter, a hustler, part carney for sure, and to use his favorite word, he was *Fantastic!*

In later years he moved to Toronto, where he introduced many dining spots that still do justice to his driving energy and enthusiastic style. They included such well-known establishments as The Irish Embassy Pub & Grill, Quinn's Steakhouse & Irish Bar, P.J. O'Brien Irish Pub & Restaurant, and Shopsy's Restaurant, Deli & Catering. Pat's family back in Ireland had been in the hospitality industry for generations, so he was no newcomer to providing what the public wanted.

It was thanks to Pat that the Dave Clark Five arrived in London, Ontario on November 3rd, 1964. Pat was the show's promoter, and made a sponsorship deal with CFPL. This second wave of the British Invasion was almost as big a tsunami as the original Beatles! The DC5 sold over one hundred million records in their career and were at or near the top of every British band popularity list. The week they arrived in London, their current hit single, Everybody Knows, was at #4 on CFPL's Fabulous Forty Survey.

I met them on the tarmac at the airport, and since we were all roughly the same age there wasn't a lot of ice to be broken. They were easy-going, well-grounded guys, with no attitude problems or pretensions of grandeur. We posed for some pictures, then we were whisked to waiting convertible limos that took us to their hotel. During the ride, we crossed the Thames River in what I was quick to point out, as their guide, was the O*ther* London. I interviewed drummer Dave Clark and organist Mike Smith during the drive.

Dave Clark was one of the savviest of the young rock stars and made sure from the band's beginnings that they kept as much of their earnings as possible. He is a very wealthy man today as a result.

The shows were of course sold out, perhaps in part because it was a real rock and roll extravaganza. On the bill beside the DC5 were U.S. singer Jimmy Soul, Toronto's David Clayton Thomas and the Shays (before he went on to stardom with Blood, Sweat & Tears), Ottawa's Esquires (forerunners of Canadian hit makers the Five Man Electrical Band), Brantford's Sandi Simms and the Diplomats and London's Johnny Stevens Sextet, the Undertakers and the Fortune Tellers.

It was a jam-packed show and all I had to do was introduce the stars to a very excited audience in the aptly-named Treasure Island Gardens. I'm sure Pat Quinn made a lot of treasure in profits from the two concerts!

Greeting the Dave Clark 5 at the London Airport prior to their live London concert.

Track 80

1967 was Canada's Centennial year. The International and Universal Exposition, or Expo 67, was a truly international event, and lived up to its title as a World's Fair. In one day alone, over 500,000 visitors would converge on the site in Montreal. More than sixty nations took part in the celebrations, showing off their national pride in the many pavilions that blossomed across the site.

The powers that be decided that our station, CFPL should play a part, by bringing the cities of London and Montreal closer together. We selected a group of high school students and loaded them with us on a chartered train to Montreal, where we put them up in hotel rooms in downtown Montreal the night before our all-day broadcast from the heart of Expo 67.

I'm relying totally on memory here, but I think our group of students numbered about twenty, and they represented all of the high schools in the city, both public and Catholic.

I'm pretty sure the whole concept was the idea of Ward Cornell, who was an ex-teacher himself. His idea, and a brilliant one at that, was to make the kids earn their way by being reporters for a day. We assigned each student a particular national pavilion, and once they had looked it over and taken notes, they prepared a script on what they had seen inside their assigned nation's showpiece.

We set up our mobile unit console on location at Expo 67, and broadcast live back to London for pretty much the entire daytime hours. Each hour at least, we had a student or two back at the microphone with their reports, and they all were proud to do their part. A magnificent promotion on several levels, we had an exciting contest to qualify to join our safari, and it grew into a real audience-building event. After all, each student in the school would be listening to hear the reports from their reporter, and all the parents and friends would be thrilled to hear live coverage from the young students as the day unfolded. And where did they listen? CFPL!

Ward and I had a special mission, which wasn't reported during the broadcast. We visited the Russian pavilion, and sampled caviar and iced vodka shots. It was a first for me, but not such a novelty for Ward, who had travelled to Russia for televised hockey matches and Olympic coverage in prior years on CBC -TV.

I think the most telling moment happened late at night as the train was taking our group back to London. Ward and I found ourselves alone in the bar car (who would have thought) sharing some conversation.

"You know Ward, you've been a great boss. You've given me such freedom to do pretty much whatever I want, and haven't acted like any kind of Program Director or GM I've ever worked with. Thanks for leaving me alone to do the best job I could!"

Ward had a somewhat gruff voice, and he leaned towards me to share his philosophy.

"As long as your ratings are good you *won't* hear from me. If things change, though, *you might!*"

Announcer: *"From smooth sailing to rough seas ahead! We'll be right back, but first, these words!"*

In that same year, 1967, a radio station in nearby Windsor, Ontario was revamping its on-air sound. CKLW was a powerhouse, 50,000-watt clear-channel station, 800 on the AM dial. They had just renamed themselves The Big Eight and implemented what was called Boss Radio, Bill Drakes' super-tight, high-energy format. They used super-short jingles, each roughly only two to three seconds. Straight to the point, they said only what needed to be said, in this case, The Big 8, CKLW! By the summer of that year, they were number one in Windsor. Nice, but not all that significant. What was much more important, they were the number one radio station in Detroit, too, just across the river. That put them on the national map in the U.S., and all but guaranteed big audiences and even bigger profits. They were programed by Paul Drew, who was a friend of my ex-Program Director in Cincinnati, Frank Ward. Frank contacted Paul with a recommendation, so that when I called for an appointment, I wasn't a total unknown.

Armed with a reel-to-reel Air Check tape in my hand, I headed to Windsor with high hopes for our meeting. After a few minutes, Paul came charging into the reception area, spun on his heels and waved over his retreating shoulder for me to follow him. Racing to keep up, I was soon in his office. There was no small talk, in fact no talk at all. He stuck his hand out for the expected tape reel, quickly threaded it onto his tape recorder, and sat down.

Out of the speakers came my suddenly outdated 1959 jingle,

"Clap Hands and Shout for Joy
Here comes that music boy
With Big Sounds, Big Sounds,
Music News and Weather Too
On the Dick Williams Show"

The elapsed time was, give or take, fifteen seconds. It felt like an hour. CKLW jingles were, as I noted, no longer than they needed to be, just two or three seconds. Mine, by comparison, seemed to last forever. From the first second, Paul was making a come on, come on, get on with it gesture with his hand. When it finished he stopped the playback, pulled the reel off the machine and shoved roughly back into my hands.

"I haven't got time for that kind of old-fashioned crap!"

He never heard a second of my voice, or what my show was all about! Within five minutes of my arrival at CKLW I was back out the front door, and heading home to London.

As I told you earlier, that jingle changed my life. And now you know… The rest of the story!)

Announcer: *"We re-join our program, now in progress!"*

Not too long after Ward's warning to me on our return from Expo 67, he moved on to become a consultant for a short period. He was then appointed to the Canadian Embassy in London, England, as Agent-General. This plum political appointment was due to his close association with the Progressive Conservative Party of Ontario.

It may have been that management at the Blackburn Empire was growing unhappy with his frequent lack of attendance at the radio stations, due to the heavy schedule of CBC TV hockey telecasts. He was away a lot in order to interview sweaty players between periods. But such things were way above my pay scale or knowledge.

Ward's successor as General Manager was a sales-oriented guy, not a programmer. His name was Bud Knight, and he had been an executive with a national gasoline company, Supertest Petroleum, based in those days in London. Bud freely admitted he knew nothing about radio, and was able to prove it with some frequency.

St. Thomas is a small city just a few minutes south of London. At that time their local station, CHLO, started to become a threat to my existence. Their only real impact on CFPL to that point had been their playing pop music after I signed off at 9 pm, but they did have a powerful signal thanks to their dial position at 680.

Seeking to take more advantage of that fact, they hired a Program Director named J. Robert Wood, whose prior experience had been at a big station in Winnipeg, CKY. Under his guidance, they bought a fresh new jingle package, hired some decent announcers, and became known as Swingin' 68. To make matters worse, they now played Top 40 music *around the clock.* As any radio DJ will tell you, teens are a fickle crowd at best. As long as they can hear the music of their choice when they want it, they're your friend for life, or until the next weekend, anyway.

With the exceptions of my evening programs, CFPL was playing a little bit of soft pop music, mixed with lots of album cuts by groups like The Ray Conniff Singers, The Ames Brothers, Frank Sinatra, Sammy Davis, Jr., and so on. Hardly what any self-respecting teenager would ever listen to voluntarily. With CHLO racking up new listeners every day, I could sense that my turf was becoming smaller and smaller.

This was confirmed soon enough. I was doing a rare in-studio show one evening, when the studio door opened and Bud Knight walked in to introduce me to our newest consultant, George Davies. I would not disparage George by saying he didn't know his job, far from it, in fact. But Bud wanted to take CFPL in a new direction, and a more sedate, informational approach on air, and many consultants would have difficulty arguing against a client's strongly-expressed desires.

Since I had unwittingly backed myself into a corner and was known as a hot-rocking, fast-talking teen DJ, my credibility as a grown-up air personality would be very hard to establish. So it wasn't too long until Bud and I had what is known in many industries as The Talk. He acknowledged that even though I still had strong ratings, they were changing directions. That has always been a part of the reality of radio, then and now. But rather than letting me go, Bud offered to move me into the Creative Services Department of the radio station, which meant that if I wanted to continue receiving a nice paycheck, I would become a copy-writer, cranking out scripts for commercials and promos all day long.

I can't say I was thrilled, but I had seen more than my share of hirings, firings, shift changes, re-assignments and the like over the years and I wasn't surprised or terribly disappointed with this turn of events. This same thing had already happened to two other long-term announcers prior to my little chat with the boss.

What did stick in my craw, however, was a comment Bud made during this discussion. He leaned back in his chair, looked at me with a sincere salesman's attitude (which of course is a contradiction in terms) and pontificated.

"After all, you wouldn't want to be a Disc Jockey at 40, would you?"

Hell yes, I would, and what kind of real radio man would ever ask such a question?

Track 83

Now Playing: Turn, Turn, Turn, by The Byrds
"To everything, turn, turn, turn.
There is a season, turn, turn, turn.
And a time to every purpose under heaven.
A time to build up, a time to break down.
A time to dance, a time to mourn"
Lyrics from The Book of Ecclesiastes, adapted by Pete
Seeger © Melody Trails Inc. © Columbia Records

I applied myself to my new job, and learned more about
what it really entailed. Working alongside me was a brash
young student from the University of Western Ontario.
Today you know him as Alan Thicke, who first reached
international fame as the patriarch of the family on the ABC-
TV comedy series Growing Pains. Al was a very funny guy,
a pretty good singer, and a talented writer even then.

When we worked together he was honing his comedy and
writing chops, and had created a character he called Pierre
La Puck, a parody of a toothless (and often witless) NHL
Hockey player. I never performed the role on air of the Ward
Cornell-style announcer interviewing him, but I would run
lines with him for a routine that sounded like this.

Interviewer: "Pierre La Puck, what was your most terrifying
moment in The Forum in Montreal, where you played for
years?"

Pierre: (In a guttural French- Canadian accent) "Well, I t'ink ma most scary time was when my girlfriend, she's *missed a period*!"

Interviewer: "She missed a *period*?"

Pierre: "Yah, she was in a traffic jam, and she missed all of da first period, and part of da second period!"

Maybe you had to be there!

Track 84

Announcer: *"Let's take a time-out here and get some black and white TV facts! We'll be right back to our story, but first...."*

At the beginning of this book I told you that I had developed a burning desire to have some kind of involvement in television. The moment I arrived in London, I had quickly contacted the management of our sister station, CFPL-TV, and started submitting ideas for television shows that perhaps I could host.

Naturally, my first submission was for an American Bandstand dance party show, which I felt would certainly be viable. Dick Clark's show was a monster in the U.S. but the idea was met with indifference in London, Ontario. Another suggestion I pitched was a folk music program. Lots of groups were selling millions of records, so there was obviously a fan base. The Kingston Trio, The Limelighters, Peter Paul and Mary, and even solo acts like Gordon Lightfoot were becoming popular. It seemed like a timely idea to me, but I didn't make the programming decisions. The people who did were not impressed and I rang up another No Sale.

In order to find out more of the technical side of the business, I worked a non-paid shift every week with the studio crew at CFPL-TV, learning how to operate the cameras, set up proper lighting, work the overhead boom-mounted microphone, learn how the film chains operated during newscasts, and even do some evening switching, the process of directing simple segments during the Late Night Show. What I quickly found out is that TV is a lot different animal, production-wise from the simplicity of radio, where most of the time the on-air guy works entirely by himself, or at most with an operator. In TV, the on-camera host or newscaster is at the front end of a long, convoluted production chain, dependent on a lot of different people to get his show on the air. And we all know the Weakest Link theory and how it works, right?

My first nibble from the TV station came from the News Department, who wanted me to interview an actress who was doing a one-woman show at London's Grand Theatre. I got to the theatre well-prepared, and huddled with the crew the station had sent to record the interview for inclusion on the 6 pm newscast. I got my makeup on, trying to apply the goopy stuff without getting it all over my shirt and sports jacket, then we waited for my interview subject. And waited. And waited. The actress never did show up, and after an hour twiddling our thumbs we all had to pack up and leave. Even had she showed up at that point, we had passed our deadline to process the film in time for the evening newscast. So there I was, all dressed up with nowhere to go. Not an auspicious start to my on-air TV career.

A few months later, though, on-air personality Paul Soles was asked to join CBC TV in Toronto to host Take 30, a position he held for many years. He was a multi-talented announcer at CFPL-TV with gobs of both radio and TV experience behind him. I was asked to be his replacement on a Sunday evening show that had been on the station's TV schedule for years. It was a charade show called Act Fast. So far, so good.

This somewhat creaky little show featured a panel of four personalities, one of whom was my radio Program Director, Geoff Bingle. To act out the charades at the heart of the show, we generally had two panelists who were seasoned theatrical actors, and there was usually was a fourth guest panelist on a rotating basis. The premise was alright, but we had a problem. Each of the panelists was *at least* twenty years older than their new host at twenty-two and there was absolutely no chemistry between any us, or among them, for that matter.

Sometimes the show aired live, and occasionally we would record a couple of shows on a given Sunday, and do a third one live to air. We always had a studio audience for our shows, but it was generally about as active as a painting. The people all had that same what-am-I-doing-on-TV look. They were usually from some small rural community and depending how successfully the panel guessed the charades, they would receive a larger or smaller cash reward for whatever project for which they were raising funds. I never knew so many area churches needed roof repairs. It seemed that every week when I would ask the leader of the group what they were going to do with the money, it was almost always going to fix a leaky roof.

 The show was shot by two monster studio cameras, the first generation of black and white RCA TV units. They were mounted on bulky pedestals with a big round steering ring that would enable them to be pushed by the cameraman to different locations on-set during the show. Each camera was equipped with a four-lens turret which could be rotated from a wide-angle view to a close-up lens, though it had to be off-air to rack the turret to interchange to the proper lens. Today, with the advent of zoom lenses, one camera can perform all the way from wide shot to close-up with the push of a simple lever.

A four-lens RCA Studio TV camera with rotating "turret." When the camera was not live on-air, the cameraman could rotate the lens array for close-up, medium, or wide-angle shots.

Remembering my visit to see Steve Allen in New York years before, I would always warm up the audience just before we began with a line Steve had used before his show.

"OK, now everybody in your row of seats hold hands and form a chain. Good! Now, would the person at the end of each row please stick your finger into the electric socket beside your seat?"

Hey, if you're going to steal a line, why not grab one from the best!

Our show would open with Camera One at the back wall of the studio on a wide-angle lens, which would show me, the panelists, and the entire studio audience sitting at the other end of the studio. Camera Two would be pre-positioned across the studio from me for the opening of the show, and would shoot me on a medium close-up lens.

Let's drop in on a particularly memorable episode of Act Fast from those days long since gone by.

The Floor Director is counting down, three, two, one, and we're live on Camera One. At this point Camera two, assigned to shoot my introduction to the show, starts to belch smoke! A tube has blown on it just as we went on-air so we are suddenly a *single*-camera show, with the one remaining camera about thirty feet away from me, locked into a wide shot. The cameras and Director are connected on intercom, and the Director gives his instructions.

"Dolly in on Dick." That means move the camera closer to the star. Usually a good thing.

The cameraman, straining with all his might, starts to push the heavy camera towards me. Like a locomotive that is slow to pick up speed, this beast begins to roll, slightly at first, then ever more quickly. I'm guessing the combined weight of camera and pedestal would be around seven hundred pounds.

By now, the camera guy is struggling to simultaneously slow the rig down, and steer it towards me to keep me on camera. Alas, he is unsuccessful, and the juggernaut plows directly into my balsa-wood desk, smashing it to pieces and knocking me backwards off my host's chair onto the studio floor! Quite a show stopper, you'll have to admit. What the audience must have thought, I have no idea.

Another show I particularly remember began normally enough, but almost as soon as we started to record the program the Floor Director started giving me the speed-up sign, twirling his finger rapidly as he stood beside the camera pointing at me. I was a little puzzled because there was no apparent need to rush through anything, and we always chatted with the various panelists in an unhurried way as I handed them their cards containing the charades they were to act out.

But the Floor Director runs the actual mechanics of the show, so we went through the first set of charades as fast as I could prod the panel on, then quickly moved to the second set for each of the panelists. I was still getting constant speed-up signals so I kept clipping along through our chores.

As we were by now into the final segment, it was time for me to act out *my* charade to end that part of the show, then interview the guest from our studio audience, wrap things up and say goodnight to the viewers. My charade was usually good for a couple of minutes, then there was a minute to chat with the audience representative, about thirty seconds to say goodnight to the panel and a thirty second roll of the credits before we went to black. That was about four minutes for the entire wrap-up. During the final commercial break, I would leave my desk and walk to the interview area where the group spokesperson and I were to chat. I never spoke to this person in advance. I was afraid if I did, they'd be thinking about what they'd already said and their responses on-air would not be natural. When the time arrived I would invite them to stand up, and position them so my shadow wasn't falling on their face. After that it was generally clear sailing to the final credits.

As we reached the twenty-second countdown re-entry mark, the Floor Director, acting on orders from the Director in the control room, yelled his instructions.

`Twenty seconds, stand by!"

This was usually followed by a quick whispered countdown backwards from ten seconds, and a hand signal of so many fingers telling me how much time remained to fill to the end of the show. It can be very tricky to get the length of the fill just right, but the ability to do so is the mark of an experienced broadcaster.

This time, instead of the normal four minutes he held up *two* hands with *six* fingers extended upwards! I'm not much at math, but I could see I would have to stretch things out an extra two minutes from what I was used to. That may not seem like much of a difference but in broadcast terms it's an eternity. Just before we went live, I asked my woman guest a question.

"Are you the President of the group, or are you the leader?"

Her reply made me start to shake. It was immediately apparent she had a *major* speech impediment that would make managing our conversation very tricky. The camera guys were of no help whatsoever because I could hear them chuckling quietly into their intercom headset microphones at my unexpected dilemma.

I was stuck in the swamp, surrounded by alligators, with no readily apparent way out. I tried to ask questions that would require the briefest yes or no answers from the woman I was interviewing. But her halting responses threw my inner clock off and I ended up not filling time to the second, but trying desperately to ease her plight and minimize any embarrassment. To put it mildly, it was a wretched time for all involved.

Somehow, we finished the show, and as the audience filed out of the studio I rushed into the master control room where the Director was positioned.

"Why was I getting all those speed up signals from you and then you made me fill with that never-ending interview from hell?"

The Director, who had been thrown into his role with very little experience or background, explained that he didn't start the back-timer at the beginning of the show, so he had no idea how much time had elapsed as we went along. They had quickly stopped the tape at the last commercial break to calculate the remaining time, which led to my six minutes in Purgatory. We watched the playback in the control room and it was just as bad as I had feared. My terrified facial expression and flustered, distracted appearance on the video just added insult to injury as I re-lived the whole wretched experience again.

On the set of CFPL TV'S "Act Fast"

Track 85

To my immense relief, Bill Brady arrived back in town and was assigned to become the new host of the show, where he continued on for several years. To mix a couple of metaphors, my shoes weren't terribly hard to fill, and I felt like a large weight had been lifted from my shoulders.

There was another weight in the wings, however. *Now*, about three years after the folk-music craze had peaked and become yesterday's news (or music), it was decided that I would host a show called Hootenanny. Not that there was any particular audience for it by then, but on we went anyway.

The Director, Peter Nott, decided to stage the show outdoors. Those big studio cameras were pushed all the way to the other end of the sprawling building, where an outdoor stage set had been erected. It was a very simple show to do, with the cameras positioned about fifty feet from the stage and locked in position due to their bulk.

Doing TV outside invites a host of little problems. One day, after we had done the rehearsal sound-checks and sat the audience down on the grass in front of the stage, I had to go back into the studio to apply a little more hair-spray. There was quite a wind blowing, and my hair was a helpless, out-of-control victim. I already had to apply a lot of makeup, especially necessary in those days of black and white TV.

When I was appropriately re-lacquered and re-plastered, I headed back outside where the Floor Director was waiting with a question.

"Do you happen to have a condom in your wallet?"

"Even if I do, what kind of question is that? What does a *condom* have to do with anything we're doing?"

"Well, this wind is playing hell with the microphone you're wearing around your neck. It's picking up a lot of wind noise, and the rubber safe will act as a shield from the breeze!"

Most of the camera crew were young, single guys, and the required prophylactic device was quickly offered up to the TV gods. I went back to the makeup room, reapplied some *more* makeup, added another blast of hairspray, pulled the condom over the head of the microphone, and headed back to the outdoor set, where the wind was still doing its thing.

The show went along fine and as the show's final credits rolled I noticed my sister Elizabeth in the audience. She was attending the University of Western Ontario and had brought a couple friends along to watch the taping of her big brother's show. She wrapped me in a big hug, then stepped back to give me a quick once-over.

"Dick, you've got a ton of hairspray on!"

I explained to her the wind had been a problem.

"Ditto with the makeup," she said.

I explained to her how important makeup was to TV hosts, especially outdoors.

"I get that," she said, "but explain to me why you've got a condom around your neck!"

A dozen smart-aleck responses jumped to the end of my tongue, but none I would want to repeat to my very own baby sister!

At the end of the summer season, Hootenanny strummed and fumbled its way to a close, and none too soon for me.

Pickin' and grinnin' on the outdoor set of the folk music show "Hootenanny" from CFPL TV. Notice all the musicians have microphone wind screens, while the host doesn't. Complications ensued!

Track 86

Now Playing: Dance, Dance, Dance, by the Beachboys
*"I gotta dance dance dance dance now the beat's really hot
right on the spot*
Dance dance dance right there on the spot
The beat's really hot
Dance dance dance now the beat's really hot"
Carl Wilson, Brian Wilson, Mike Love© Universal Music
Publishing Group

About four years after I had submitted my proposal for a TV
Dance Party show, the powers that be at CFPL-TV decided it
was finally time to air one locally. Better late than never, I
suppose, but by the time Wingding! took to the London
airwaves Hullabaloo and Shindig had faded to black and
American Bandstand was just a shadow of its former self,
cut back from a show every weekday to a lone airing on
Saturday.

We went on the air with an in-studio, bona fide, on-air sock
hop, complete with Go-Go Dancers wearing the iconic knee-
high white patent-leather boots, which were, by then, way
out of fashion with the kids. But it was a fun show to do, and
the Director, John Lackie, showed off his chops by pre-
taping the kids dancing to the 45's during rehearsal, then
intercutting to them live when the show was on air. That
allowed him to do quick cuts between live and taped action,
effectively doubling our camera coverage during the show

from just two to four. That not only looked good, but added a visual momentum to the show.

One of our first guest bands was The Guess Who, with their featured vocalist Burton Cummings. They were a really hard-working band that had a gig as the house band on the weekly CBC-TV show called Let's Go. They had yet to break out with their first hit, These Eyes, but you could definitely hear something special in their music.

We did the usual rehearsal sound-check and the guys showed up wearing outsized hockey sweaters. When the rehearsal ended, I expected them to change into the kind of matching suits most bands in those days would wear for a TV appearance. Nothing doing! They were part of the new, casual look bands were starting to affect and they went on live wearing the same clothes as when they arrived.

They were definitely part of a trend, though. You don't see many musical acts wearing matching outfits these days, except for military bands and church choirs.

Wingding! was pretty much the only TV exposure available for local London teen bands, and it became a status symbol to have appeared on the show. We didn't have the equipment or expertise to put bands on the air live, so they would set up their equipment in our loading dock. Microphones were arranged to record a performance that would later be played back while the bands mimed their way through the live show. Milli Vanilli was far from the first act to fake its way through a performance!

Not only was it the first time playing on TV for almost every young band, it was also the first time many of them had actually heard a recording of themselves, as the soon-to-be-ubiquitous portable tape recorders were still in the future.

Wingding! was ground breaking in its own local way, but was doomed to failure. Not only was the concept out of date, but the TV studios were located far away from any bus routes, making it very difficult for our young audience of dancers to make it to the tapings.

Promotional Support for CFPL TV's "Wingding" Dance Party"

Track 87

There is something both compelling and unsettling about seeing someone walking down the street talking to himself. In London, as in many cities, downtown shopping began to decline as a result of the proliferation of suburban shopping mall complexes. Someone in the sales department of CFPL-TV decided to do an on-location shoot in the heart of the city to promote shopping downtown in the core. I was asked to do the on-camera work for this promotional commercial but what seemed like a good idea on paper took more than a few takes to complete.

First, they had to set up a jib crane, a counterbalanced long boom pole with a compact TV camera at the end. This camera was raised to about fifteen feet above the street, and located about half a block away from where I would appear on-screen. The idea was that I would walk towards the camera from a distance in one long, uninterrupted shot, gesturing and talking to it as I got closer and closer. I was wired with a tiny in-ear headset, and a wireless, cordless microphone pinned to my suit jacket.

Between where I started to walk and where the camera was stationed was an intersection I had to cross while continuing to talk and look at the camera. I wasn't able to use a TelePrompTer to read the script, so I'd had to memorize it. Walk, talk, pace myself, keep from tripping on the sidewalk and avoid getting run over in the crosswalk. For a guy who has difficulty walking and chewing gum at the same time, that was quite a tall order and I was pretty sure we were in for a long afternoon. But as things turned out, I wasn't the main problem.

What caused endless re-takes was the traffic, on the road and on the sidewalk. While you're looking upwards into a camera in the distance, trying to make sure you're communicating effectively to the eventual audience, you still have to dodge oncoming pedestrians, many of whom aren't particularly looking where they're going. At least getting bumped into by a wayward pedestrian wasn't life-threatening (unless he'd happened to see Hootenanny).

Not so with the vehicles driving through the intersection I had to cross. Some of the drivers took notice of the strange man in the suit talking to himself and gave me a wide berth. But others cut right in front of me to swing around the corner as I was trying to cross the street. I also had to note the changing of the traffic signals and try to time myself to allow a steady walk towards the camera, with no pauses for red lights.

More troublesome to me were the buses. They were tall enough that if I was too close to the intersection when they arrived, they would obscure my line of sight to the camera. Stop and start over. If I timed it wrong I would end up jumping out of their way as they pulled into the intersection. Stop and start over. More than once, as I made it across the road without being picked off by municipal transit's finest, a clueless pedestrian would stumble off the curb and either bump into me or make me side-step them to avoid a collision. Stop and start over. Did I mention I was wearing heavy TV makeup? So I also had to maintain my concentration as people would stop and stare at this weirdo in a suit with his face covered in pancake makeup, staring into the distance while he walked down the street talking to himself. That wasn't the kind of natural pedestrian action we were looking for, that's for sure. We probably tried thirty times before everything worked in one continuous take, without me either flubbing my lines or being almost crushed by a passing bus. Doncha just love show business!

Track 88

Announcer: *"Return with us now to those thrilling days of yesteryear!"* The Lone Ranger Radio Drama on WXYZ, Detroit

After writing commercial scripts for CFPL-AM for several months, I left the business full time for about a year. I was determined to keep my hand in radio, but until appropriate opportunities presented themselves I needed to earn a living. I formed a Company called Total Image Productions, or TIP, to produce radio jingles and radio station contests. I offered a turnkey package to subscribers, with a monthly contest, scripts, and all the production aids necessary to air an exciting new, attention-getting contest every month. All the related introductions and supporting materials were voiced and produced by me, and customized with the subscribing station's call letters and slogans.

I also had some luck in selling several large Canadian companies custom-produced jingles for use across the country. Musical jingles are proven sales boosters and the right one can help make or break a company or product. TM Productions was (and is) a large company in Dallas, providing music products to stations across North America. The beauty of using this firm was that they had a library vault filled with jingle background music that they had already written, scored and produced for companies such as Lone Star Beer in Texas. The brewery would have paid for the initial recording of the backing tracks, and for lyrics and musical scoring, plus the studio rentals necessary to lay down the instrumental beds. Then TM would assemble their crew of singers, play back the master tape, and add voices and lyrics to the multi-track recordings.

TM sold the rights to the finished product, but not to the music alone. That meant that once they finished and sold a specific jingle, the music tracks were still available. Smaller customers could pay a much-reduced price to TM, and have the jingles *re-sung*, using the existing musical backgrounds. Since the production company had already been paid for creating the instrumental tracks, anything they made with a re-sing was gravy for them. They simply had to call in some singers, pop them into the studio with the new lyrics I had written for my client, and voila, a completely new jingle was created in a "pre-fab" flash.

Steps were taken to ensure there was no duplication of backgrounds in the same market, but beyond that the opportunities were endless.

I then joined a company called Shannon Services, a full-service sales promotion agency that also offered in-house print production, screen printing, photography, art design and writing. As their Sales Promotion Manager, I learned a whole new facet of the advertising industry. After I arrived, Shannon Services added Audio-Visual production to their capacity, and produced some very exciting presentations for large companies in the Toronto market.

One of the first places I called on to drum up new business was CFPL Radio. Like most salesmen know, the first prospects you approach are friends and family, a sales concept as old as the hills. Knowing that CFPL was about to celebrate fifty years as a broadcasting icon in the London market, I saw an opportunity for a company like Shannon Services to act as a full-service agency for the ongoing event, handling all the print, promotion and billboard advertising on their behalf. If I could convince them to give TIP the job of handling their 50th Anniversary contests as well, I'd have a real one-two winner.

I soon found myself sitting across from Bud Knight, the man who had pulled me off the air and demoted me a few months before. I was glad now that I hadn't made much of a scene or a fuss at the time, because we were able to talk in a very friendly manner. I think there is probably no one easier to sell to than a salesman when you have a product of obvious value, and once I had laid out my plans, Bud quickly agreed to my proposal to step in for an annual contract. Then he made my prospects even sweeter.

"You know," he said, "with a bit of water under the bridge now, we've got some weekend radio shows to fill. How would you like to do them?"

Salesman to salesman. No one's immune to the right kind of bait, and so began a new chapter in my life!

Track 89

"I tell you, I'm never going to stop. I'm not interested in rusting away." Dick Biondi, still on the air at WMJK Chicago, playing rock 'n' roll.

CFPL Radio, London Ontario (Again!) 1973 Playlist:
"Bad, Bad Leroy Brown" Jim Croce
"Killing Me Softly With His Song" Roberta Flack
"My Love" Paul McCartney and Wings
"Crocodile Rock" Elton John
"You're So Vain" Carly Simon
"Touch Me in the Morning" Diana Ross
"The Night the Lights Went Out In Georgia" Vicki Lawrence
"Playground in My Mind" Clint Holmes

Now Playing: W.O.L.D., by Harry Chapin
"Hello honey, it's me
What did you think when you heard me back on the radio?
What did the kids say when they knew
It was their long lost daddy-o?
Remember how we listened to the radio
And I said "That's the place to be"
W.O.L.D. (I Am the Morning DJ) Harry F. Chapin © Story Songs Ltd.

I now found myself in the best of both my professional worlds. I was back behind the microphone at CFPL-AM, I had a solid deal to create all kinds of new on-air goings on, for the anniversary and other things, and I still had a lucrative full-time job in the sales promotion business. What did it matter if I was busy every day of the week, juggling all kinds of balls to keep them all in the air? I was working every day, then coming to the station at night to create and produce CFPL's 50th Anniversary promotions and contests. It sure made for a whirlwind life, but it also took a heavy toll on my marriage.

By this point in the evolution of radio, operators were pretty much a thing of the past. Since the advent of tape cartridges, all the commercials could easily be aired by a single guy, following a tight format. The same schedule precluded DJs playing the songs of their choice. The Music Director was fully in control now, creating playlists from which a DJ varied only at extreme peril. This led to stations sounding far more homogenous than they had in prior years, with the on-air staff working more as a team with a theme than a collection of individuals (which is generally a good thing, by the way.) In the new scheme of things, there was less individualism but more of an overall station 'feel'.

One of my first challenges was to let our listeners know that CFPL-AM was going to be celebrating a big event in its life. That had to be followed up by promotions designed to lure new listeners by using *external* media. To get things rolling, I contacted TM in Dallas and had them score and produce a phrase we incorporated into all their promotions: *We've Only Just Begun.* Similar to Al Jolson's "You ain't heard nothing yet," this one line from the Carpenters summed up the promise of things to come. (Just as an interesting footnote, We've Only Just Begun was originally produced as a singing jingle for a bank commercial and became a hit in a song-length version, reversing the newer trend of hit songs becoming backgrounds for commercials.)

To promote the fact that CFPL was a full-service radio station, offering lots of things beyond music, the on-air positioning statement we used was "CFPL Says It All." That was a succinct way of summing up that if listeners wanted news, sports, commentary, the farm report, the latest weather and the Open Line call-in program to air their comments, we had them covered with the spoken word as well as the hit music they knew they could rely upon.

Supporting these on-air efforts, Shannon Services provided artwork and design for billboards across the city, re-enforcing the slogans. We also offered free car window decals with the same artwork. By displaying the decal, you could be chosen a winner if you were spotted with the CFPL 50th Anniversary sticker in your car's rear window. It may seem like a small thing, but in a community like London in those days, radio rivalries could be fierce, and a surprising number of loyal listeners were happy to display their allegiance on their vehicles. Great advertising – and pretty much free, too!

Shannon Services also produced a month-long Cash Calendar insert for the London Free Press that was distributed all over town. By listening each day and filling in spaces in the print piece, daily, weekly and monthly prizes could be won. All these promotions were put into place to entice new listeners to the station.

Sometimes, the contests worked *too* well! One of them was called Look in the Book and every hour the DJ would announce a specific page from the London telephone directory. The first person on that page to call in when we announced each hour's telephone-book page would win a small cash prize of $9.80 that marked the station's position on the dial. But the jocks were also given a sealed envelope for each hour of a program. Inside the envelope was the name and phone number of one person on the designated page. If that person happened to call, he or she would win $980.00! That sounded pretty exciting but the odds against it were pretty big. Who could have guessed that on one Sunday shift we had not one, but *two* winners of the big prize! That was close to two thousand dollars of the annual promotion budget out the door in just one day. But you can be sure people all over town were talking about the big winners on CFPL Radio.

Behind the controls of the CFPL Radio Master Control Board, when the station had by and large dispensed with operators, due to the introduction of DJ-friendly tape cartridges, which simplified day-to-day operations.

For a really visible promotional tool the station arranged for the rental of a Bell helicopter and dubbed it the C-F-P-Licopter. We used it for both traffic spotting through the week during morning and afternoon drive times, but on weekends we got to do beach reports from nearby resorts Port Stanley and Grand Bend. We had lots of fun flying in the chopper. We would orbit over the town and at a specific time do a quick beach report, then fly to the other location. While we were orbiting over Grand Bend one day, waiting for our time to go live with our report, I convinced the pilot to do a low-level run up The Cut, where the Ausable River flows into Lake Huron. We were just above mast height to avoid sailboats that might be moored in the river when something unusual on the ground caught my eye. Over the intercom, I yelled to the pilot to hover and crank in some left rudder. As the machine rotated, we both saw a young couple in the grassy dunes below us, naked as jaybirds.

I asked the pilot to dip the nose forward and I grabbed a small P.A. microphone attached to a speaker under our glass bubble dome. With the downdraft of our rotors beating the grass down with a vengeance, the amorous couple were completely exposed! I couldn't resist the temptation to make the young lovers' adventure even more memorable by offering a comment.

"Have a happy day from your friends at CFPL," I shouted, and away we flew.

Another summer promotion we ran at Grand Bend invited listeners to spell out our call letters on the beautiful sandy beaches. We arranged for a spotter on the ground to contact the lucky winner, and the prize was a ride the next weekend in the helicopter. When we landed at the Grand Bend International Airport and Shoe Repair the next week to pick up our winner for the promised ride, it turned out to be a ten-year-old boy.

I hopped out, the youngster hopped in, and the helicopter headed up and out for a quick flight around the area. When it returned a few minutes later, the passenger looked a little green around the gills, and quickly scampered out of the machine and under the spinning blades. As I was strapping myself in, I asked him if he had enjoyed his flight. Before he could answer, the pilot spoke up.

"Well when we got out over the lake, the leading edge of the rotors got hit by a gust of wind and we bounced around pretty good. I guess it gave the boy quite a scare."

As he was relating this to me, he increased power to the blades for lift-off and the machine began to shake, tossing us around inside the cockpit while we were still on the ground. He quickly cut the power and shut the motor down.

"That gust must have knocked the blades out of position," he said. "Just hang on a second." He grabbed a hammer from his tool kit, and gave a resounding whack to each of the big blades in turn. Apparently satisfied, he climbed back into the cockpit.

"That likely knocked them back into the proper place. I'd guess we're pretty much good to go!"

"Likely" and "guess" are not the kind of words to give comfort to someone who has just seen a very complicated flying machine fine-tuned with a hammer. Not exactly a confidence-builder, co-pilot-wise. But away we flew, problem-free, so I guess that's how it's done.

I have mentioned the legendary Stork Club in Port Stanley
and I was lucky enough to be part of the last radio broadcast
from their thirteen-thousand-square-foot ballroom. Although
the room was nowhere nearly as packed as it had been
during the Big Band years, when people thronged to see the
hottest groups of the era, we still had a respectable crowd on
hand for the broadcast as Lionel Thorton, a former CFPL
Radio salesman, raised his baton to the Casa Royal Orchestra
facing him.

At exactly the top of the hour, I cued Lionel, and the band hit
the down beat, then faded behind me as I did my best Old
Time Studio Announcer introduction.

*"Now, from the world-famous Stork Club in Port Stanley,
overlooking the shimmering waves of beautiful Lake Erie,
CFPL Radio is proud to present Lionel Thorton and the
Casa Royal Orchestra. Join us as their lovely vocalist
approaches the microphone to kick off our broadcast, with a
song made popular by Frank Sinatra! Here's the classic All
The Way!"*

What an incredibly nostalgic broadcast that was, and I was
proud to have been a part of what quickly became history. It
was a real shame not long after that balmy summer evening
when the Stork Club was heavily damaged by a fire that
began in a nearby dumpster. The damage was too expensive
to repair, and what had been Port Stanley's major tourist

draw for many years was eventually demolished. It was replaced by a beachside housing area where the dancehall once proudly stood.

Track 92

Now Playing: You Turn Me On I'm A Radio, by Joni
Mitchell
"You're driving into town
With a dark cloud above you
Dial in the number
Who's bound to love you?
Oh honey you turn me on
I'm a radio"
© Joni Mitchell/Crazy Crow Music/Siquomb Music,
Sony/ATV Music Publishing LLC

Joe Duchesne was the morning man at CJBK Radio, a new
station that was rapidly making inroads in the market, and he
was the driving force behind their presence and their
audience penetration. As a morning man, he was really the
Guy Next Door, with a smooth voice, lots of natural wit, and
superb skills when he interacted with listeners on the studio
telephone line. His timing was impeccable, and it was clear
he loved what he did.

He called me one day at Shannon Services and asked if I
would like to come into his studio and do his show with him.
Just sit and talk about the good old days of my early time in
radio. Hey, why not! I grabbed a few of my trusty old drop-
ins and musical jingles, including the Clap Hands and Shout
for Joy jingle that lost me that great job opportunity at
CKLW, and I joined him behind the microphones in the pre-
dawn darkness. Joe was the perfect host, and let me supply

most of the punch lines, even though he could just as easily have one-upped me every time. He really put me at ease, and we passed the three hours interacting with each other as if we had worked together for years. Joe had a laugh that was so genuine and delightful that it was little surprise he was such a popular new force in the London radio market.

I also got to talk on-air with some of my former listeners from more than a decade earlier, and of course these calls were recorded and then aired as Joe sailed effortlessly through his program. I really felt relaxed, and very much at home in these bright, modern surroundings. Too soon the show was over, but the hook had been firmly set again and I realized I had to get back into a full-time radio career somehow, even if it meant moving or taking a pay cut.

Track 93

"The times, the people, the music, the station all came together to create something bigger than the sum of its parts." Bruce Morrow, "Cousin Brucie" on 77 WABC New York

CJBK London, 1978 Playlist:
"Shadow Dancing" Andy Gibb
"Night Fever" Bee Gees
"You Light up My Life" Debbie Boone
"Stayin' Alive" Bee Gees
"Kiss You All Over" Exile
"How Deep Is Your Love" Bee Gees
"Baby Come Back" Player
"(Love Is) Thicker Than Water" Andy Gibb
"Boogie Oogie Oogie" A Taste of Honey
"Three Times a Lady" Commodores
"Grease" Frankie Valli

Now Playing: On the Radio, by Donna Summer
"But they said it really loud
They said it on the air
On the radio
Whoa, oh, oh, oh
On the radio"
Michael Omartian, Donna Summer © Universal Music Corporation

As things turned out, I didn't have long to wait. I got a call from Rick Richardson, the owner and General Manager of CJBK. We arranged for a lunch meeting, which stretched into late afternoon and involved martinis. Several martinis. Rick was never one to beat around the bush, and shortly after the first round of silver bullets hit the table, he asked me to come to work for him, doing the afternoon drive show. We wrote some facts and figures on cocktail napkins, and I liked the deal he was offering. He even threw in an extremely generous signing bonus to seal the deal, large enough to put a down payment on a condo townhouse for the newly-divorced guy he had just hired. We shook hands on the deal, man to man.

Very elated with the agreement, I called Joe Duchesne at home to share the good news with him. He was happy for me, but cautionary, too.

"Dick, you've given up a pretty secure career in sales to come back to radio, which you know as well as anybody is notorious for here-today, gone-tomorrow jobs. But I wish you well, buddy. Welcome back to the monkey house."

Rick couriered a written contract to me the next day and after a quick once-over I resigned my position, then sent Rick's contract to my lawyer just to have him look over the fine print. I suppose I might have reversed that order just to be safe, but Rick's word was good enough for me.

Several days later I sat in on the evening show to get familiar with the new equipment and controls I would be working with, all of which was state of the art. There were no turntables in the studio at all. Everything was on carts. Just off to my left were six individual cartridge machines. Each tape cartridge contained either a song, jingle, commercial, News 'sounder' or whatever other element might be needed. Each time you triggered your next cart, a clock in front of you reset to zero seconds and began to count upwards; one, two, three, etc. At the end of each jingle or commercial, a light above your head flashed on to alert you that the cart was finished.

With the music carts, thirty seconds before the song was about to end a bright light flashed over your head, then at ten seconds the light turned on steadily to notify you in no uncertain terms that your music was running out!

With all these warning lights, you could load up your next inserts into the five machines that were not playing anything. Once you went into a commercial break, you could record calls from listeners while the spots were playing, and just punch in the next cartridge as each commercial ended, flowing from one to the other in sequence. It's actually harder to describe the process than it was to execute it on air. All of the songs and spots were recorded and compressed to the same output level, so the volume controls on the control board stayed open and untouched. Everything had been made as idiot-proof as possible. Of course, as a wise old codger once told me, the odds of succeeding at that are slim and none.

"You can't make *anything* idiot-proof because idiots are so ingenious."

He must have worked in radio.

Everything about this station was top-flight. The engineering staff, headed by a mild-mannered gentleman named Jeff Guy, had everything so finely tuned that whether they realized it or not, the listeners heard a beautifully-processed signal with a ton of punch and presence. The studio itself was very ergonomically designed with everything in place for ease of operation. This attention to detail allowed the on-air guys to concentrate on their presentation, rather than having to worry about any technical glitches. One whole wall of the studio was filled with hundreds of music carts, while all of the commercials were stored right behind the DJ in a spinning rack, so the on-air jock could grab his spots easily, then put them back without even leaving his chair.

Taking it easy for a moment between on-air activities.

Cliff Jackson in the CJBK Control Room. The entire studio wall behind him stored hundreds of hits from the tightly-controlled playlists. To his left, the 6 cartridge machines which played back jingles, music and commercials. In the foreground, "carts" that had been played.

Track 94

Now Playing: Pilot of the Airwaves, by Charlie Dore
"Pilot of the airwaves
"Here is my request
You don't have to play it
But I hope you'll do your best
I've been listening to your show on the radio
And you seem like a friend to me"
Charlie Dore, © Warner/Chappell Music, Inc.

With one flick of a switch, the on-air personality could instantly start a tape machine in record mode, which also muted the on-air monitors so any incoming call to the station's Listener Line could be captured with the complete two sides of the conversation between DJ and the listener automatically balanced at the same volume. A very important consideration. That's where the lighting displays mentioned above came into play. When the warning lights flashed, the jock would know he had to wrap up his phone call and get back on the air without delay. The call, now captured on tape, could be edited and quickly spliced together to delete any unnecessary chatter. It was also a way to improve the quality of the final call.

I remember a caller asking me a personal question while I was busy getting ready for something, and I didn't have an instant snappy comeback. Caught off guard, I asked the caller to hold on for a minute while I loaded up my next commercials. I rammed my spots into the machines, then

300

suddenly the answer came to me. I think we've all had that I-should-have-said-this moment after the fact, but I could do something about it. With the tape continuing to record, I replied to the question. Then I did a quick set of cuts and splices to the tape and I was ready with an edited version of the conversation with no long pause in the middle. It turned out to be one of my better bits, I think.

Listener: *"How much does the average DJ make?"*

Me: *"I don't know. You'll have to ask an average DJ!"*

That's also how stations handle so-called instant requests. Did you ever wonder how it can be that a listener can ask for a song on the air, and within a second it is playing while the DJ and his listener are still talking on the phone? It's simple as can be. The entire call is recorded, then played back. The DJ knows that the call runs, say twenty seconds, and that the introduction music before the vocalist sings the vocal line is fifteen seconds. He hits the playback tape, the Hot Clock starts to count upwards, and when it hits five seconds, he hits the cartridge with the requested song. It's just math. The call ends, the vocal begins. But to the listener it's magic! In today's world, with digital technology, and drag and drop audiofiles, it is even easier.

Here's a brief clip of mornings on-air flying solo:

AUDIO/VIDEO: CJBK 1980

After my first evening learning the controls and basic format of the station, I was officially back on the air! No question I was a bit rocky, and I made several mistakes during the shift. but nothing earth-shatteringly out of line. At 6 pm when my shift ended, though, the Bat-Phone in the studio lit up. That's the private unpublished studio telephone line. When it rings, it's usually not good news. I picked it up and it wasn't Commissioner Gordon.

"Rick. My office. Now!"

Prior to his involvement with radio, Rick had been a sailor and had served on the Royal Yacht. He could swear like a salty dog when he was annoyed, and he was plenty annoyed now. I walked into his office and he was standing behind his desk, obviously very irritated. He threw a thick sheaf of paper towards me, along with some choice epithets. A quick look revealed the former were legal documents and the latter were the result of the former.

It didn't take more than reading the first paragraph to realize that my lawyer had modified almost everything Rick and I had settled on in our Martini Meeting a few days earlier. He had inserted a higher salary number than we had agreed on, more vacation time, more this and more that. To make matters worse, he had done it and mailed the contract directly to my new boss without even telling me.

I was almost as upset as Rick, and for the same reasons. He had offered a fair deal and I had accepted. And now some pencil-pushing Perry Mason wannabe had spoiled the whole thing. If Rick blamed me and thought I was trying to manipulate him, my return to radio would be over after one shift. But at this point there didn't seem to be a lot I could do about it and I felt like the cartoon coyote who is sitting on a branch while busily sawing it out from under him.

But this was not the first time a lawyer had annoyed my new boss, and to my great fortune he accepted my assurances that I didn't know anything about any changes and was more than happy with the original agreement. We stroked out the offending clauses, corrected the figures, made sure there was nothing in the document we hadn't agreed on earlier, and finally signed the amended version. We may possibly have had a few more martinis.

Remote broadcasts for CJBK

Track 96

Even with the contract out of the way, I was still the new kid on the block, and had a few more kinks to work out to get myself locked into the format. Remember my mentioning earlier that I got to play Gordon Lightfoot lots more over the years? One afternoon, without even thinking, I rammed in the cart of his Wreck of the Edmund Fitzgerald. A monster song for Gordon, but a l-o-n-g one! Even the edited version for radio stations was almost six minutes. As luck would have it, the song started at about 4:57, and I had to fade out of the song at 5 pm for our drive-time newscast. At which point the ship hadn't even started to break up, musically speaking. By the time I realized my mistake it was too late to do anything but fade the record and intro the news.

*"You know, I always get that **sinking** feeling when I play that song, but we know how it turned out, right? News is next on CJBK!"*

Our playlist was referred to as being tight, with a limited song list. Generally speaking, we rotated through our current top songs in around three hours. To slow the rotation down a little, past hits would be inserted during the mid-day hours, although they were never called oldies. When the Bee Gees became incredibly popular during the Saturday Night Fever craze, it seemed some days that about every third song would be one of theirs.

We did a lot of wild promotions for the station. One of the more interesting ones was the Annual CJBK Bikini Contest. The perfect promotion for the summer, right? But CJBK had a better idea. We did ours in the dead of winter, when bikinis were generally just a memory of summers gone by. We encouraged our young female listeners to come to the studios dressed in their best bikini beach wear, and model it for an appreciative audience of DJs. Of which, I probably don't have to note, there was always an ample supply for this promotion. (Wonder why.)

CJBK·129
RADIO LONDON

SEPTEMBER 21, 1978

DICK WILLIAMS
PLAYS LONDON'S BEST MUSIC
10 - 2 p.m. on **CJBK · 129**

Track 97

One afternoon CJBK's studio door banged open and our evening jock strode in, fully duded in the latest disco garb, the big wide-brimmed hat, three-piece vested suit, gleaming shoes and a shawl thrown fashionably across his shoulder. He was one cooool cat. He tossed a small plastic baggie on the console.

"Try that, my man!"

Inside the package were a couple of home-rolled joints. Marijuana, ganja, reefer, weed, whatever you called it there was plenty around, even though in those days possession was still a serious offence. I quickly tucked the baggie into my pocket and did the rest of my show in mild anticipation of a pleasant high afterwards. But before any fun and games, after the program I was scheduled to take our station vehicle out on the streets and hand out prizes to listeners displaying a bright yellow and red CJBK sticker on their rear bumper. Every day a different DJ would be out looking for winners, and we had station envelopes containing cash prizes ranging from twenty dollars to as high as one hundred dollars.

When on patrol, the idea was to pull over the lucky winner by flashing our vehicle's lights. Once they had stopped, we would approach with tape recorder in hand to interview our latest lucky listener. These tapes would then be edited and played back on-air, often quite a few times. We had accumulated a big library of these tapes and had a Bumper

Sticker Winner cart that was played every hour, making it sound as though we were constantly giving away money!

This particular day I picked up my clipboard to record the winner's name and address, put the envelope with the cash prize inside my pants pocket, and rolled out of the station parking lot. A few minutes later I looked over at the car to my right. There was a big guy behind the wheel, and in the rear side window hung a freshly-pressed police uniform shirt. I figured he was probably on his way to the Cop Shop to check in for his evening shift. Pushed by a sudden gust of inspiration, I signalled with great care and slid back into the lane behind him before flashing my lights to get his attention. He obviously recognized our canary-coloured van with the flashing light on top, as he pulled around the corner onto a side street and parked at the curb. I climbed out of the van, chuckled at the cleverness of my little idea, clicked on my recorder and strode up to his car as I spoke into the microphone.

"I've been pulled over by the police before, but today the tables are turned and *I'm pulling over a policeman!* Hi there, sir, I'm Dick Williams from CJBK and can I ask you to get out of your car?"

He smiled and unfolded himself from his vehicle. Remember I said he was a big guy? Add intimidating to the description. We were now standing face to face, with only the microphone between us.

"I notice you're displaying a CJBK bumper sticker and guess what I have for you?"

At that point, I reached into my pocket and pulled out the envelope….*and* the baggie! It fluttered to the ground and I realized I had just made a huge mistake! Say, why don't I pull over a cop while I'm holding. What can possibly go wrong? Not your brightest move ever, Dick. They say God looks out for fools, drunkards and idiots. In this case I had two out of three, and Divine intercession looked to be the only hope I had to escape being hauled off to jail.

The cop looked at me. I looked back, with a gulp. He looked down at the baggie, then back up at me. I was still gulping. He looked down again but I was afraid to acknowledge the illegal substance at my feet by following his gaze. So when he brought his eyes back up again, mine were right where I'd left them. Have you ever been given the hard eye by a cop? Let me tell you, it can be pretty frightening. Especially when you've been caught in the act. I was one hundred per cent sure young Richard was heading off to the hoosegow, the victim of his own twisted sense of humor.

Luckily for me, the cop had a sense of humor, too. His glare turned into a smile as he nodded towards the baggie on the ground and the envelope in my hand.

"Which one do you want me to take?" he asked with a grin.

I stuffed the envelope into his big mitt and as he drove away thanked whatever special angel watches over dumb-assed DJs. I picked the baggie up off the ground and drove off myself. But in a different direction, thank the Lord.

Track 98

CJBK bikini contests were held in the winter months but our softball games were strictly a summertime thing. We would accept challenges from groups across the city and play at least one game a week at local diamonds throughout the summer. It was a fun way to meet our listeners, and we never had any trouble recruiting enough players. We deliberately didn't take the games seriously, and were always looking for ways to inject a little humor into the events.

One gag was to let the other team get ahead by a few runs, then on a pre-arranged signal, when our team got a base hit with a man in scoring position, *our entire team* would run beside him and across home plate. This netted us multiple runs on one hit, or so we would claim because the opposing team couldn't tag all of our runners.

Another one has likely been around since Abner Doubleday played the game. We would prepare a baseball-sized grapefruit with a coat of white paint and at the right moment our so-called coach would walk out to the mound, along with the catcher, to have a word with the pitcher. The catcher would trade his grapefruit for the real ball, leaving our secret weapon in the pitcher's glove. A quick windup and the pitcher would then lob it across the plate. He made sure it was such a hittable pitch that few people missed it. When the player at bat hit the grapefruit it would explode in a great shower of pulp and juice. Hilarity would ensue.

There was one evening though, when the joke was on me. I had laid down a bunt and was racing towards first base, looking back over my shoulder to home plate to see if I could beat the ball to first. As any little-league coach will tell you, watch where you're going. I didn't, and for my trouble ran directly into a pie-plate filled with whipped cream, wielded by the first baseman! I saw the amusement factor in it, but more than the memory lingered on. I wasn't wearing a ball cap and the heat of the day turned the whipped cream in my hair and on my clothes rancid and sour. There was no question I was not the most popular person to sit next to in a nearby pub, where both teams later celebrated our on-field adventures.

CJBK·129
RADIO LONDON
APRIL 14, 1978

DICK WILLIAMS
WITH A CHEER FROM DALLAS
ON CJBK-129

Pictured with two of the Dallas Cowboy Cheerleaders

Track 99

After the first ratings period of my new show, and a visit from the consultant, it looked like I would be a better fit for the mid-day slot in the station's line up. I didn't have the rich, powerful male voice of most afternoon drive DJs, and at the age of thirty-six or so I was too old to attract the teen-age after-school listeners. There was only one Dick Clark, after all. After some consideration, I accepted the move, not that I had that many options anyway.

Consultants were visiting us on a twice-a-year basis, listening to each of the jocks and passing on their thoughts and insights to not only Rick, but also to his Sales Manager and the Program Director. As far as the DJs were concerned, we could generally figure out when the consultants were in town, holed up in a downtown hotel room to monitor all of us, so we all tried extra hard to do our best on-air work.

However there was always another factor that we knew would come out of their visits.

If you are hired to critique a radio station (or any other business for that matter), the assumption going in is that the money will show some results, ie: your advice will improve things, especially the bottom line.

"Your guys are great! Don't change a thing!" just isn't on the table.

There has to be something that could be better, and in my experience almost every consultant zeroed in on pretty much the same thing; how much time did the DJs spend talking? So, if on his last visit the consultant's report indicated we were talking too much, the jocks would keep their chatter brief when they thought they were being monitored. Almost without fail, the report this time would knock the jocks on the same issue, but in reverse.

"Your DJs aren't doing anything except time and temperature. You need to tell them to talk it up more and show more personality." Duh. That's exactly what he didn't like the last time. This cycle would repeat itself over and over because it perpetuated the myth that consultants were indispensable, and they could always answer criticisms that we were just doing what they had recommended by simply saying we weren't doing it right.

Generally speaking, the better the management at the station, the less real use the consultants were. But to their credit, most senior managers would stop well short of unconditional support for a consultant's recommendations, adopting the parts they thought would be useful, while leaving the rest aside.

Track 100

Announcer: *"Dick hangs out with the Hell's Angels and goes to prison! Plus some high-flying action! Our story continues, after these words!"*

CJBK·129
RADIO LONDON

MAY 17, 1979

DICK WILLIAMS
10 a.m. - 2 p.m.

JIM CONNELL
2 p.m. - 6 p.m.

JOE DUSHANE
6 a.m. - 10 a.m.

CJBK'S ALL - STAR
TEAM

Being at CJBK offered me another opportunity to broaden my broadcasting profile. I was able to try my hand as an interviewer for our award-winning talk program on Sunday mornings, Dialogue. Bob Smith was the program's Producer and he allowed me the opportunity to hone my skills. This kind of program was something I hadn't tried before, and I was able to interview doctors, lawyers and Indian chiefs, authors and politicians, saints and scoundrels. If three men in a tub had come dub a dub dubbing on by, I would have interviewed them, too. There is something very satisfying about doing a good interview, one that engages both the host and the guest while it entertains and informs the audience.

On a trip to San Francisco with my eight-year-old son DJ, I dropped a tape recorder and some cassettes in my travel bags. Before we drove down to San Diego to see my old buddy Mel Hall, DJ and I took the recorder to Alcatraz, the island prison that sits in the middle of San Francisco Bay. I was able to interview some guides from the National Park Service who were on duty there, and got a private tour that included some areas that are not generally seen by the public.

In San Diego, DJ and I stayed in Mission Beach, close to the area where I had spent much of my time while I was at KDEO. Out looking for dinner one night, we watched in surprise as the door to a restaurant was slammed open and a very annoyed group of Hell's Angels poured onto the sidewalk. I guess the tape recorder made me feel like a genuine intrepid reporter, because I stepped up and asked them what was going on.

"Dude didn't want to serve us, told us we would upset the people eating there. What a load of …."

In for a penny, in for a pound. I found myself asking another question.

"I'm a radio reporter and I'm wondering if you would mind if we talked a bit about the Hell's Angels."

"There's a bar just up the street. If you want to, come on along."

I'm sure it wasn't the first time these guys had been refused service, as the Hell's Angels have a well-deserved reputation that is more than scary. But once inside the biker bar the guy I had talked to turned out to be a very articulate college graduate, and the interview unfolded smoothly. He gave me a very good insight into life inside their motorcycle club and their circle of friends, and I got a look at our society from a whole new perspective. It was fascinating, and made for a very good interview, but even after talking with my new 'friend' for a while I would still be upset if a crowd of them came into a restaurant where I was eating.

Another memorable interview involved Canada's famed Snowbirds, officially known as the Canadian Forces 431 Air Demonstration Squadron. These highly-trained aerobatic pilots were professional to the core and I managed to ride with them twice, marvelling at their skill each time. Since my brother John had trained a few of them to fly, he was able to pull some strings and get me a ride alongside a pilot who would give me the full treatment. The normal press tour flights are exciting on their own, though limited to non-aerobatic flying, just a bit of speed and some shallow turns and banks. But shortly after takeoff, my pilot broke away from the group and we did some fully- aerobatic flying on our own before rejoining the rest of the team to land together as a group.

For a fully aerobatic in-cockpit look at the Snowbird's precision flying, I highly recommend spending a half-hour watching the link below. Not for the faint of heart but a real thrill ride! Notice how tightly the group is spaced as they fly through some turbulent summer conditions. Come right back, though, because there's lots more excitement ahead!

AUDIO/VIDEO: Canadian Forces Snowbirds Aerobatic Formation Flying

As much fun as it was to be on our own, rolling and tumbling through the skies, it was also quite a thrill to be a part of the formation, flying at speeds of four hundred miles per hour and no further apart than six feet, wingtip to wingtip!

I also had a chance to interview stunt pilot legend Art Scholl. I hitched a ride with him, and conducted the interview later. It was quite a flight even though there were three of us in his tiny, two-person Super Chipmunk aircraft. I sat in the front seat, Art behind me in the pilot's seat. Art's dog Aileron, a tiny terrier, sat on a shelf Art had installed for him just over his left shoulder. I enjoyed our ride immensely and Art performed only positive-G manoeuvers that would push us *into* our seats, so Aileron didn't have to be strapped in. When I looked into my rear-view mirror as Art rolled inverted over the top of a loop, there was Aileron, relaxed as could be, just enjoying the ride!

We landed the amazingly-nimble little stunt plane and as we taxied back to the flight line Art opened the canopy and Aileron walked out on the wing. Finding the right spot, be sat down looking straight ahead, enjoying the wind in his face as the prop-wash streamed over him. I don't know as I've ever seen a happier dog or, when I looked back into the mirror at myself, a happier passenger. What an experience!

I felt a real affinity for pilots (and still do), not just because of my Father and brother, but because I knew almost all of them were doing what they loved, and being paid for it as well. Just like me. What a life!

Track 102

Since we're still on a sidebar tangential to the main story, let me tell you another aviation-based tale or two. I really wanted to record a documentary-style interview with jet pilots for Dialogue. It took several phone calls and letters to get the proper credentials, but I wound up taking a special orientation course at Trenton, Ontario. Tests were given at its completion, and it was a very detailed instruction program. It included spending time in a high-altitude pressure chamber, simulating explosive decompression at, say, thirty thousand feet. One of our exercises required us to take off our oxygen masks inside the simulator. Without a mask, since almost all of the oxygen had been removed from the chamber, you soon became disoriented due to oxygen deprivation, feeling woozy, intoxicated, or passing out. Trained observers in the enclosure closely monitored everyone to make sure no one was injured.

We were trained in the operation of ejection seats in both the CF-104 and CF-5 jets, and taught how to carry out an emergency ground egress. It was comforting to know that if you screwed up due to nervousness or inexperience you could be fatally burned by the rocket seat, or be thrown hundreds of feet into the air without the comfort of a parachute landing to look forward to. The course was no laughing matter, and was taken very seriously.

Much time was spend detailing what to do in the event your pilot said the magic words.

"Eject! Eject! Eject!"

That would be all you would hear from him, because immediately after yelling that order he would pull *his* ejection seat handles and be very forcibly pushed out of the aircraft by a powerful rocket literally strapped to his butt. With luck, it was possible to survive an in-flight emergency, *if everything worked as designed,* with nothing more than compression fractures in your spine from the jolt of the rocket boost.

When the pilot gives the eject signal, it is not a suggestion, it's an order that is not to be taken the least bit lightly. That's why we novices had the details of the procedure drilled into us. We were trained to keep both our hands and legs close to our bodies in order to avoid breaking bones as the seat was catapulted upwards through the thick, clear canopy. Or, more precisely, where it had been milliseconds before. As just a passenger, you were told in no uncertain terms to react instantly and without thought to the Eject command, because if you were still in the aircraft a second later you would be talking to yourself. They had a simple reason for urging a pilot not to wait around for a passenger if things went to extremes.

"Reduce the death toll by one" was both the goal and the injunction. A seat ejection from a combat jet is a race for life, and pilots are very competitive people!

Dick's "Hero Shot" beside the Canadian Forces CF-5 fighter trainer in Cold Lake Alberta, just prior to an aerial combat Fighter Weapons duel. From his back seat position, he was able to break the sound barrier, and record an audio documentary which you can hear on this site!

Announcer: *"High-speed dicing with death on the way, as our show continues to take off!"*

Now Playing: Danger Zone, by Kenny Loggins
"Revvin' up your engine
Listen to her howlin' roar
Metal under tension
Beggin' you to touch and go
Highway to the Danger Zone
Ride into the Danger Zone"
Loggins, Moroder, Whitlock © Sony/ATV Harmony, WB Music Corp.

One extra bit of instruction in Trenton offered tips on how to survive an ejection in the wilds of northern Alberta, potentially useful information given that our next stop was in that western province, at the airbase in the aptly-named Cold Lake. Having now completed the High Altitude Indoctrination (HAI) course, I was flown to the base, where my brother John (call sign Jock), was stationed. As the pilots say, time to strap on an airplane.

Most first-time riders became nauseated shortly after takeoff, and in the kind of air-combat operation we had scheduled for the next day that would mean a wasted flight for two aircraft, and the loss of a lot of money, time and effort. The plan was to begin with a supersonic run just to familiarize me with the local area, flight procedures and the high-G environment. If I was going to be airsick, unconscious, or both on my first flight, better it should be a short familiarization ride.

On the flight line, John helped me into the rear cockpit of his CF5. Strapping in involved attaching myself to the plane in nine very specific ways, including seat harness, maritime lanyard, normal and emergency oxygen, helmet interphone connection and G suit. Failure to do any of these checks both properly and in the correct order could prove fatal.

Once we were both strapped in, fully connected, and ready to go on our familiarization flight, we removed the seat and canopy ejector safety pins, and were on our way. I turned on my recorder to document the events that were about to take place. I had strapped a brick-sized recorder to the knee of my flight suit, and plugged the inputs into the two-way intercom of the fighter. What a thrill to finally experience this once-in-a-lifetime event!

As we taxied to the end of the active runway, John filled me in with his own version of the instruction course at Trenton. I was all ears.

"Do exactly what I tell you at all times and absolutely nothing else. Keep your hands and feet off everything, but you can follow me through gently on the controls. I can overpower you if need be. I've got the strength of ten men and I'll know how serious the problem is! You've heard this before, but if I say '*Eject, Eject, Eject,*' adopt the ejection position, raise the handles and punch out. Do not wait for a second invitation, and no RSVP is required."

Yes, sir, brother Jock, sir.

We received takeoff clearance and John taxied us into position on the runway, released the brakes and advanced both throttles to full afterburner, calling out the numbers as we increased towards our take-off speed of one hundred and ninety-knots.

At about ten knots short of that marker, the aircraft began to throw itself from side to side so violently that I could see my brother's helmet hitting the canopy with each left-to-right cycle, and hitting it *hard*. I was being thrown around, too, with the added advantage of having no idea at all what was happening. Were we going to leave the ground or not? Would we ever get out of the plane alive? It was difficult to see anything around me because of the terrible vibrations that seemed to be shaking the craft apart. With the huge stresses being put on the airframe, the instruments on the dashboard in front of me suddenly popped out of their mountings! Talk about a confidence booster.

John had training and knowledge that I lacked, including what to do in such a situation. He immediately chopped both throttles to idle and stood hard on the brakes while deploying the drag-chute that quickly blossomed behind us. Doing their part, the control tower scrambled fire-trucks and an ambulance to race to the runway, which is standard operating procedure in this sort of emergency.

As the aircraft slowed through about fifty knots, John entered the high speed cut-off, the vibration ceased entirely, and the plane rolled smoothly over the tarmac. As soon as it came to a stop he shut down both engines, set the parking brake and yelled instructions to me.

"Replace your safety pins for the canopy and ejection seat and get out of the plane as fast as you can!"

We had no working intercom, but I could hear him yelling from the front seat. He was out of his straps and on the ground in a few seconds, since this was something he had done hundreds of times before. I was still fumbling with my harness and it wasn't until I stood up that he realized why I had taken so long to get out. I was holding a complete set of "cockpit instruments" that had shaken themselves loose during our rocky ride and landed in my lap.

"Is it always like this?" I asked, only half kidding. Just then two screaming fire trucks pulled up and although they were not needed I have to say it was comforting to see them regardless.

To put this bronco ride in perspective, the entire event from take-off roll to full stop might have been thirty seconds at the most. The violent oscillations had released the record button on my machine, so I wasn't able to capture any play-by-play or after-the-moment chatter. It was later determined that a damping device in the nose wheel shimmy damper had been installed improperly. The aircraft damage was assessed at three hundred thousand dollars after some of the instruments were opened up revealing further damage not immediately visible to external inspection. You have to wonder what kind of slap on the wrist you get when you seriously break a piece of government property because you screwed up on an installation.

It could have been a very bad day, but brother John just shrugged it off.

"Listen, Dick, any airplane ride you walk away from is a good one, so we really didn't do too badly!"

Sure, if you say so. My knees were still knocking.

"But now I've got to grab another plane and get us airborne again."

It's the same as when a rider has been thrown from his horse. You can become spooked by the fall, or you can get up, seize the reins and get right back in the saddle again. We opted for the latter. This time, the shimmy damper properly dampered the shimmy and we lifted off the ground and blasted into The Wild Blue Yonder. After a couple of quick touch and go landings, we were both ready to call it a day and get ready for The Good Stuff coming up in the morning.

Now Playing: Excerpts from "Jet Jock" Documentary from
C.F.B. Cold Lake, Alberta

Dick: *"Recently I flew faster than the speed of sound in the
cockpit of a Canadian Forces CF5... Inside the cockpit
canopy, the roar of a screaming jet engine is muffled by the
hard plastic pilot's helmet. Wearing this self-contained gear
you become akin to a man from space, as your eyes are
shaded and protected by a bug-eyed face visor, your mouth
and nose covered with an oxygen mask....Come fly with
me!"*

Pilot's voice: "Jock" Williams: *"OK, power's coming
up...ninety percent both sides, temperatures are good, oil
pressure, hydraulic pressure all right. We go! One...two
good burner lights...aircraft accelerating OK...one hundred
and sixty knots...aft stick, and we're airborne! Gear's up,
flaps are coming."*

To hear portions of this broadcast, go to:
AUDIO/VIDEO: Jet Jock (Part 1)

"I feel the need for speed!" Tom Cruise in Top Gun

The next day, with John once again in the front seat and me
in the rear of another CF-5 fighter, I was allowed to fly in an
aerial combat dog fight. From the time the fight began with
the words to our adversary aircraft, Fight's On, we pitched

and rolled in every direction through the skies, enduring up to seven G's (or seven times the force of gravity) for brief periods of time. To give you an idea of how stressful that condition is, imagine six people of your weight sitting on your chest. If your head is of average size it weighs about thirteen pounds. At seven G's it would be as hard to move as if it weighed ninety-one pounds.

I felt my field of vision contracting as the G's increased, narrowing until it was all I could do to see straight in front of me. Even with a G-suit compressing around my stomach and upper legs to slow the pooling of blood in my lower legs and feet, I had to remember my training to grunt hard to stay conscious and keep the blood flowing to my brain. As tough as the flight was physically, it was wonderfully exhilarating, and no amount of training can fully prepare you for this kind of ride. As I mentioned, many inexperienced back-seat passengers are very prone to passing out during these periods of extreme physical stress. I'm pleased that I stayed awake for every thrilling second of it.

To add to the intensity of the combat, we frequently found ourselves pulling negative G's as well, hanging suspended in our straps as we rolled upside down. The blood would rush to our heads, as we were often twisting and turning at the same time. After severe fights of this nature, pilots often return with bloodshot eyes from ruptured capillaries in the eye. It is said that an hour of manoeuvering in that form of simulated combat is the equivalent of a full day's work digging ditches.

During this flight I recorded the grunts, groans and intercom information, along with John's explanations during the combat with his commentary during our flight. After several engagements, we finally closed down with the words, Knock It Off. This means end the combat, disengage, and regroup for the flight back to base. Let me put you in my seat to let you hear how the dogfight happened,"

AUDIO/VIDEO: Jet Jock (Part 2)

As an aside, even though the dogfight is still an important part of a pilot's training, in today's warfare most kills of enemy aircraft are the result of the pilot firing a missile from many miles away, identifying his target on sophisticated cockpit radars when they are still too far away to see. Modern fire-and-forget missiles have their targets designated by the computer and do the rest on their own when they are launched off the firing rails.

A dogfight really is a last-ditch duel to the death after all the missiles have been fired, and if you're locked in close-range combat at this stage, you are in serious difficulty. It does not happen often, but often enough that it preserves the last vestige of the idea that pilots are knights of the air, the last warriors to do battle one on one in the high, clean air.

For video shot inside an F-5, showing some of the views from where I sat, check out:
F5 Performance Demo & Touch and Go Landing

This is a perfect video of an F-5 in a dogfight to show what it is like in aerial combat:
F5 Dogfight Sequence

Here are some F-5 Pilots demonstrating their "Go-fast ability" in the Swiss Alps, this will give you an idea of this nimble fighter aircraft:

F5s In The Alps

During my visit to Cold Lake, I was also able to fly in the plane dubbed the Missile With A Man, the CF-104 Starfighter, which looked for all the world like a giant rocket with two stubby little wings and a bubble canopy on top. With the aircraft still in use as a fighter then by the Canadian Forces, a two seat trainer version had also been developed. I was fortunate enough to have clearance to hitch a ride in this powerful machine for a mission on Cold Lake's Training and Gunnery Range.

The razor-thin-winged fighter aircraft was the first fighter capable of sustained speed at twice the speed of sound at altitudes of thirty thousand feet.

During my one-hour flight, we dropped some simulated bombs on ground targets and also made several strafing passes to fire the 20 mm. Vulcan Gatling Gun, which has a rate of fire of six thousand rounds per minute. With our hard-hat helmets, it was impossible to hear the gun firing, but to a listener outside the aircraft, it sounds just like a buzz-saw, with a continuous ripping sound! It was fascinating to watch the impacts of exploding earth as the pilot "walked" the hail of bullets right into his targets on the ground.

We wrapped up the day with a high-speed Mach 1.3 low-level run, Mach 1 being the speed of sound. That meant we were travelling at one thousand, four hundred and sixty four feet per second…at tree-top heights! This thrilling rocket ride culminated with a pull-up into a vertical climb, taking us from ground level to thirty-thousand feet in a mere thirty seconds. Levelling the wings after this demonstration, the pilot had the last word over the intercom.

"Just think…I get paid to do this sort of stuff!"

I interviewed my brother John at length after our dog-fight, and portions of the interview and documentary I produced back in the CJBK studios were played on the CBS Radio Network, as well as our own Dialogue program.

For a great view from where I sat in the CF 104, click here:
F104 Backseat Supersonic Flight

For an exterior view of the CF 104 in action, watch:
F104 Airshow Performance

Here's a back-seat look during a low-altitude "trip" in a F104:
F104 Starfighter Low Level Flight Nellis AFB to Pheonix

Track 106

Announcer: *"Just ahead, a move to mornings and a wake-up call! We return to our story, now in progress."*

To begin my mid-day shift at CJBK, Joe Duchesne and I would have a morning chat that would effectively let us hand over the baton in our daily radio relay. It was always fun to chat with him on-air. At about 9:50, I would settle into the news booth across a glass window looking straight at him, and away we would go.

"Well, Tall One, what's on your show today?" I would tease a few of the songs coming right up, and usually give a little clue to some kind of offbeat man-bites-dog story I had dug out of the wire service news we had received that morning. In the business such tidbits are called kickers, and are frequently the last stories in newscasts, offering a look at the lighter side of what's happening.

One morning Joe threw me a curve-ball. We said our usual good mornings to each other, and then he just sat there. No more talk. Not a word. Nothing. He was obviously not going to give me any help, and I finally had to break the silence.

"Aren't you going to ask me what's on my show today, Joe?"

"No...I listened to your show yesterday. Not interested!"

335

I wish the audience could have seen his ear-to-ear smile.

Another talent that made him such an outstanding entertainer was his ability to work the phones and Joe was on the telephone almost constantly when the music was playing, recording *everything*. When a listener called in, Joe wouldn't respond immediately to whatever the comments were. He would wait a beat or two, and sure enough, almost always they would add another comment that was even better. If Joe had jumped in the line would never have been uttered, but his timing was perfection and he got some of his best bits that way.

Like many DJ's, Joe wanted to be more than just a morning man and had found a small radio station for sale in the resort village of Huntsville, Ontario, CFBK. Our management was aware of his interest in buying the station and kept upping the ante to keep him (and his high ratings) in London. They even went so far as to suggest *they* would pay for a full-time manager to run his station, allowing Joe to stay behind the microphone at CJBK.

That wasn't what he wanted, though, and we got the news one day that Joe had turned in his resignation. The hunt for a suitable replacement was on, and it was just about impossible to find the right person to fill his very large radio shoes. Predictably, we went through two new hosts as the ratings accelerated downwards.

One of the morning hosts was so off the mark that I went to Rick Richardson and told him I would like to take a crack at the shift myself. Nothing ventured, nothing gained, but maybe I should have remembered that old line....be careful what you wish for because you just might get it.

What I did get was the shift, and a lovely bonus perk Rick arranged, the use of a shiny new red Corvette. Nice wheels!

Track 107

Radio morning show hosts are a unique bunch. They have to be at the peak of their game when most of their listeners are trying to burrow back under the covers or are wandering around like coffee zombies. Most morning DJs go to bed quite early, and that doesn't exactly make for a sizzling social life. Nor do you have the luxury of sleeping in. The morning show is the most important and generally profitable shift of the day, and it takes a passel of personality and a pile of preparation to make it work. Unlike other shifts, where the format is music-driven, this time slot has to have everything you can deliver; local presence, listener interaction, fun and games, ongoing humor and all the stuff broadcasters call housekeeping; keeping the listener up to date on time, temperature, news, weather and sports. And all of it has to be incorporated into a highly compressed time frame.

You can't just show up and wing it, you have to hit the air knowing pretty much exactly when you are going to use each joke, when you will be teeing up the next newscast, or where in each hour you'll be doing a funny bit to keep the audience amused. People need to get their information in a hurry, and they expect the same kind of presentation at the same high intensity every morning. You can have good days and better days, but there is no room ever for a bad day on a morning show. Sure, it does happen, but when you stumble you do so under the brightest spotlight of the day.

The only plus side to all this preparation is that the same bits that you did in the 6am hour can be repeated during the 8am hour. The audience is constantly shifting rapidly, as people rise and shine, and the turnover as they leave for work is very quick. So you can do the same thing with the 7am jokes – go for another laugh in the 9am hour. But if you want to be a successful morning show host, they'd better be *worth* repeating. Moving all this along is the host, whose overall job it is to deliver the show in a way that sounds like he's happy to share a coffee with you for a few minutes, and hasn't a care in the world. Even though he's on a hot seat and in a pressure cooker at the same time. To practice enough to sound unrehearsed is the key, and that takes a lot of hard work. I found that I spent almost as much time prepping for my show as I did doing it on air!

On the first morning of my new show, I arrived at the station at five in the morning, eager for my six o'clock start. I wandered into the newsroom feeling quite proud of my early-morning discipline, only to find our News Director had already been hard at work for more than an hour, writing the morning newscasts. At least I wasn't alone in the station.

I was OK being an early riser while the novelty of the new job lasted. But once I got settled in, I found it difficult to get used to getting up *every* weekday in time to be at work at 5. I was disappointed to see how long it was taking me to get used to it. One morning I put the rooster question to Gord Harris, the News Director, a long-time veteran of the morning radio wars.

"Man, it's really hard to get rolling at this time of the morning. Does it get easier as you go along?"

"Not so's you'd notice. No matter how long you do it, it's still the middle of the night when you have to climb out of the sack, and every time it's just a little bit tougher to haul yourself to the vertical. I've been doing it for years and I still ask myself 'why' every morning!"

But the real answer is the same for just about everyone on morning drive: "because that's where the biggest audience is". There's nothing like prime time.

Track 108

"FM radio will overtake AM by 1975." Harvard University study, 1961

With every listener survey period (known as The Book), it was duly noted that our competition, an FM station playing Classic Rock, was gaining audience. The clarity of the FM signal compared to AM was blaringly obvious, and the listener shift to FM across North America was something all Top 40 AM stations were experiencing. Music on AM radio had long been the kind you could carry in your pocket in a transistor radio. FM was designed to go straight to the brain with crystal-clear sound and little if any radio interference. Teenagers especially felt it made more of a statement to punch an FM station on their car radio. In those days FM rock was heating up the airwaves even while it was becoming the coolest format around. The early DJs had more room to program album cuts, longer songs and a more eclectic mix. However hard we worked to make the content solid, there wasn't anything that could make our AM signal sound any better, which was already a super-crisp bright sound but still no match for FM.
The writing was on the wall and sooner or later listener drain was going cut huge chunks out of AM radio audiences if something wasn't done.

One of the attempts to forestall the inevitable was something called The Morning Zoo format. Taking a page from morning television shows like Good Morning America and

Today, morning radio went from single hosts to either co-hosts or even a team of people if the budget could carry it. CJBK was quick to get on the bandwagon and Rick called me into his office to announce that I was going to be the first-ever co-host of a morning show in London. My partner was to be Judy Savoy, a former local TV Weather Lady, (to use the term at that time). In a brilliant fit of creativity, programming dubbed it Good Morning London.

Judy had done some hosting on my old station, CFPL-AM 980, so she wasn't a novice at radio. But her natural inclination ran to the mature, calmly-presented CBC Radio style of broadcasting. She had a very quick mind and was always upbeat, both on and off the air. Just the thing for morning radio, in theory. Neither of us had ever worked with a co-host, however, and Judy had no experience in the highly-structured, rapid-paced, demanding morning format. It took us quite a while to get used to each other and make our interaction sound as natural as possible. And worrying about that made it tougher when we had to deal with the kind of unexpected things that morning drive-time can throw at a host.

Before Judy, I knew how and when my jokes would end. Now, I had to pre-explain to her where I was going with a story, so she knew the direction to take for perhaps an *extra* punch line at the payoff. All this took time and understanding on both our parts. However, once Judy figured out how the dance steps worked, she got better at it all the time.

Her natural zaniness was best shown when the city decided to drastically change the pickup times on all of the garbage routes and we came up with a comedy bit to suit. I would put on some crazy background music and make like an announcer.

"Now ..... here's the Garbage Lady!"

Judy had come up with a rough character voice and would deliver it in a pronounced Bronx accent.

"Hey, things are picking up in Zone A today! Picking up! Ha, ha...that's a good one. Today's your day, Zone A, for getting that trash out to the curb! Hey Dick, Am I too late for the garbage?"

I would punch in a cart with sounds of garbage cans being tossed around.

"No, Hop in!"

Not Burns and Allen, maybe, but the listeners seemed to enjoy our humor.

Judy was also a pretty fair singer, and she and I decided to record a home-made jingle, sung over the backing of a Philharmonic orchestra playing Handel's Hallelujah Chorus. Of course, *our* version was a little different. Those of you of a musical bent, feel free to sing along. Whatever happens it can't sound any worse than Long Tall Texan.

"Dick and Judy, Dick and Judy, Dick a-and Ju-dy,!"
Who said it wasn't a classy show?

One of our news staff noted one day that Sports is the Toy Store of Life, and another of our daily bits was called Sports Shorts. It gave us the opportunity to take a quick look at the funny side of playing games. It always began with a group of guys yelling Sports Shorts! That was immediately followed by a terrible rendition of Take Me Out to the Ball Game performed by Phil Music and His Tijuana Pit Band. Played slightly off key and in a burlesque manner, it set the stage for some unusual stories, including one Judy reminded me of when I was writing this book.

That morning, after the band swung into raucous music, I went through a few off-the-wall sports stories I had prepared, then wrapped things up with a slightly twisted teaser.

"George Schwartz of the New York Yankees is reported on the disabled list today. Turns out he's suffering from a bad case of hemorrhoids!" Like there might be a good case?

Then we rolled right into the next song, a Dionne Warwick hit currently riding the charts. I introduced the record over the opening run-up to the vocal, then spoke the fateful words.

"I Know I'll Never Love This Way Again. Come to think of it, neither will George Schwartz!"

Judy absolutely lost it, and laughed like a happy lunatic, fighting to keep from falling on the floor. She was so out of control that she forgot to kill her microphone, and that made for chaos in the control room, too. I love live radio!

Since the morning show is so important to any station, there was lots of fine tuning to be done, almost on a daily basis. Every time our microphones went on we were being recorded on a skimmer tape, so called because it would skim over the commercials and other distractions and record only what we said and did on air. That meant our entire show could be listened to in about twenty minutes in our post-show debriefings with the Program Director, who would critique the good, the bad, and the occasionally ugly. The meetings generally would be about an hour in length, as we broke down and reviewed that day's show. Not unlike what NFL teams do the day after their Sunday TV Games, but without the smell of liniment.

Judy and I were really clicking and on a roll when she told me in confidence one morning that she was not only leaving the station, but leaving town altogether. Just when it was finally coming together! Her husband had taken a position in his church ministry that involved moving to the Maritimes. I knew I was going to miss her, but the hunt for a new co-host began.

CJBK
1290
RADIO LONDON

MARCH 13, 1981

LISTEN TO . . .
GOODMORNING LONDON
with
**DICK WILLIAMS AND
JUDY SAVOY**
on

CJBK
1290
RADIO LONDON

Outdoor advertising for Good Morning London with Judy Savoy

Track 109

I didn't have very much input into the choice of either of my two co-hosts, and it was decided a CFPL-FM employee would take over Judy's position. Her name was Janice Zolf, and one of her close relatives was Larry Zolf, a popular CBC Radio and TV commentator known for his biting wit. Janice had been doing an evening show 'down the street' at CFPL-FM 96, and was also known as the Queen of Clubs because of her interest in and coverage of local jazz clubs. Her style was distinctly influenced by this kind of music and her program was very laid-back and cool. Where Judy was like a nimble sports car, Janice was more like a smooth-riding, expensive sedan.

The quick transition from her past experience to the hurly-burly tempo of morning mania certainly put her adaptability to the test, and since her listening habits had been shaped by the somewhat staid style of CBC Radio, that's where her comfort zone lay as a broadcaster. So it was back to the drawing board again, with more meetings and tape critiques to help us build a better flow and interaction between us.

Track 110

Now Playing: Midnight Choir (Mogen David), by Larry
Gatlin &The Gatlin Brothers
"Will they have Mogen David in Heaven?
Dear Lord, we'd all like to know
Will they have Mogen David in Heaven, sweet Jesus?
If they don't, who the hell wants to go?"
Lyrics Larry Gatlin, © Sony/ATV Music Publishing LLC

Around this same general time, I heard from my pal Joe
Duchesne, who had his hands full with his new station in
Huntsville, Ontario (think Mayberry RFD, but with a lot of
millionaires out on the many nearby lakes in their
Architectural Digest cottages). As a newly-hatched
entrepreneur, he had to not only manage every facet of the
station business, he had to supervise sales and promotion and
play Program Director, too, trying to keep an inexperienced
young staff of DJs in line. On top of that full-time job, and
then some, he also had to do the morning show. It's no
wonder he always had a funny tale or two to share. Hoping
to hear the latest, I asked him how things were going.

"Well, Tall One, let me tell you about what it's like in real
radio. One of our clients called me a couple days ago, and he
was mad from top to bottom. Threatened to stop all his
advertising with us. He's a car dealer, and about the biggest
account we have. Turns out one of my DJs played that
Midnight Choir Mogen David song by Larry Gatlin, and the
client didn't like it. Not at all. So the man said he wanted to

349

meet with me in his offices, as soon as humanly possible. That did not sound good to me.

"But I went in and told the DJ he could never play that song on my station, then went over to the client's with our sales rep to see if we could mend some fences. He had our station playing on his radio, and he left no doubt that might not continue. We had to eat a couple of helpings of humble pie, and promise the DJ had been sufficiently chastised that such a sacrilegious thing would never be heard on our airwaves again. That seemed to sooth the client's ruffled feathers, and when he suggested we kneel in prayer I was ready to hit the floor without hesitation.

"We've done some good work here today, gentlemen, and I believe this mistake has taught us all a lesson," he says. "Let us close our eyes and pray together." We were almost home free, kneeling on the floor in prayerful communion, when I hear the first notes of the next song begin. And of all the things that might have come on, well, you can guess which one it was. If that DJ had been in the room I would have clubbed him with a bottle of Mogen David. There was nothing left to say, and nothing to do but just stand up and get out of there."

Life in small-town radio.

Track 111

Radio survives on revenues from commercials, and making sure they get on the air as promised in the broadcasting contract is a very serious issue. In the midst of working through our very demanding show one day, I somehow missed playing a spot from one of our sponsors. We seldom heard what was being broadcast when our microphones were off because we were constantly recording the off-air listener calls we needed for the show while attending to all the other plates we had to keep spinning at the same time. Confident I had played all the carts required, because I always had, I signed the commercial log in the studio verifying they had all aired. But as later checks of the logger tapes showed (they are tapes recorded at a very slow speed to keep a record of everything that airs on the station) one spot in particular had not, in fact, been played. That is a very serious omission, and was rightly taken seriously by management. But perhaps too much so.

A make-up broadcast of the spot several additional times for free and an abject apology from the DJ to the client is usually enough to calm the troubled waters, but that's not quite what happened. Instead, I was called into the Sales Manager's darkened office Monday right after our show, for a one-sentence, one-sided conversation.

"We need the keys to the car." I was fired.

There was no question that was because of a lot more than a missed spot, as serious as that was. In hindsight (and to a certain extent, at the time) it was plain to see it was just an excuse, and the station was looking for a reason to bring in somebody new. In shock at the cold and sudden way I was let go, I had to leave the Corvette in the parking lot and hitch a ride home from one of the other jocks. Talk about your symbolism.

By the way, a couple of weeks later the Sales Manager called me at home and offered to let me pick up the station's lease for the Corvette if I would like to. Talk about rubbing salt in the wound while still twisting the knife! My response to his offer wasn't anatomically possible.

The next morning the firing was front-page news, citing *Broadcast Irregularities* as the reason for putting me on the street, in this case literally. The station ended the next morning's newscasts saying the same thing and it seemed to me they wanted people to think I was a thief or a pervert or God knows what. I knew the truth, that they were just tired of my voice, but I didn't want to get into a mud-slinging contest with the station management.

I came to find out that most people who knew the real story thought the whole thing was ridiculous, including Vern Furber, who owned CHLO-AM in St. Thomas, a smaller city just a few miles from London. He offered me *their* morning show if I wanted it. The pay was comparable to what I had been making, so the decision was easy. Plus, it meant that I could stay in London, continue to ply my trade and be near my son DJ as he grew up, rather than moving out of the market looking for a job.

I went to a labor relations lawyer to see if I had a case against what I considered unfair dismissal. He told me I could probably win a suit against my former bosses, but it might take a year or longer for the matter to work its way through the courts. Plus, since I almost immediately found alternate employment, I didn't lose any money to speak of and it would be hard to get any significant damages. He went on to say that if getting even was what was motivating me my case was strong, but I would probably be happier in the long run if I just shrugged it off and got on with my life. They sound like wise words now, and they did then, too. I decided to heed his advice.

Track 112

"Just stay on the wheel and you come back on top again."
Legendary deejay Bobby Mitchell

CHLO AM St. Thomas, Ontario, 1981 Playlist:
"Endless Love" Diana Ross & Lionel Richie
"Lady" Kenny Rogers
"Kiss on My List" Hall & Oates
"I Love a Rainy Night" Eddie Rabbitt
"9 to 5" Dolly Parton
"Being with You" Smokey Robinson

Now Playing: That's Why God Made the Radio, by The
Beach Boys
"Capturing memories from afar
In my car
That's why God made the radio
So tune right in, everywhere you go
That's why God made the radio"
Brian Wilson, Mike Love © Capitol Records

Embarking on this new chapter in my career, I started each
morning with an extra half-hour commute in darkness to
neighbouring St. Thomas, and once again became a 'disc'
jockey. CHLO had their commercials on tape cartridges, but
all the music was still on 45 RPM records. In some ways, it
felt like coming home. Vern had bought the station as is, and
clearly hadn't spent any money on upgrades to the studios,
so it really was back to basics after the gleaming studios and

state-of-the-art technical surroundings I had become used to at CJBK.

In addition, since its glory years in the 60s when it had a booming signal at 680 on the AM dial, CHLO had moved up to the much weaker position of 1570, almost as far to the right as you could tune. While their signal could be heard in London, it was a very weak one compared to the local stations and we were in a tenuous situation at best, ratings-wise.

I was to do the morning show with a local DJ named Bob Williams. In another stunning flash of creativity, the show was called Williams and Williams. Bob's actual last name was Hammersley, but that wasn't considered a radio name, so Williams and Williams it was.

It was a pleasure to work with him right from the start because we were two peas in a pod and could sense from the first morning where to jump in, or where to let the other host fly on his own. It was a fun gig, and I am convinced would have been very big in a bigger market.

But we weren't, and it was quickly apparent that paying two hosts for one show was not nearly as cost-effective or practical as splitting them up. So we became Williams in the Morning and Williams in the Afternoon. We bought some nice snappy jingles to that effect, along with a few other station jingles, too.

Once a week, Bob and I would get together in a recording studio and do thirty or forty segments together, which would be aired over the course of a week. Every day, we would play back these two-voice segments on *both* our shows, which made both good programming and economic sense, giving the station two strong bookends in our broadcast day.

With Bob's help and experience, we culled our playlists of Favorites of Yesterday and Today to blend soft favorites of yesteryear with the soft current hits on the charts. It had a nice sound on-air, rather like todays Adult Contemporary FM stations.

Shortly before April Fool's day one year, one of the other DJs got creative with his tape and razor blade and made up a new April Fool's jingle. One of the new Dallas jingles we had bought to spice up our on-air sound had the following lyrics:

"We're the station you'll always remember
With the music you'll never forget....
1570-CHLO"

On April Fool's morning, when I punched in that jingle, here's what listeners heard:

*"We're the station you'll never **remember***
*With the music you'll **forget**...*
1570-CHLO"

Announcer: *"Stick around for more fun and games! More of our story when we come right back after these words!"*

Track 113

Just on the outskirts of St. Thomas is a huge psychiatric hospital, originally built to house 5,000 patients. During WW II, it became a Royal Canadian Air Force training base, then resumed its regular role when peace returned. St. Thomas Psych, as most people called it, was known far and wide.

A couple of DJs took advantage of the place's notoriety to stage a rather elaborate hoax. They pre-recorded a supposed radio show onto an audio cassette, then they inserted this mini-drama into the player built into their car's dashboard. Time for the road show to begin. They started cruising around the region, looking for an unsuspecting hitchhiker. In those more carefree days it didn't take them long to find their target on the side of the road. Stopping to pick him up, they placed their unsuspecting victim in between them on the front bench seat and resumed their drive.

Then, the fun began. Each of the guys had a role to play, and off they went. One developed a twitch in his arm, which kept flapping into the side of their passenger. The other began to frequently clear his throat and make strange noises. The hitchhiker had to be wondering what he'd gotten into when suddenly the driver stopped coughing and made a suggestion.

"Let's see what's happening on the radio," he said as he switched on the pre-recorded cassette in the dash player.

357

A few seconds of music followed, then the song faded out to be replaced by the introduction to CHLO's newscasts.

"CHLO news at 5. Police are urging everyone in the St. Thomas area to be on the lookout for two escaped residents from the St. Thomas Psychiatric Hospital. One of the escapees has a twitch in his left arm, and the other one is reported to have a nervous habit of clearing his throat!"

There's a lesson there, kids: Never accept a ride from strangers.

Track 114

Announcer: *"Thanks for hanging in there! Now, back to our story!"*

Our mid-day DJ was one of those guys blessed with a million-dollar voice, and a fine sense of humor, too. Once he got on a roll, however, Bill sometimes didn't know how to turn it off. He would be talking over the introduction to a song, tell a joke, and then start to tell another one! By then he would be talking over the vocal, which is pretty much radio's biggest no-no.

I had spoken to him several times about this, and how bad it sounded. Finally, I wrote him a formal, documenting memo of the problem and brought it into the control room. Essentially what I instructed him to do was tell his jokes, then play the music, and *never talk over any more songs!* Harsh as it was, I insisted he sign the document, and warned him that if he screwed up more than two times more (anyone can make a mistake- once), he would be subject to dismissal.

Signed document in hand, I was about to leave the room when the next record began to play. Bill opened his microphone, talked over the intro, and was still talking when the record's vocals began. Strike two. The next day was a Saturday, and I got a call from the station while I was at home. One of the jocks told me Bill appeared to be off his meds and was punching the walls and acting erratically. I asked the guy to put Bill on the line.

"Bill, buddy. I think you need a rest. You head on home and I will have a full severance package prepared for you. Just leave your key at the station and consider this as your last day."

I had never had to fire a fellow on-air performer, and I did not like it at all. Bill left for home, and left me thinking that being a Program Director was not a fun job at all. But Bill didn't seem to mind. During my morning show on Monday he called up to ask me what time I wanted him in the station for his show. I reminded him what had happened on Saturday, and that he was no longer employed at the station.

"You sure?"

"Pretty much."

And so much for poor old Bill, who may still be talking over intros somewhere, hopefully when the Program Director isn't listening.

Track 115

Announcer: *"Just ahead, a medical miracle!"*

During my time at CHLO I had to pay the price for years of skiing that had worn down my left kneecap, and I underwent arthroscopic surgery to correct the painful result. Dean Shavalier was a well-known ex-newsman from CFPL who was working as a Public Relations Officer for the hospital where my procedure was performed. When I woke from the anaesthetic, the first thing I saw, clipped to the sheet which covered me, was a sandwich baggie containing two shrivelled-looking walnuts which he had glued together. It contained a note from Doctor Dean.

"While you were under the knife we gave you a two-for-one special. We didn't think you'd be needing these any more, but you can keep them for a souvenir."

Funny, Dean. Very funny.

Track 116

Announcer: *"Coming up, everything old is new again! Our story continues!"*

CHLO's owner once explained his habit of constantly looking for something new to offer his listeners and improve his station's share in the competitive London radio market.

"Dick, I'm like a hungry hooker. I want to go where the crowds are!"

As a result, we changed formats frequently in a search for a more money-making, crowd-pleasing, on-air sound. It was almost a Format of the Day approach, and it led to a format called The Music of Your Life!

Track 117

CHLO St. Thomas (Part 2), 1983 Playlist:

"Peg O' My Heart" The Harmonicats
"Buttons And Bows" Dinah Shore
"Cruising Down the River" Russ Morgan
"Ghost Riders in the Sky" Vaughn Monroe
"Some Enchanted Evening" Perry Como
"That Lucky Old Sun" Frankie Laine
"Rum and Coca-Cola" The Andrews Sisters
"Sentimental Journey" Les Brown & Doris Day

Now Playing: Stardust, by Nat King Cole
"Love is now the stardust of yesterday,
The music of the years gone by."
Carmichael, Parish

"The dimensions of the radio are truly to be treasured."
CBS Radio Commentator Charles Osgood

To say this new format was a change of pace would be a vast understatement. The syndicated package was the brainchild of Al Ham, a former recording executive who realized that the songs he wanted to listen to weren't being played on the radio anymore. He compiled a list of the music he missed, recorded hundreds of tracks onto hour-long reel-to-reel tapes for broadcasters, and made the results available to stations for airplay around the clock.

The songs were hits by well-known artists of the Forties and Fifties, mixed in with big band standards from the Second World War. There was no room for personal picks, and very little contribution required from the announcer. Plus, the developers of the format wanted programmed silence of a couple of seconds between songs. That's known in the business as dead air, and is a cardinal sin. For anyone coming from a Top Forty background with super-tight production values, those seconds seemed to take forever. And all the announcer really had to do was recap the songs you had played and make sure the tapes kept turning.

This positioning statements, or liners, added even more atmosphere to the Nineteen Forties-era time-warp.

"Soft as Velvet, Smooth as Silk, The Music of Your Life Continues on CHLO."

Not the music of *my* life! It sounded more suited to a funeral, actually.

This kind of format was appealing as a band aid solution for ailing stations, and was intended to increase a minimal audience to something more respectable, in a demographic group that conceivably had more money to spend than other, younger target groups. The beauty of it was that little outside promotion was needed. Word of mouth spread quickly among the listeners, who would call their friends to promote the station.

"Maisie, there's a radio station that's playing *our* kind of music. None of that noisy stuff the kids listen to. You should try it out yourself!"

We did receive quite a few hand-written letters from listeners, and a fair amount of phone calls from the targeted seniors. Bear in mind, however, the *youngest* listener we would be catering to would have been in their sixties at that time. Depending on their ages, some of the younger folks were known to refer to the format as The Music of Your Mother's Life, or even your Grandmother's. Dynamic it was not.

I remember one of our newsmen poking his head into the studio, waving what he introduced as the Obituary column of the newspaper.

"Dick! Dick! We lost fourteen listeners yesterday!" It was funny, but oh so true, too. I had visions of myself doing my show from a rocking chair in some not-to-distant future. I wasn't ready to rush into old age off the air, and the same went for my on-air life. As much as I loved her, I didn't want it to be my Mother's.

But if you want to work in radio you have to take the job that's there, until something better comes along. *If* something better comes along.

Track 118

"It doesn't end with telling the time and introducing records."
Cousin Brucie 77 WABC

CIQM FM London, 1984 Playlist:
"That's What Friends Are For" Dionne Warwick and Friends
"Say You, Say Me" Lionel Richie
"I Miss You" Klymaxx
"On My Own" Patti Labelle and Michael McDonald
"Broken Wings" Mr. Mister
"How Will I Know" Whitney Houston
"Friends and Lovers" Carl Anderson and Gloria Loring

Now Playing: Nothing's Gonna Stop Us Now, by Starship
"And we can build this dream together
Standing strong forever
Nothing's gonna stop us now"
Albert Hammond, Diane Warren © RealSongs, Universal Music Publishing Group

As I was lamenting my fading youth, I got an invitation out of the blue to bring my career back to London. There was a brand new FM station in town and they wanted me to do the mid-day shift.

General Manager Gord Hume I knew, and the Program Director of CKSL-AM and the new CIQM-FM was a guy named Jerry Stevens who had been my Program Director back when I was at CJBK. I had done a lot of interviews then, and they apparently wanted somebody with skills in that area. I guess my reputation preceded me, and radio is, after all, a fairly small and interconnected clique of people.

I liked the idea of coming back to the big city, and I loved the idea of being able to sleep in past four in the morning. Five or six years of that had been more than enough. I knew I was taking on a professional challenge when I took the job, but I had no way of knowing what I had really let myself in for.

With FM stations ruling the airwaves these days, it is interesting to note that when it was announced applications would be accepted for the 103.1 FM frequency and radio station licence, only *one group* responded. FM was huge in promise but still finding its way commercially. There was a distinct lack of competitors, likely because no other broadcasting group was prepared to sustain the steep financial costs of building a brand new station in an already-busy market.

On top of that, the new operators had to agree to a long list of promises and restrictions, just to be allowed on the air. In those days the government body overseeing Canadian broadcasting, the Canadian Radio and Television Commission (CRTC), had very specific rules about what you could and could not play on an FM station, and a pretty solid if flawed idea as to what else you should be doing. So the new CIQM-FM had to promise to play fifty-one per cent *non-hit music*! If a song had charted any higher than number forty on any music chart it would be considered a hit and subject to restriction. On top of that, thirty-five per cent of our music had to be CanCon - Canadian Content.

That would appear to be good for Canadian artists like my old pal Gord Lightfoot, but his songs like The Wreck of the Edmund Fitzgerald were considered hits since they had charted in the Top Ten in North America. So if we wanted Gord, we had to play his songs that didn't chart so well. That left us playing second-rate or third-rate, unfamiliar songs instead of the first-class material that actually sold records and attracted listeners. I guess that made sense to somebody in Ottawa, but damned if we could figure out what it was supposed to do except make it a lot harder for us to do our primary job of entertaining our listeners. Our tax dollars at work!

In order to maintain our license, we had to allocate a specific amount of hours for the presentation of Spoken Word programs, Foreground Music programs, News and Public Affairs programs and the like. We also had to spend twenty-eight thousand dollars a year promoting local musicians, and promise an investment of forty-five thousand for new and improved digital recording equipment over the next five years.

If that's what the CRTC wanted, why bless their pointy little heads we gave it to them. We went so far as to have our very own station poet, with his own show. We recorded many classical selections from the London Symphony Orchestra, live on location. We aired film reviews, restaurant reviews, public affairs shows, whatever our News Department could conjure up to comply with our promised commitment to The Arts.

We also aired an esoteric Sunday evening classical music show, geared exclusively to the cognoscenti and hosted by the proprietor of a local record store that sported a collection of rare and unique recordings, many of which were available only at his shop in those days before eBay and Amazon. It turned out to be a pretty much full-blown commercial for his business, and the playlist was not exactly what you'd call mainstream classical. But it helped us meet the mandate, so more power to him.

These specialized programs couldn't be buried in late evening hours, but had to be sprinkled into the 6 am to 6 pm listening timeframe. Stations still have to go through this initiation period, until they can successfully make the case that the burdens imposed by the very obligations *they themselves agreed to in order to get the licence* are preventing their getting enough listeners to survive until the restrictions are reduced. In other words, to get an FM license, you had to *over-promise*, then *under-perform*. To get the CIQM-FM franchise the company had made lavish promises, telling the CRTC whatever they wanted to hear. The fact that the resulting format was a money-losing dog would only matter down the road when they applied to have the restrictions lifted. The results were predictable. With a very poor local signal, and saddled with perhaps the most restrictive Promise of Performance many broadcast experts had ever seen, we introduced ourselves to London radio and waited to see just how bad things would get.

Gord and Jerry had proven their credentials over the years, and taken a second-rate CKSL from an also-ran Top Forty station to a real contender in the marketplace. They had imported some big-time voices and Gord had talked the wealthy owners into relocating from a run-down, old fashioned set of studios in an old office building to a new home in the prestigious City Centre complex in the heart of the city, with spacious studios, great studio gear, and a top-flight News team.

CIQM, though, was the somewhat overlooked newborn second child, still trying to find itself, and was crammed into tiny quarters that must have been somebody's after-thought.

"Oh yeah, the FM station. Almost forgot about that. Hey Charlie, clean out that broom closet, willya?"

But inside the control room waited a pair of Compact Disc playback units, the very latest in technology and a brand experience for me. They were still such a novelty that we would frequently promote them when introducing a song.

"Here's Harry Nees and the Hip Replacements singing I Only Have Thighs for You - on Compact Disc."

Announcer: *"On the way, more of the perks and perils of live radio!"*

From the beginning, we identified ourselves on air as Canada's First AFM station. What this was supposed to mean was initially any listener's guess, but after several weeks it was identified as Adult FM. My contribution was to deliver a seventy-five-minute talk program daily, called Mid-Day Magazine. Seventy-five minutes, plus just a few seconds more. It was that precise. The CRTC hired entry-level flunkies to randomly audit the station, and use a stopwatch to time any program suspected of being a time bandit.

To do a similar talk show on CBC Radio, the host would have a dedicated Producer, a couple of research assistants to provide background material and interview questions, a board operator to insert commercials and deal with the time delay necessary for any live talk show, and a Guest Booker to find interesting people to interview on the show.

Yeah, sure. I had a staff of only three, me, myself, and I. Always scrambling for content, I contacted every book publisher in Canada to let them know their touring authors were welcome on my show. I also contacted people I believed could perform well on a radio show. Lots of professionals really know their chosen field, but freeze up when the red light goes on. I lined up a veterinarian, a travel agent, several psychics, a lawyer, a general practice physician, and a fashion consultant to join me on the show on a rotating, ongoing basis.

My fashion consultant was a lady named Mary McEllister. I had worked with her previously, producing her commercials for her London store called Green Gables when I was at CHLO. I knew she had the gift of the gab and would make a fine guest. A woman of impeccable taste, she shocked a lot of people when she later agreed to become my wife.

I asked each of my regular guests to come prepared with a lead sheet of questions I could ask them during their appearance. That way they didn't have to worry about being caught off guard, and a relaxed guest is likely to be a more entertaining guest. This also took a great deal of prep work out of my hands. I always told them to save this sheet in their records, and after a year or so, we would just re-do the complete show.

In due course, the authors started to drop in for interviews, which again let me off the hook from constantly trying to book fresh voices. Generally, the book-flogging authors were very busy during their tours, and would try to schedule several different interviews at as many stations in town as possible. Sometimes I would have to pre-record their interviews for later broadcast.

I think the most bewildering but incredibly funny interview I ever conducted was with the late Canadian actor, writer, playwright, composer and comedian, Don Harron, who was perhaps even better known as Charlie Farquharson, his character on the perennial hit American TV show Hee Haw.

Charlie was the rumpled farmer from Northern Ontario (or pretty much rural anywhere) who sported a tattered sweater and a three-day growth of beard.

Don was then touring to tout his newest book, Charlie Farquharson's Unyverse (sic). And the interview was the most confusing half-hour I had ever spent on the air. I would ask *Don*, the actor a question, and *Charlie*, the master of malapropism, would respond. When I would ask *Charlie* a question, *Don* would respond in a mellow, mature voice, as naturally as though there were no shenanigans going on at all.

It's generally a good idea to let a professional comedian have the last word, and I gave it to Don when I asked him what he thought was the best part of his book. Charlie replied:

"Well, son, here's the thing about my book. I think you should just rip out one page at a time and read it in the bathroom. **Then you can put it behind you!***"*

I hope you won't be tempted to do that at home with this book!

You can view an old video of Charlie in action on "Hee Haw" at:
Hee Haw - Comedy
One of my most memorable interviews, (which I had to tape) was with Canada's foremost author, Pierre Berton, a prolific writer with many best-sellers to his credit. He was currently on tour promoting his latest book, Vimy a detailed account of the bravery of the Canadian soldiers who, against all odds

in 1917, valiantly seized the German bastion at Vimy Ridge on the Western Front during World War One.

Pierre was a broadcasting icon, and had been an interviewer himself, on his own long-running national interview show. He was a stickler for detail and always well-prepared for his guests. A towering presence both physically and on the literary front, he expected the same attention to detail from would-be hosts interviewing *him*. Or else. He was famous for not suffering fools gladly. As far as he was concerned, you had better have read his whole book and not just the dust-jacket, or he was known to walk out of the studio in the middle of a live interview. Or worse, stay and berate the host.

I understood his preference, but I received his thick book only a day before he was to arrive in my recording studio and there was no way I was staying up all night to read it. Instead, I quickly skimmed it and picked out some random portions that would prompt a question carefully worded so Pierre could answer with a lengthy reply. I figured that put me on the track for a successful chat with him.

"Mr. Berton, you state in your book, that blah, blah, blah, blah. Could you elaborate on that for our listeners?"

That would usually take him a few minutes, at which point I would repeat the exercise with a new quote.

The studio we were using was equipped with a very complex control board, similar to what you would see in a multi-track recording facility. Since it had all kinds of knobs and dials, channel-selectors, equalization and compression controls and other bells and whistles, it was far more complex a piece of equipment than needed to record a simple two-microphone interview. But it was what I had access to, and I had to make the most of it.

It wasn't an easy interview at first. I'm sure that every author gets bored answering the same questions time after time, and Pierre was a big enough star that he had enormous bluster-power working for him. He was a big man, too, solid and imposing, and as I said he had no patience for fools. During the first four or five questions I could sense he was testing me, checking to see how I reacted under pressure. He wouldn't really engage, and his early responses were short and mumbled. He wouldn't make eye contact with me, either, and that can be pretty disconcerting when you are trying to connect with someone.

But once he was convinced I had actually read his book (some of it, anyway) and wasn't some charlatan who didn't know anything about the art of interviewing, his posture shifted and he began to loosen up. For the rest of the interview he was charming and talkative and shared a lot of insights about his book and the people and places in it.

After about forty-five minutes, I wrapped things up, thanked Mr. Berton and turned the microphones off. Just to be sure the sound levels were OK, I spun the tape back to the beginning of our interview, then punched play. Nothing but tape hiss. Apparently the microphones had for some reason failed to pass along to the tape recorder what they had heard. It took only a few moments to realize someone had been fooling around with the multitude of dials and knobs and mistakenly shut off the input into the tape machine.

I was almost out of my mind. To have this happen with any interview (and it does happen) is a disastrous waste of time for all concerned. And with Pierre Berton? Bad enough I had failed to operate the equipment properly, but I had plainly wasted his time. He always had plenty of interviews to do when he came to London and his people kept him on a tight schedule. I decided to throw caution to the winds anyway.

"Mr. Burton, I'm so terribly sorry, but you can see what my problem is. I know you are very busy but is there any chance we could redo the interview at some other time?"

I braced myself for an explosion (that suffering fools gladly business, again). Instead, he leaned back into his chair and gave me a big grin.

"You took the time to do your homework, so let's make time to redo it now. Maybe this time I'll give you better answers! Will that work for you?"

It certainly would, we redid the entire piece and I think it was much better the second time around.

A few weeks later I interviewed Vickie Gabereau, another CBC Radio and TV personality/interviewer. Coincidentally, her dad was a close friend of Pierre Berton, and she grew up with him as a frequent guest in her family's home. She too had written a book. (What is it about radio hosts writing books, anyway?)

Before I started to record my interview with her, I related the story about my mishap with Pierre. She started to laugh and said she was going to tell me a story I would enjoy. I sat back, looking forward to some happy family anecdote or insightful analysis of the Great Man. I guess in a way I got both. As I have said, the Berton family had been part of her life for many years, and they had shared many happy memories.

"I was assigned to interview him once on national radio, and didn't bother to read the book he was touting. I figured I knew him well enough to get away with some casual questions. But as soon as he realized I was faking it, he got right up and walked out of the studio!"

Apparently I had been even luckier than I'd thought. (Just for the record, Vickie, for all her national reputation as a broadcaster, was a horrible interview subject. You'd be surprised at how many like her are.)

Then there are the interviews that veer ninety degrees away from where you thought you were going. Like the one with the female head of an exciting new clothing line that was growing by leaps and bounds. Not only was she a local success story, but her status as a female CEO had brought her additional media attention. To make sure the interview went as smoothly as possible, I sat down beforehand and wrote out a long list of questions for her, all designed to elicit positive responses and keep her talking.

I should have known strange winds were blowing when she passed by me into the booth where her portion of the interview would take place, separated from me by a big glass window. This was really not the most comfortable setting for a guest. With both of us in the same room we wouldn't need headphones, which can be intimidating and uncomfortable. But nobody had taken that into consideration when setting up this studio.

As she squeezed by me, she nodded and gave me a wink.

"Hey Dick, you know that story about the lady that goes to the dentist? When she is in the chair and the dentist picks up his drill, she grabs him by the balls, and says 'We aren't going to hurt each other, are we?' Your interview's going to be like that, right?" I could see under her bravado she was terrified of doing the interview, and had obviously medicated herself with some stress reducer before coming to the station.

"No need to worry, this will be the easiest interview you'll ever have in your life! Just relax and let's have a nice chat. Pretend you're in your living room."

In the booth, she took off her shoes and socks and sat cross legged on the guest chair in a yoga pose. I hoped she felt as relaxed as she looked. I turned on the microphones, which put us on the air live, and tee'd up the show with a quick synopsis of the history of the company. Then I gave my guest a glowing introduction and launched into my first question. Remember now, we're live not recorded, because what can possibly go wrong?

"With such a large and growing company now, what do you think was the most important thing in making your success possible?"

"Horseshoes!"

I knew her company made a lot of products, but I hadn't seen any horseshoes in the catalogue. Nor had there been any reference to horses in her bio. Puzzled, I asked the question again. Same response.

"So horseshoes were the most important factor in your success? How so?"

"I must have had golden horseshoes up my ass!"

As success story interview quotes go, they don't get much better than that.

Track 121

Lawyers were the one profession I had difficulty getting repeat performances from. Not hard to explain, really. What lawyer worth his salt would give up an hour's billing time in his office for a non-paying guest role on the radio? I knew several glib, silver-tongued guys who would have been superb studio guests, but they always had something better to do. Or so they said!

My own lawyer was one of them but at least he put me in touch with someone else he said was a student of the law. It was the student part that worried me. Remember Professor Irwin Corey, who used to appear on the Ed Sullivan Show dressed in a disheveled suit, hair all standing on end, tie askew, and wearing running shoes? That's the spitting image of my on-air legal expert. (For younger readers, think Doc Brown in Back to the Future.)

But he was the best I could do, he helped fill the allotted time, and he came prepared with his notes to guide me through the interview. One particular show the topic under discussion was Representation by Population, which grew from the observation that a thinly-populated province like Manitoba had an equal say in constitutional matters with the much more populated province of Ontario. Reading from the notes he had supplied, I asked him why that was, expecting a lengthy (and predictably boring) response.

As he started to talk, I shut off my microphone, stood up, and started to file some records and commercials away, to make ready for the following DJ. It was common practice near the end of a shift, and I would be sat down again in time to ask the next question. We were on a seven-second digital delay, but I had never had occasion to actually ever use it. Suddenly, a short sentence leaped out at me from whatever it was he had been saying.

"Frankly, sometimes I feel like a (N-word) in my own country!"

My arms were filled with a stack of albums but I dropped them on the floor and dove for the Dump Switch that would prevent the last seven seconds from being broadcast. Too late. The seven seconds of safety net had expired. Surprise, surprise, the phones lit up instantly. And to make matters worse, we still had to continue the show to fill the time commitment, or face retribution from the CRTC. I couldn't even toss him out of the studio (or the nearest window), and had to carry on as though nothing had happened.

When the show was finally over, I told him not to leave the station.

"Don't go too far, I'm going to need a retraction from you for what you said! Go sit in the lobby for a few minutes and we'll record it after I clear up in here."

He gave me a puzzled look as if he had no idea why he would have to do a retraction, but followed my instructions and went to the lobby. I found him there a few minutes later and I walked him back to an empty recording studio where he sat down and waited while I got ready to record his apology. Then I started the tape rolling and cued him to start.

"Earlier today I said I feel like a (N-word) in my own country."

I just stared at him through the glass, slowly shaking my head.

"I don't think that's quite going to do it," I said.

"No?"

"No."

"Well, what should I say?"

"How about starting with something like, earlier today I inadvertently slighted a minority group in Canada. Then say you're sorry, you didn't mean to say it and you'll never do it again."

It didn't occur to me until later that me having to give legal advice to him didn't say anything good about his legal expertise, whatever that was. As he left the station I had one final reminder why I'd have been better off had I never found him.

"Does this mean you won't want me back again?" You think?

Mary McEllister, my Fashion Specialist, turned out to be a standout guest who sounded great on-air. She was very relaxed, could respond to any question at length, and had fun chatting as if I was a close friend, (which at *that* point, I wasn't.) But she was almost always within seconds of air-time when she arrived at the studio. I would be fighting off a panic attack when she would breeze into the studios while the opening theme was playing, pass me a sheet of questions to ask during the show, pull on a set of headphones, turn on her own microphone, and start the interview as if she had been sitting in place for hours waiting for the show to begin.

The crazy thing is, she would bring in samples of things she would be talking about, like shoes, some fluffy new winter earmuffs, or maybe a new padded bra. This is radio, remember, not the TV Shopping Channel. But there she'd be, talking about her products as though everyone could see them. Which, in a way, they could, because she was such a good talker.

Because she would arrive with her props in a large carrying case, I started to call her The Bag Lady on the air, and she became a popular addition to the show. Her on-air success certainly did her business no harm because her interview time was essentially a free full-length commercial for her store. And in an ironic twist, *she wasn't even a paying sponsor on the station!*

Mary told me that when she got back to her store after doing the show there would be calls from men wanting to buy some of the articles she had talked about on that day's program. She even got a call from a guy asking her to put away a set of the fuzzy earmuffs she had been describing on Mid-Day Magazine. Apparently his voice on the phone sounded like he was in an echo chamber, and she asked where he was calling from.

"I'm in a drain sewer doing some repairs for the London Public Utilities Commission!"

Shades of Ed Norton, for those of you who are lucky enough to have seen recall Jackie Gleason's Honeymooners.

Knowing Mary was in control of her part of the show, I stood up one day while she was talking and once again started to file away carts and LP's to keep the studio clutter to a minimum. Just like I had with the lawyer. In my opinion it didn't make any difference to the on-air sound of the station, because she was filling the time very capably. But she's a person who likes to look everyone in the eye when she's having a conversation and I wasn't playing by the rules (though I know better now).

She has never admitted whether it was revenge for being ignored or just her being playful, but I almost dropped the records I was sorting when I hear her voice darken and go up several decibels.

"Dick, you're not paying attention to me!" Ooops! I grabbed my headphones, stuck my face in front of my microphone and flipped it on.

"Mary, I'm hanging on your every word!" That was the right answer as an interviewer, and a pretty good strategy for a husband, too.

Dick and his wife, Mary McEllister, in Toronto to accept Telemedia's "Announcer of the Year" award.

Announcer: *"Still lots more to come. Things really start to look up, and help is on the way."*

"When the Corporations took over, that was really the end of our kind of radio." Progressive rock pioneer Dusty Street

After about two years of this talk-heavy format, the station was sold from local owners to a large Quebec-based media giant called Telemedia. Changes quickly followed, as is usually the case in radio. First, we were able to convince the CRTC that we were stuck in limbo with the restrictive, over-regulated Promises of Performance we had made in order to get our licence. Thankfully for all concerned, that wasn't too hard to do. At that point, the station was losing over $500,000 per year, although it may have been a nice tax write-off for the original owners. Both Gord Hume and Jerry Stevens were soon replaced with Braden Doerr, our new General Manager, and Barry Smith, a long-time friend and experienced Program Director.

Many of the talk elements were quickly discarded, the non-hits disappeared, and we hired some slick consultants, Bohn and Associates. They rapidly introduced a very homogenous, ballad-heavy Adult Contemporary format on what they now billed as Q103 rather than the stuffy CIQM, 103.1 FM, as we had formerly called ourselves. A lovely set of jingles accompanied the change, and almost overnight we started to build a large audience.

"In my day, everything came from my belly button and seat of the pants. Today, everything is done from research." Early Top 40 radio executive George Wilson

None of this was done by chance. Many dollars were invested in Focus Groups of our listeners, to give us up-to-the-moment details of what songs they liked, which artists they preferred, and which songs they didn't care for. Also, daily Call Out research was initiated, and we polled our listeners off-air each evening to keep our fingers on the pulse of the audience almost minute-by-minute.

Within months, our tightly-scripted, music-intensive format started to give us a huge numbers in the Time Spent Listening category, and we began to tout ourselves as The At Work Network. Offices across the area started to play the station over their office speakers, exposing more and more people to our smooth sounds. To keep the consistency identical throughout the day, we were supplied with "Liners," pre-tested slogans that re-enforced our role.

"Not too hard, not too soft. We're the station everyone at work can agree on! We're London's office favorite, Q103."

Amazingly, our audience almost tripled in a year. That kind of growth is almost unheard-of in radio these days. Another break came our way when CKO, an all-news network, went off the air and out of business.. Telemedia and our local management moved quickly, obtaining the rights to change our frequency and power to CKO's former London position, 97.5 on the FM dial. We gained a power increase, a much better dial position and a new antenna placement on a much higher tower. At the same time, we rebranded ourselves again.

"You're listening to Q97.5, London's EZ Rock."

Here's an audio sample of the smooth sound of Adult Contemporary afternoon radio on "The At-Work Network":
AUDIO/VIDEO: Q 97 5 Adult Contemporary

Announcer: *"Stand by for digital doings! Coming up, we'll show you how a DJ can be in two places at once!"*

"The radio of my youth ... is now a quaint memory replaced by computer hard drives." Former TV talk show host Phil Donahue.

"It is entirely possible that the medium market Program Director of today will have to deal with some form of computerization (in the future)." Bob Paiva, accurately looking into the future in his 1983 book "The Program Director's Handbook."

During this time in my career, computers became the backbone of our entire on-air operation and turntables and tape recorders became relics of the past. All we had to do was record all our commercials and jingles into the computer system, then add all the music we might need. Once you got used to it, life was a lot simpler for everyone involved. The entire show sat on the monitor screen, and once the first event was fired, the system could run on cruise control, sequencing everything automatically, until it was told to stop. Then the on-air DJ would do whatever was required, live on air, before restarting the pre-programmed next item.

A separate software program would allow the jock to record upcoming parts of his show while music was playing live, on-air. That was called voice tracking. He would simply skip to the first element where he would normally be called on to say something, then hit record on the screen and record *just his voice*. It would then be played back automatically when that part of the program was reached in real time. He could basically drop in whatever he wanted, wherever he wanted. Then, in Auto-Record mode, the program would automatically sequence to the next time he was to speak and the process would be repeated. The neatest thing about it was that it also allowed you to record a different show from the one you were broadcasting at the time.

With practice, a bare-bones, six-hour voice-tracked segment could be recorded in as little as thirty minutes, for playback up to a week later. All of this could be done at the same time as the announcer was on-air, doing a live show. All this multi-tasking helped keep costs in line for the station's programing budget, and make sure that sparsely-heard segments like the overnight show could still sound really good.
If it sounded like there was a warm body behind the microphone, there didn't actually need to *be* one.

Minor changes to the master logs of music and commercials could be made by simply inserting an element, such as a specific commercial or a piece of music, with just a few simple key-strokes on the computer.

I had purchased digital recording equipment for my home as soon as good-quality components were available at a reasonable price. I knew my business would continue to change and I wanted to be part of it. With my home studio I was able to produce and record the voice tracks for a four-hour weekend program called The Saturday Special, then *email* the audiofiles directly to the Production Department at the station, where they would be inserted sequentially into Saturday's digitized programing.

That's a long way from slapping a 45 on a turntable and turning a microphone on to share your dulcet tones with the world.

Q97.5 Control Room (previous two pictures)

Track 125

Announcer: *"A change in the wings! There's more to come, but first this little tale."*

While studios were changing from CD's to PC's, one of our newsmen decided he was ready for a change, too. After much soul-searching, he became convinced he was meant to be a woman, and wanted to have his body changed appropriately. I had known him for years, and there was no question he faced a tough battle ahead in his chosen path. In order to qualify for a full-blown sex change operation, he had to live full-time as a female. It wasn't something he could do just when it was convenient, it had to be all the time.

So he arrived for work one day in full makeup and wig and wearing a woman's dress, and carried on with his regular shift as usual. I have to admit it was always a little disconcerting when he came in for his newscasts in feminine attire, sat down across from me in the news/interview studio, arranged the headset over his dark black wig, and read the news in a very deep, masculine, authoritative voice.

I had no problem with his choice because people are people, whatever their gender. It certainly took a great deal of courage to make this mid-life course correction, and my friend handled it well, although he later decided (before the operation) that maybe it wasn't such a good idea after all and he continues to live as a man.

Track 126

Announcer: *"From FM to AM again. That's coming up, but now, back to our regularly scheduled program."*

"The freshening of the air sound will be a constant objective."
WOR-FM positioning statement.

CKSL Oldies 1410, 1998 Playlist:
"I Want to Hold Your Hand" The Beatles
"She Loves You" The Beatles
"Hello, Dolly!" Louis Armstrong
"Oh, Pretty Woman" Roy Orbison
"I Get Around" The Beach Boys
"Everybody Loves Somebody" Dean Martin
"My Guy" Mary Wells
"We'll Sing in the Sunshine" Gale Garnett
"Last Kiss" J. Frank Wilson and the Cavaliers
"Where Did Our Love Go" The Supremes

Now Playing: Right Back Where We Started From, by
Maxine Nightingale
"Ooo and it's alright and it's comin' 'long
We got to get right back to where we started from
Love is good, love can be strong
We got to get right back to where we started from"
Vincent Edwards, Pierre Tubbs © United Artists

At this time our two-station group of stations merged with CJBK-AM and BX93-FM, the area's biggest country music station, and our entire so-called cluster consolidated in the same building from which I had been fired a few years earlier. With *four* stations occupying the space which had been designed for just two stations a few years before, we were all cramped into a congested area. In the beginning, I felt that our two Telemedia stations were looked on as intruders, but over time, things smoothed out.

CKSL had just abandoned a very expensive exercise with a spoken word format called News Talk for the 90s. Since our new sister station CJBK already had a similar talk format, it was decided that it would be worthwhile to go after the niche for Oldies music. I had been asked to voice track the mid-day show on the Oldies station, in addition to my existing show on EZ Rock, and was glad to do so. Since I had already prepared to present one radio show per day, it didn't take much more to cover the second one, too. Nor did it take much time, as I explained earlier. I got a chance to get back into the Personality Radio style of presentation, and quite enjoyed bringing back the songs I had aired way back in the Fifties and Sixties.

There was never any reason to believe that an Oldies format would be a smashing success in the London AM market, or in any market, for that matter. Talk stations were flourishing on the AM bandwidth but there was room for only so many. Across North America, many AM stations were 'going black' by turning off their transmitters and locking the doors, as local and corporate owners cut their losses and walked away. AM radio had become an outdated way to listen to music. With little or no money available for promotion, The

Oldies format was, at best, a holding pattern while corporate management looked for different formats to fill older listener's needs and attract sponsorship dollars.

Change was once more in the wind when our cluster was acquired by another broadcasting conglomerate, Toronto's Standard Radio. That was kind of a wakeup call for me. I realized that my days on a youthful-sounding FM station were dwindling. I was now in my sixties and nearing retirement, not exactly the kind of persona relevant to a younger audience. With that in mind, I wasn't entirely surprised to be called into the Operations Manager's office one day, and be told that I would be leaving Q97.5.

Before I could consider the consequences of unemployment, I was offered the job of host of a morning show on Oldies 1410. I would be doing the show live and also be in charge of scheduling the music, merging the commercial logs with the music logs, and carefully timing the almost totally automated station to fill its twenty-four-hour broadcast day.

What had been a fun, part-time shift was now quite a different realty. I had no experience in the complexities of the technically-demanding process of programing a radio station in the digital age. Sure, I knew how to run programs on-air as a DJ, but I had never experienced the difficulties of making an entire station manageable by programing one from the ground up.

I'll spare you the details, but it was a very steep learning curve. So much to do, so little time took on a whole new meaning for me. I often felt the same way I had felt in my earliest days in radio, some forty or more years ago. But with many consultations with another seasoned veteran at the station, Chris Harding, I was able to cobble together a day-to-day station that would be unattended from 10 am when it went into automation mode, until 6 am the next morning. On weekends, we went into automatic mode at 10 am Friday and the station had no live person in the control room until the following Monday morning at 6 am. What I learned through this process made life a bit easier when I had to learn to program and schedule my own radio station! (Another tee-up! I couldn't resist!)

Back to the Oldies, and the hits just keep on coming! Non Stop memories, commercial free, with The Tall One and "The Greatest Hits of All Time!
AUDIO/VIDEO: Oldies 1410, London

Track 127

"If you're good, you'll always work somewhere. If not, you'll learn to do something else." Former WKBW DJ Fred Klestine

CKSL Oldies 1410, 2000 Playlist:
"Are You Sincere" Andy Williams
"Can Anyone Explain" Ames Brothers
"Shangri-La" Vic Dana
"Happy Heart" Andy Williams
"Moments to Remember" Four Lads
"How Little We Know" Frank Sinatra
"Java" Al Hurt
"Lisbon Antiqua" Les Baxter
"Ruby" Harmonicats
"Mack the Knife" Louis Armstrong

Now Playing: Can Anyone Explain (No! No! No!), by Ella Fitzgerald
"Can anyone explain the wonder of love?
No! No! No!
But now that you and I are sharing a sigh
We know, yes, we know"
Benny Benjamin, George © Warner/Chappell Music, Inc.

It wasn't long until our new corporate owners decreed a new format for Oldies 1410. We were to drop all the Oldies and replace them with all the mellow hits of the Fifties and Sixties, plus a few current songs from The Great American

Songbook re-sung by modern artists like Michael Bublé, Rod Stewart, and Diana Krall. Sure, whatever you say. All we had to do was totally update our digitized playlist by entering all the new songs into the computer while deleting all the Oldies.

It was a very tedious and time-consuming prospect to enter close to four thousand songs, and accurately time and categorize them into the computer system. Each song had to be recorded in real-time as well, not ripped as is done today with Ipods and Ipads and such. Once again, we were starting from the ground up and looking for a totally new audience, which likely would not be a large one in any case. Over the years, successive owners had not maintained the station's broadcasting towers and radial ground lines, which under normal circumstances would be buried in outward-radiating lines under the earth around the transmission towers. The land over these cables had eroded, leaving the cables exposed, so the signal was not even reaching many parts of the city we were tasked with covering, but transmitting directly upwards into space instead!

I was fortunate to know of a true radio gentleman, Lyman Potts, who at one point in his long career had headed up the Canadian Talent Library. Years earlier, in an ironic set of circumstances, Lyman had been part of the team when CKSL went on the air in the 1950s. He was an invaluable help with our most difficult programing needs, namely Canadian Content. Lyman was able to supply me with hundreds of beautifully-recorded cuts to augment the few Canadian songs that fit into our newly-evolving playlist, and I will be forever grateful to him.

After a few months of totally revamping the format of the station, we had created a very smooth, (if not very relevant) sound. But we had a devil of a time attracting listeners to the format. I was reminded of the words of my old GM at CFPL, Ward Cornell, those many years ago.

"We're making twenty people in London extremely happy."

It was another format that time had passed by, with an older audience that had grown out of the bait of listening to AM radio and preferred its own recorded music, or the very poorly-programed FM station in the region that played a somewhat similar style of music, with much better sound reproduction.

The Music of Your Mother's Life didn't make the cut and once again it was back to Oldies 1410!

Before we do, have a listen to AM Radio mornings with "Great Songs and Great Memories!
AUDIO/VIDEO: AM1410

Track 128

"Make the best of it while you can ... have fun and keep those experiences close to your heart, then take all your winnings and run like a bitch". Legendary CHUM Toronto DJ the late Terry Steele

Over the years I had been up and down and sometimes sideways, and at a time when I should have been coasting on some relaxing final laps of my radio career, I found myself working harder than ever, with technology that was still new to me.

There were some discussions with the station brass and I finally decided to call it a day. I couldn't have done it at a better time. Mary and I spend our winters in Key West, Florida, but to do my *last* show, I had to drive forty-five minutes through a raging snowstorm from our newly-renovated home in Port Stanley, south of London on Lake Erie. That sealed the deal that we had made the right decision. I signed off the last show with my usual extro.

"That's my story in words and music. I'm Dick Williams, and thanks for listening all these years."

I cleared out my office, threw away most of the dozens of CDs containing my on-air gimmicks and finally hung up my headphones. At my retirement party, guess what? I got the proverbial watch! Yep, at a period in life when time generally doesn't have to be accounted for much, that's the default departing fare-thee-well gift. I appreciated the gesture, and it really was time to go. The next day Mary and I flew to Key West to begin the next phase of our lives, but not before I shared a few words of wisdom with my friends and colleagues.

"I loved every minute of it, and if you love what you do, you never work a day in your life!"

Track 129

Announcer: *"Still to come, life after radio- the wonderful world of voiceovers. Stick around, we'll be right back!"*

"Radio used to be more show than business. Now it's more business than show." Jerry Del Colliano, Publisher of Inside Radio

Now playing: Love's In Need of Love Today, by Stevie Wonder
"Good morn or evening friends
Here's your friendly announcer
I have serious news to pass on to everybody"
Stevie Wonder © EMI Music Publishing

Years before my retirement, I had been retained to do a series of voiceovers for an old friend from my time at Shannon Services. Up to this point I had been hiring a sound technician and renting a studio to produce any audio tracks I needed on my own, but my friend made a good suggestion.

"You know, if you build an in-home studio, it will pay for itself in a hurry and save you a lot of money!"

I took his advice, and true to form, he was right. Within a few months I had paid off the cost of building the studio and equipping myself with the microphones, amplifiers, and reel-to reel, multi-track tape machines that would let me voice and fully produce finished narrations and commercials.

I was then hired by CKO Radio, an All-News Network, to produce and voice commercials for several of their dozen stations across Canada. This gave me a nice base to expand upon, and shortly after I was also hired as the booth announcer for CFPL-TV in London, where I had toiled in front of their cameras years before.

CKO at the time was state of the art. They would send scripts via a form of teletype machine which would instantly forward them to me as soon as they were typed and addressed. I would then rush down to my basement studio, record the spots, and courier them to the stations. Turnaround times would be within two days. Today, with computers and the internet, turnaround deadlines have been trimmed to as little as an hour or so after receiving the script.

With CFPL-TV, which shortly became known as The New PL, things got a little tense when I realized that I was pretty much the *only* on-air voice they were using. When I watched the station I would cringe, because if they played four commercials back-to-back, I would be the announcer on all of the spots! Not a good thing.

Another problem was a weekly set of sixty-second commercials called En Route, which involved reading five different ten-second spots sandwiched back to back after an intro and extro of ten seconds. Since TV times are crucial and split-second timing is required, I had to read the scripts at the same time as I kept an eye on my stop-watch. They had to come in at exactly fifty-nine seconds, no exceptions! As I would reach the fifty-second mark, the pressure would be on to either speed up or slow down to hit the time just right. Too often, I would get to the last few words and flub them. With tape, there was no quick and easy way to edit the goof, so I would have to spin back the tape and re-read the spot over and over and over, until I *finally* got a proper read of the exact length.

But with my investment in a computer and a very primitive piece of audio recording software, I eliminated my timing difficulties once and for all. I could quickly edit any mistake out of the file I had recorded, then either time-compress or time-expand the audiofile to fit exactly 59 seconds. The savings in time spent recording made it well worth the switch to digital recording.

A bit of audio magic for you to sample, with digital recording produced for a radio station in Europe: AUDIO/VIDEO: Dick Williams Radio Imaging Video

Over the years, I hooked up with several other computer-connected voiceover artists and we collectively became The Silver-Tongued Devils. I introduced the group to producers in Canada and the U.S. as optional voices, both male and female, young and old, for radio and TV spots all over the continent. For more than fifteen years, I've voiced thousands of spots with these people, and even though I have contact with them daily, most of them I have never met in person.

That has had some interesting consequences. One of my female voices, Natasha, was headquartered for a few years in the Turks and Caicos Islands. When she was on vacation in Canada a few years ago, we arranged to meet face-to-face in Port Stanley, where I have my Canadian studio. As I was standing on the appointed corner at the appointed hour, I realized I had no idea who to look for. And a law-abiding single guy on a street corner has to be careful how he deals with ladies passing by. No telling what kind of trouble you might get into. After watching the passersby for several minutes, I noticed a young lady looking at me with a curious expression on her face. She came a little closer before speaking.

"Are you Dick?"

I must have had the same look on my face too! We had performed together on hundreds of two-voice commercials, but had never seen each other! That's how isolated from each other people can be on these multiple-voice commercials.

With the advent of major, industry-wide cost cutting, automation, syndication and programs beamed to radio stations, many stations today have *no* live, local announcers on staff anymore, other than the morning programs. (And there are a growing number of stations who have even dumped them!) So there's a pressing need for announcer voices to record local commercials. It is also much cheaper to pay a disembodied voice a per-commercial price, or a monthly retainer fee, than to pay a full-time announcer's wages. Plus there are no health benefits, sick time, or vacation issues. All of which is a bonus to self-employed voices using the internet as a delivery system to radio and TV stations everywhere!

Over the years, my voice has been heard on Sirius XM Radio, the American Armed Forces Radio Network, and for a three-year period was the daily radio voice promoting The New York Daily Challenge, a black-owned newspaper in Brooklyn. These ads were aired on 1010 WINS in New York, the most listened-to AM radio station in North America. Of course, for every one of those grand projects we did a dozen for small and medium markets all over America. I also produce commercials for the syndicated Oldies radio program, Shake Rattle Showtime, heard on about thirty stations across North America. I recently completed my U.S. Perfect Fifty when I was hired to voice a commercial for a tiny station that aired it in the only state I had not yet been heard in, the Treasure State, beautiful Montana.
Here are some of the talented voices I have the pleasure of working with for clients across North America:

AUDIO/VIDEO: Silver Tongued Devils

Dick Williams Voice Talent

DICK WILLIAMS VOICE TALENT offers Radio and Television stations all over North America rapid turnaround for commercials, promos, ID's, stagers and imaging, to position your station as the dominant leader in your market.

We're your first choice for commercial production, and corporate voice work.

Our stable of "Silver Tongued Devils" can deliver your message with maximum impact and offer you a variety of styles, one of which can fit you like a glove.

Please listen to our Demo Commercials, Radio and TV Imaging and much more. We know you'll get the message, loud and clear!

HOME
ABOUT US
SAMPLES
CONTACT US
GREAT SPOTS
VIDEOS
RADIO IMAGING

Have a listen to the Silver Tongued Devils yourself!

Track 131

It is still quite amazing to me that in the course of any given day a voiceover person can do work for stations anywhere in the world. I've done produced station-breaks for radio stations in Holland, Australia, South Africa and several in Britain. My wife Mary's is the voice you hear if you board the elevator in the Burj Khalifa, which stands at two thousand, two hundred and seventeen feet high in Dubai. On the day it was completed it became the tallest building in the world, and Mary is waiting to talk to you!

No two days are ever alike, and it's always a marvellous challenge to deliver what the client needs.

One interesting project was providing the voice for a GPS System installed in rental cars in Britain and several other countries of the E.U. The project itself was pretty boring.

"Turn Left in seven hunded meters."

"Turn Left in six hundred meters."

I live for the day I will climb into a car and listen to me tell me where to drive.

With time, I was able to purchase a large library of background music, timed to fifteen-, thirty- and sixty-second lengths to use behind commercials, as well as an extensive sound effects library. That gives me access to almost any effect I might need to add to produced spots. From the crack of a baseball bat to the rumble of far-off storms, I have all kinds of sounds stored on a hard drive I can take with me anywhere. And with a multi-track software package, any number of voices, music tracks and sound effects can be assembled for any kind of production, from the most basic to the truly elaborate.

Track 132

"*Basically, radio hasn't changed over the years. Despite all the technical improvements, it still boils down to a man or a woman and a microphone, playing music, sharing stories, talking about issues - communicating with an audience.*"
Casey Kasem

Now Playing: Changes in Latitudes, Changes in Attitudes, by Jimmy Buffett
"*It's those changes in latitudes
Changes in attitudes
Nothing remains quite the same.
With all of our running and all of our cunning
If we couldn't laugh, we would all go insane.*"
Buffett © ABC Records

Six months of the year, Mary and I live in the Southernmost City of America. Of course, recording in Key West can a bit of a struggle. The two mile by four mile size means the whole island is on final approach to the airport, and it is a busy travel destination. As the planes pass overhead, as one just did a second ago, they are at a height of about two hundred feet over my studio/living room. The island is also home to an enormous rooster colony, and let me tell you they don't just crow at sunrise! Throw in passing dogs, un-muffled Harleys, motor scooters, the always-present dueling chain-saws, leaf-blowers and wood chippers, and the ambiance is anything but friendly to audio recording. A sonic paradise it is not.

That makes recording a real challenge, and involves lots of pauses and editing to end up with a quiet finished product. Add to this mix the nearby location of a Naval Air Station, with the heavy rumble of high-performance Super Hornets, Tomcats, Eagles, and other military aircraft adding to the din.

On an early pre-Christmas visit to Key West, I had just got my recording studio up and running. We were listening to one of the local stations where a syndicated radio show called Delilah was playing carols. We had also aired the program at Q97.5 back in London. When they broke for commercials, I heard my voice on a spot I had recorded back in Canada just two or three days before. It was quite wrenching to hear it so soon, hundreds of miles away in another country.

Always looking for interesting projects, I called up the Manager of a local FM Radio station, Key 93 as it was then known, and asked if I could come out and make her an offer. My wife Mary and I were both dressed in shorts and hopped on our bicycles, which we use to get around the island, to ride out to the station. With the quickly-changing weather patterns of the Keys, we found ourselves in the middle of an unexpected torrential tropical storm, and were soaked to the skin by the time we finally reached the station. Leaving trails like two snails behind us, we dripped our way into the lobby to meet the Manager.

Ignoring our obvious wet-to-the-bone condition, I explained to her that I could offer her fully-produced commercials that would make her station sound a lot better without breaking the bank. I knew I had a good product and I thought I had a pretty good sales pitch, but something else must have put her off. If it wasn't my Bermuda shorts and balloon-tire bike, it can only have been my sad and soggy appearance, the only time I ever tried to make a sale looking like a twice-drowned rat. Whatever it was, she passed on the proposal and Mary and I rode off back to Casa Williams, wetter but wiser than when we had left.

Track 133

Now Playing: The Wreck of the Edmund Fitzgerald, by
Gordon Lightfoot

"The legend lives on from the Chippewa on down
Of the big lake they call Gitche Gumee
The lake, it is said, never gives up her dead
When the skies of November turn gloomy"
© Moose Music Ltd. /Early Morning Music Ltd.

I've never been able to get away from this song! Having
played it so many times, even thinking about it causes the
lyrics to loop around in my brain and repeat themselves over
and over. My friends in Florida have heard my story about
Gord begging me years ago to play his music, and how I
eventually had to play it to the point where it has been
burned into my brain.

Enter the Schooner Wharf Bar. It's been here since 1984,
and definitely qualifies as a local's bar. It's located on the
site of an old shrimp factory, right on the water. All the usual
suspects can be found there, frequently accompanied by their
dogs, and you often see parrots perched on bar-side patrons'
shoulders. It's an open-air place, and a great spot to kick
back and hoist a few adult beverages.

On almost any given afternoon, the entertainment is supplied
by Michael McCloud, a laid-back singer who perches on his
stool for a five-hour stint of music. He usually includes The
Wreck of the Edmond Fitzgerald at some point in the daily

festivities. My buddies know how much the song affects me, and at least twice a week one of them will call me mid-afternoon. When I pick up the phone, the culprit will point his cell phone towards the bar, and all I can hear is *that song* being played in the background. Then they hang up, while the song continues to spin in my brain for the rest of the day. Thanks for the memories, Gord.

Track 134

A few years ago, I read with interest about a local historian, Bruce Neff. He had set himself the goal of producing a series of local Key West Historic Marker Tour audio features, which can be used by tourists exploring the City of Key West.

You can get a look at this website here: www.kwhmt.org

You can also see a few videos of Bruce's work at my website www.southernmostradio.net/tourism

Bruce refers to me as a Voice of History, which I take as the ultimate compliment. It has been a pleasure to work with him. To date, I've probably voiced about seventy of these features, in addition to a couple of very interesting video projects about the architectural styles of the city, and another video promoting Key West tourism. It has been a fascinating glimpse into the rich history of Cayo Hueso or Bone Island as the island was once known. I really wanted to give back to this marvelous, unique island known as The Last Resort or The End of the Road, so I offered Bruce my services to record the details at each of the sites. These recordings will play on long after I've shuffled off, and for that I'll always feel I've made some sort of permanent mark for posterity in Key West.

Two of the markers really stood out in my memory as I was doing my narrations. One was for The Cable Hut, which stands right next to the Southernmost Point. With Bruce's permission, allow me to quote from his script.

"This hut was installed to protect the connection between the land line in Key West and the 120-mile-long underwater telegraph cable running to Havana, Cuba. A few years earlier, through cables like the ones this concrete hut was protecting, on Christmas Day in 1900, the first international phone call was made. John W. Atkins called to Cuba, testing to see if it would be possible for voices to be heard through the telegraph lines. After a long silence, Cuba answered in Spanish, with a simple *'I don't understand you.'* The cable hut still stands today as a monument to remind us how international communication truly started."

Another Historic Marker Script concerns itself with the Great Fire of 1886. Again, allow me to use Bruce Neff's script to illustrate a fascinating chapter of intrigue in The Conch Republic. Here, word for word, is an insight into what really happened.

"At 2:00 am on the morning of April 1, 1886, the most devastating fire in Key West's history was ignited in a small coffee shop next to the San Carlos Institute. This fire was more than an accident! There is evidence that this blaze, costing two million dollars in property damage in 1886, *was set by the Spanish Empire to try to shut down Key West!*

"At the time of the historic blaze, the Spanish Empire was entrenched in a revolution against the Cuban people. The Cuban Revolutionaries depended on Key West for the majority of financial support, to keep their soldiers able to fight against the Spanish. Add this to the fact that Spain had to sell Cuban tobacco to the Key West cigar factories in order to fund their own troops, and it created a vicious circle of each side being funded by Key West.

"It made sense for the Spanish Empire to shut down the Key West Cigar Industry to make sure that the funding for the revolutionaries was put to an end. They had other places they could sell their tobacco, but the Cuban revolutionaries had no other single place that contributed anywhere near the support that Key West did.

"The blaze was ignited very symbolically next to the San Carlos Institute, the club erected by the cigar manufacturers and the focal point of the Cuban society in Key West. The fire ravaged the downtown area, burning down eighteen major cigar factories, six hundred and fourteen houses and government warehouses. Our only steam fire engine was off in New York being fixed at this time, another suspicious coincidence, which explains why it took twelve hours for the fire to burn itself out.

"There are 3 large factors which really add to the intrigue of this destructive fire. The first is that the blaze was actually extinguished on Whitehead Street in the early morning, but against prevailing winds the fire miraculously *re-ignited* on Duval Street, targeting major cigar factories. The second factor is that the following morning, there was a Spanish flotilla waiting just offshore to take all of the newly unemployed Cuban workers back to Cuba. The third is that it was reported by the Tobacco Leaf, a paper printed back then solely for the tobacco industry, that an article ran in Havana *the day prior* to the blaze, touting that Key West had burnt down.

"This fire truly was one of the worst Key West had ever seen and with all of the circumstantial and suspicious evidence surrounding it, it's easy for one to draw the logical conclusion. Hopefully, through in-depth research and with a little luck, concrete evidence will be found to finally prove this blaze was no mere accident."

Which just goes to show you, there are fascinating stories everywhere, to say the least!

Track 135

Another facet of voice-for-hire folks like me is the recording of Audiobooks. There's a booming business for this off-shoot of publishing, and these projects can take days to complete. I'm sure you can imagine this if you've ever read a chapter aloud to a child before bedtime. The pay for this sort of project is by finished hour of audio recorded, which involves a lot of editing time and intense concentration to complete the task.

You also have to learn to check your personal feelings at the studio door when you make yourself available to record commercials for anyone who wants your voice on their TV or radio spot. I've voiced spots for the Johnny Cochrane law firm, as well as campaign commercials for Senator Lindsay Graham.

A challenging aspect of this type of work is called, voice acting. Often, a sponsor doesn't want a typical, booming *announcer* voice, but a more subtle character read of the script. It might be the voice of an imaginary grandfather, someone brimming over with joy, or just a man-on-the-street treatment of the script supplied. We're often called upon to deliver the script with instructions referring to other performers.

"Make it sound like Morgan Freeman, or do you have anyone who sounds like Donald Sutherland?"

Of course these two individuals are fine actors first and foremost, and professionally trained in both stage and film delivery. With good reason, they're already in demand for National TV commercials, and paid great money just to sound like themselves. I suspect that sooner or later a lawsuit will be filed by someone trying to stop such impersonations in commercials and I think it will be very interesting to see what happens if and when it comes to pass.

Home Studio

Announcer: *"There's more to come, but first these words!"*

When faced with these kinds of challenges in voice acting, I reached back into my past. I would frequently send an audiofile of me doing a voice acting job to my long-time friend, Mel Hall back in San Diego. Mel by that time had already made a name for himself in Los Angeles, and with his great pipes and keen ear was well-established in the voiceover business. His critiques were a big help to me.

After years of trying to sound like an announcer, with the deep voice, resonant phrasing and smooth polished delivery, I had to make the transition to an entirely new path, where I needed to sound like anything *but* an announcer. It was not the easiest thing I have ever done.

On an industry website, Mel added his comments to my personal profile in a tribute of sorts.

"I've worked with this lad since he was in his teens, and am proud to see his progress in this field. I'm glad he followed my advice and changed from his tight-fitting Jockey underwear to looser-fitting boxer shorts. It makes all the difference in the world!"

I'll take what praise I can get.

Track 137

"Good evening, ladies and gentleman. My name is Orson Welles. I am an actor. I am a writer. I am a producer. I am a director. I am a magician. I appear onstage and on the radio. Why are there so many of me and so few of you?"
Orson Welles

My pal Mel really knew his stuff. He had once been hired to produce a commercial starring the late Orson Welles. Orson himself had been an actor, director and voiceover artist of international fame. His in-studio temper tantrums had driven many would-be directors into paroxysms of fear. He was famous for not accepting direction in any manner. When Mel first hit the intercom to comment on Orson's treatment of the script, the larger-than-life character began his usual tirade against those with enough temerity to question him.

While he ranted, Mel asked the engineer of the session to close Orson's microphone and he went into the studio for a private, one-on-one chat. He picked up Orson's script, and read it aloud, in a pitch-perfect imitation of what he wanted, *in Orson's voice*!

"Mr. Wells, that's what I'm looking for. Now the decision is yours. You can sit and argue with me about it and waste both your time and mine. But if I were you, I would just do it the way I did, take the money and you can be out of here in about two minutes."

Welles pondered for a moment before replying.

"I see your point," he finally said. "Nice read, by the way. Furthermore, I want you to direct me anytime I'm asked to record a commercial script!"

Rosebud.

Mel Hall, Voice Actor and director. The man who taught Orson Welles a thing or two about how to read a commercial.

Track 138

Announcer: *"Life in the tropics and the sound heard round the world! That's next as we continue!"*

"The Internet is the new FM radio. This is where the future is." Early FM rock format announcer Dwight Douglas

Southernmost Radio, 2011 Playlist:
"Margaritaville" Jimmy Buffet"
 "Key Largo" Berty Higgins
"Blow Me Down To Cayo Hueso" Scott Kirby
"Tropical Vacation" Tropical Soul
"At The End of U.S.1" Trop Rock Junkies
"Shady Lives in Sunny Places" Sunny Jim White
"Conch Republic Song" Michael McCloud
"Living on Key West Time" Howard Livingston
 "Sand & Sun" A1A
"Life Is Better In Flip Flops" Tiki Thom
 "Frozen Drinks" Billy Mitchell

www.southernmostradio.net

Now Playing: Give Me a Bar to Steer By, by Clint Bullard
"Give me a bar to steer by
On an island afar that's nearby
The glow of the neon puts me on a course for
The Beer Guy
Give me a Bar
Who needs a star?

When you've got a bar to steer by!"
Clint Bullard © Texas Bone Music

You can't spend much time in Key West listening to the
modern-day troubadours who entertain tourists and locals
without hearing plenty of what is called Tropical Rock, or
Trop Rock by its fans. It's on the menu at most of the
watering holes that dot this island. Technically, I suppose, it
contains elements of the Jamaican steel band sound,
Calypso, Country, Rock and Roll, Reggae, and Zydeco.
Jimmy Buffett pretty much started the trend when he sang
for tips near the waterfront many years ago.

I had the good fortune to live next to two of Key West's
outstanding performers, Clint Bullard and Scott Kirby, each
of whom have lived, written and sung in these tropical
climes for years. On one memorable birthday cruise with
these two balladeers, our sailboat became stuck on a sandbar
just off the island. I thought we might have to toss an empty
bottle overboard with a Save Our Ship note inside since we
appeared to be marooned. Fortunately, at that moment there
were lots of empty bottles around from which to choose.

Over those years we all became good friends, and have
shared more than a few drinks at the Hog's Breath, The
Smokin' Tuna, and the Tiki Bar at the Galleon Resort, while
enjoying Key West's fabled sunsets on the Gulf of Mexico.
What a life they lead, playing their own music for happy
fans, and being paid to do so!

Trop Rock songs are pretty much focused on fishing,
drinking, boating, drinking, relaxing, drinking and generally
carousing. You could pretty much sum up the genre by

saying it is music by which you can grow old disgracefully. Can I get an amen?

Track 139

I was talking to one of my clients one day, the Owner/Manager/Program Director/Sales Manager of a small AM radio station in upstate Florida, and happened to ask him about why he had decided to stream his signal on-line through the internet.

"Why not? The price is peanuts, the sound is vastly superior to AM radio, it is broadcast in stereo, and you can hear it all over the world!"

As much as they may sound like terrestrial counterparts, a lot of streaming audio Internet radio stations have a very different focus. Traditional AM and FM radio stations *broadcast* to large segments of the listening public with well-defined formats like Oldies, Adult Contemporary, Country, or Classic Rock.

But streaming audio stations tend to focus on much smaller slices of the potential audience. In contrast to the earth-bound stations, what they do is better referred to as *narrowcasting*.

To draw a comparison, it is like the difference between an Ear, Nose and Throat specialist and someone who specializes only in noses, or maybe just nostrils, or even just the left nostril. But the more specialized you get, the smaller your potential patient base becomes. Or your listening base in the case of streaming audio.

Track 140

The seed had been firmly planted and I knew I wanted to be involved in this new kind of 'casting. I contacted an ex-Creative Director of CFPL in London, who I had worked with at both CJBK and CHLO. He had already purchased a complete radio automation software program, and was very experienced in making it work flawlessly.

It didn't hurt my goals that he wanted to get involved in a streaming audio radio station himself, so we quickly put our heads together and agreed to a format and Call Sign.

Southernmost Radio was a no-brainer. Since we had both lived through Oldies formats, we knew we didn't want to do another round of *that*. How often can you twist again, like you did last summer? Given the rest of our musical preferences, the inevitable format was Hits of the Seventies, Eighties and Trop Rock!

Rob Mitchell, my First Mate on this venture, had an extensive music library of the mainstream music we needed, and I started to contact everyone I knew in Key West to get them on board by supplying us with access to all their CDs. Little by little, our Trop Rock library swelled to over one thousand titles, and when we combined these songs with close to three thousand Top 40 hits from the 70s and 80s we had created a hybrid station that stood apart from anything else to date. When you consider that most FM terrestrial-based stations only play about four hundred songs in their rotation, we offered *ten times* more well-researched music.

Our feeling was that a steady, round-the-clock rotation of nothing but Trop Rock would be too much of a good thing, so we arranged the software to automatically insert a Buffett-style title about every third song. Then we added specialty programs to add some spice to our programs, so that Thursday Nights became Thunderstruck Thursdays with Classic Rock hits. Fridays we offered Absolutely 80s, on Saturday we air Saturday Night at the Seventies, and on Sundays we roll a six-hour segment called The Buffett Buffet.

That one probably explains itself. It contains one hundred per cent, unadulterated, not-from-concentrate Trop Rock. Come back for second helpings! Sunday evenings, we present Jammin' Sundays with Jawaiian, (think Hawaiian Reggae), Calypso, Ska, and Reggae.

Next, we designed podcasts, or as we called them, Tropcasts, giving our listeners Trop Rock On Demand. This one-hour weekly program features all Trop Rock, and lets me host the show from our Tiki Hut Bar in the Tropics, complete with background bar-crowd sound effects. Essentially, no matter what time zone the listener is in, they can experience their own musical sunset so that it's always Five O'Clock Somewhere.

With the addition of specially-crafted Trop Rock Jingles that invite the listeners to *Let the World Turn Slow on Southernmost Radio,* we offer a station that can be heard anywhere in the world! It was especially neat to fire up my laptop in a condo overlooking Waikiki Beach and hear our little station pumping out the beachside beat!

When I point out to people that Southernmost Radio is commercial-free I generally add another revealing comment.

"We didn't plan it that way, it just happened!"

Seriously, this whole adventure is a labor of love, and if it makes one person happy, as they used to say at the end of the old Lone Ranger radio shows,

"My job here is done, Tonto!"

Try it now for a taste of the Tropics. Go to www.southernmostradio.net and turn up the volume!

Track 141

Announcer: *"The Keys are a breeze! Plus, a close shave causes an accident! On the way, more great memories, but first…"*

It's a long way from London to Key West, and it may be worth a few words to explain how we washed up on that particular shore. My wife Mary has always loved the place, and her enthusiasm for the island was very contagious. On my first visit there, I didn't know exactly what to expect but it didn't take long for me to be won over. We were wandering down Duval Street, the main street of this quirky town. It is just over a mile in length and runs north to south, from the Gulf of Mexico to the Atlantic Ocean. During a typical Duval Crawl, you'll see plenty of t-shirt shops, of course, but world-famous pubs and bars like Sloppy Joes, Jimmy Buffett's Margaritaville, Fogarty's, Rick's Café, and Irish Kevin's. Add to this the ever-present Conch Trains and Trolleys, Pedicabs, Pepto-Bismol-pink taxis, skateboarders, and wide-eyed tourists from around the globe, more than a few of which are holding what we call go-cups as they make their way along the sidewalks. You can imagine what they contain.

The first sight that really caught my eye was a local riding along on a balloon-tired bike with high-rise handlebars. Sitting on the right handgrip was a brilliant green parrot, while on the left was an equally bright red one. Sailors reading this account will realize the birds are living navigation beacons.

A few moments later we saw a German shepherd sitting on the gas tank of a passing Harley, happily wearing a WW I flying helmet and goggles. Quirky and unique, just like Key West. I felt like I had found a new home. These people weren't looking for attention as much as they were just expressing themselves and enjoying life in the tropics, where every night is a Party in Paradise.

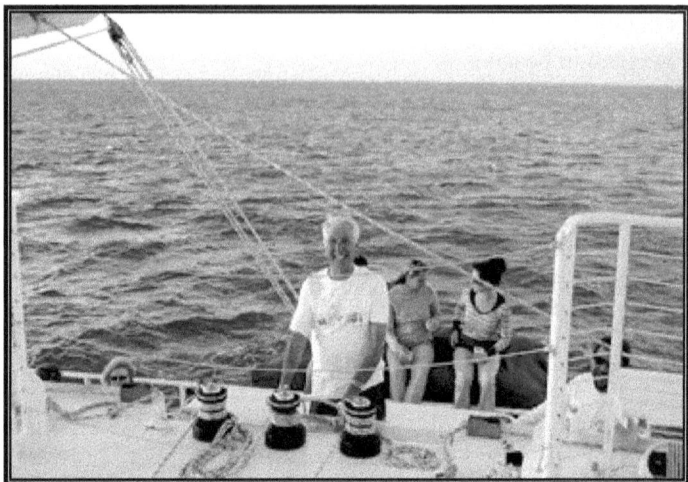

At the helm of a sunset catamaran cruise in Key West: Commotion on the Ocean!

Track 142

Even though this is a book about radio, I can't pass up this opportunity to relate a newspaper story from the local Key West Citizen a few years ago. I can only compare what follows to a newscaster wrapping up his news summary with this story as a kicker, so perhaps it could be a radio news story as well (with a lot of editing).

It seems there was a young lady driving her vehicle into Key West on the Overseas Highway. Something happened, she caused an accident, and was subsequently arrested. Instead of concentrating on where she was going, she had been intent on getting ready for a hot date. As she drove to an evening get-together with a new flame, she was also busily trimming the foliage on her private parts, below the belt-line. Thus distracted, her mind wasn't exactly razor-sharp. Multi-tasking, sure, but this was ridiculous. To further complicate the narrative, her ex-husband had actually been *steering* the car at the time of the accident, from the right-hand side of the pickup truck. Two people in the vehicle they hit were slightly injured in the mishap.

To make matters worse, this same well-groomed woman had been convicted of driving under the influence just the day before. Her licence was already under suspension, (for the sixth time) and the car had been ordered impounded. She was charged with driving with a revoked licence, reckless driving, leaving the scene of a wreck with injuries and driving with no insurance.

According to the arrest affidavit, the trooper asked her afterward why she didn't hit the brakes when she saw the SUV. She answered candidly.

"I told you, I was shaving."

An attending police officer backed up her story.

"If I wasn't there, I wouldn't have believed it."

People around here often insist there's something in the water in the Keys. There are times when I am convinced they are right. Only in Key West!

Track 143

Announcer: *"We're back with more of our story! Don't touch that dial... you don't know where it's been!"*

"Radio is full of surprises. Stay tuned." WABC programing genius Rick Sklar's last line in "Rockin' America"

"We've turned an art into a science."
Veteran programmer/DJ Tom Shovan on radio in a 1983 interview

Now Playing: Radio Ga Ga, by Queen
"Let's hope you never leave, old friend
Like all good things, on you we depend
You had your time, you had the power
You've yet to have your finest hour"
Roger Taylor/ Roger Aitken © EMI Music Publishing

A few years ago I was asked to speak about radio to a group of students enrolled in a Community College Radio Arts program, which would graduate them as broadcasters-to-be. I began by telling a story that Jack Nixon, almost my partner in the ill-fated car wash of yesteryear, used to tell his classes at his first lecture of the year when he taught this same course.

Jack would ask the students to take careful notes, then recite the ingredients and instructions to make a lovely pot roast.

Sooner or later, one of the students would ask the obvious question.

"Why are you telling us a pot roast recipe in a broadcasting class?"

"You're not going to make much money in this business, so you better know how to stretch your income by putting together a healthy meal that will last you a week."

That is bottom-line, practical thinking at its best, and it also reminded the students that if they were lucky enough to find a career in broadcasting they needed to find satisfaction in something besides money. My audience was not impressed. As I went on, sharing the skills I'd learned in an adult lifetime behind a microphone, it became quite apparent that none of the students was really paying very much attention. I was sharing information that could help them find success in their chosen field but to my surprise, they didn't seem to care. Finally giving up, I asked if anyone had any questions to ask, hoping to stimulate a little dialogue that way. Not gonna happen. They just sat there, obviously bored to tears.

This was doubly sad for me, because I entered this business with a burning enthusiasm and love for what I wanted to do more than anything else in my life. And here was a room full of people who supposedly wanted to follow in my footsteps but were acting like they were only there for lack of anything better to do. It occurred to me that of this entire class, perhaps only one or two graduates would even land an entry-level job in the field. And with the kind of attitude they showed me, they wouldn't be able to keep those. What a shame.

But the industry has changed and is changing so much they might not have been able to get jobs even if they had been interested. In my day, there were always small-town radio stations looking for hungry young announcers, but that market is all but gone. Nor are there as many of the low-budget, low rent stations that might have paid starvation wages but at least gave you the opportunity to learn your craft. Small-market radio can rely on automation or syndicated programing, so the pipeline doesn't allow anyone the opportunity to earn while they learn.

With the advent of voice-tracking, one DJ can do a program for multiple radio stations, some clear across the country, eliminating even more jobs for new, untested Community College grads. There are no more live overnight shows, either, where young broadcasters can ply their trade. Overnights are now all automated by the multi-tasking and voice-tracking I described earlier.

To make matters worse, there is little or no job security in radio anymore. For most people, it is not a career with a future. As I write this, a major Canadian broadcaster has just laid off eighty employees, and you can be sure this annual purging at fiscal year-end will be matched by many of their competitors. Tragically, the bean counters who run radio today have totally lost sight of what made radio great in the first place- the personalities who drew listeners into their worlds. The magic of that kind of radio has been totally forgotten by accountants who don't know how to account for talent in their ledgers. All they want is cash flow, and they will do almost anything to get it, including abandoning the very people who created the profits in the first place.

To add insult to injury, many of the long-time broadcasters tossed on the street are at an age where when they will likely never get another job in radio, which in most cases is all they know. I know how lucky I was to have come through all the changes I weathered in radio with so few skinned knees. I am not exaggerating when I say that almost every single person I ever worked with or for in radio has by now been escorted out of the buildings where they served so loyally.

Track 144

"For years everyone looked toward the demise of radio when television came along. Before that, they thought talking movies might eliminate radio as well. But radio just keeps getting stronger." Host of American Top 40, Casey Kasem

Radio's future may seldom have looked so bleak, but people have been predicting the demise of radio since it began. Remember the opening quote in this book, from the genius Thomas Edison?

"The radio craze ... will soon fade."

He was right about light bulbs, but wrong about radio. So were the people who thought television would be the death of radio. It wasn't. Satellite Radio was another threat that hasn't made as much of an impact as most predicted. Digital Radio came and went without notice, which is even stranger when you consider that many AM stations stayed on the air looking forward to a day when all stations were to migrate to Digital Frequency Bands in order to create a level playing-field for everybody. MTV was supposed to make radio obsolete, too, but it's still here. Gutted, largely stripped of personality, but still there, waiting to see what comes next.

And now we have the Ipod, the Walkman, the Ipad, Pandora, Spotify and other music delivery systems, such as the ever-proliferating streaming audio on the World Wide Web. Terrestrial radio stations continue to exist, and I'm almost positive there is a future for the immediacy, portability, and rapid response that local radio can bring. In an emergency, where's the absolute first place you turn to? While the TV news crews are spending precious minutes setting up their remote feeds from a breaking story, they are constantly scooped by instant reports from sophisticated radio reporters, armed with compact digital systems that can feed their stories live via cellphone with studio-quality sound.

Sure, the corporate structures continue to drive small stations off the air, but lately some major conglomerates such as Clear Channel Communications have begun to hive off many of their smaller assets. At one point they controlled eight hundred and thirty radio stations but have sold off more than five hundred and forty of their smaller-market stations. Some of them have gone back to Mom and Pop entrepreneurs who might re-launch more local programing or even come up with an entirely new format that might sweep the country the way early Top Forty did back in the Nineteen Fifties.

Nobody knows the future, but surely there's nothing wrong with hoping for a resurgence of Personality Radio and a trend away from formulaic, copy-cat electronic programing. We can be pretty sure whatever evolves will be exciting, and maybe something we've never heard before.

Think about the renewed interest in Talk Radio, especially in America. Many stations have flipped their AM talk shows over to their FM sister stations to build on already-strong audience numbers. There's nothing to say some other format might not come along and do the same thing.

Track 145

Announcer: *"We hope you've enjoyed yourself, but now it's time to say goodbye! Thanks for listening!"*

"I see by the old clock on the wall...there's a dead fly." Old-time radio comedy skit

"May you live to be a hundred, and me a hundred minus a day, so I'll never know good people like you have passed away. Peace, love, truth and soul." Frankie Crocker, WMCA

"Keep on rockin', because in this world you really rock ONCE!" Jerry Blavat, WFIL, WIBG

"Keep your feet on the ground and keep reaching for the stars." Casey Kasem, KRLA

Now Playing: Clap Hands, Closing Theme
"Hey now, that's our show
Looks like we got to go
Williams says 'Bye Bye'
Hope to see you by and by
Tune us in another day
On the Dick Williams Show!"
© Commercial Recording Company Dallas Texas

How do you sum up the impact you may have in almost sixty years of broadcasting? What professional epitaph is appropriate? I have wrestled with this question for some time as I made my way through my life in the pages of this manuscript, and I think I can best turn the answer over to someone else.

I was at a birthday party for two friends a few years ago, and standing in a long line to get a pair of cocktails from the bar. Beside me was a woman of, as the French say, a certain age. She kept looking at me with a puzzled expression on her face and was quite obviously trying to place where she knew me from. Her attention was getting uncomfortable but a light finally dawned in her eyes and she leaned towards me. *"Excuse me, but didn't you used to be Dick Williams?"*

That's my story in words and music. Thanks for listening, and thanks for reading!

Acknowledgements

".....I owe thanks to the people who have listened to me over the years, who tuned in on the radio. They have given me a warmth and loyalty that I've never been able to repay. The way they have reached out to me has certainly been the highlight of my life." Ernie Harwell, Major League Sports announcer and fifty-five-year Voice of the Detroit Tigers

First, I have to thank my wife Mary for her contributions to this book, both on and off air. She not only has heard all of my stories innumerable times, but had to suffer through me re-reading them to her yet again as I progressed through the book.

Thanks as well to my first wife, Debbie, who I know loved her time in radio, and to my son DJ, who inherited the love of the medium from both of us. I hope these stories will continue to strengthen the love between us.

I find it hard to think I would ever say thank you to a lawyer. But he's a personal friend of ours, Bob Beccarea, and it was he who first suggested I write these stories down. Thanks, Consiglieri! If you think he had a bad idea, take it up with him!

I also have to tip my transmitter to two of my mentors who forever will be my inspiration. Frank Ward, my Program Director at WSAI, and my friend Mel Hall, both of whom are now broadcasting in Heaven and likely still arguing about who has the deeper and ballsier voice.

Thanks also to another dear-departed friend from Key West, Albin Krebs, a graduate of the Columbia University School of Journalism, where he won a Pulitzer traveling fellowship for travel and study in Europe. He ended his career in Journalism at The New York Times. He referred to me as Tonsils, and would constantly badger me to stick to the facts whenever I wrote something. I'm sorry if I didn't strictly adhere to his dictum throughout my career. Albin, please don't get your thong in an uproar!

For the background on a young Frank Ward, and Tom Clay, I thank Steve Cichon of Buffalo Stories LLC.

All of the great quotes from radio legends included in this book were supplied by Dale Patterson of Rock Radio Scrapbook, which spotlights the Golden Age of Top Forty Radio in words, sounds and images. Dale's superb website is www.rockradioscrapbook.ca

I also want to recognize a man who for years has been the biggest collector of radio air-checks I know, and who helped a lot with the preparation of this book. Charlie Ritenburg is a good friend and has even been known to do a little broadcasting himself from time to time. Charlie has his own radio station, but that's another story entirely, and for another day. Recently, Charlie became a new summertime neighbor in Port Stanley, so perhaps we'll do some broadcasts together here. Thanks for keeping the memories alive, Charlie!

Appreciation is also due to Ken McKinnon, Ward Cornell, Rick Richardson, Vern Furber, Jerry Stevens, and Gord Hume, who allowed me the opportunity to appear on their respective radio stations.

And more than one big pat on the back is due to Rob Mitchell, my partner in Southernmost Radio. He's put in more hours than I even want to consider, making our streaming audio radio station a vibrant listening experience. He also did a fabulous job designing our website and keeping the site curated on a daily basis.

I would like to express my fond thanks to Brenda Page, too, who came up with one of the few control room shots of me at CJBK. Brenda was CJBK's most ardent fan, and in later years, a very dear friend.

Thanks to Peter Goodall, the photographer, for the Seventies-era portrait of a much younger guy with much darker hair.

Speaking of photographs, sincere thanks to Jeff Guy, who made me sound so good for all those many years I had the pleasure of working with him. Jeff was kind enough to supply shots of the CJBK control room. He also was instrumental in setting up my recording studio years ago, and was his usual meticulous self. In the Small World category, a shout-out to Jeff's son Kent, who allowed me unlimited access to the pictures and documentation of my time at CFPL, so many years ago. His pictures are labelled with the notation: ***

I would like to document my appreciation of Barry Arnott, of the Archives and Research Collections Centre, Western University, London, Ontario for his help and invaluable access to many of the pictures featured in the visual collection of this book. Barry was able to pore through the million-plus negatives in their files to find many of the needles in the haystack. I really appreciate his efforts and those of his co-workers. Well done! Those pictures are labelled with the notation: +++

To James Reaney, well-known columnist of the London Free Press for over a quarter century, a special shout-out for his enthusiastic contributions and support in not only sorting through his memories and files for past documentation, but for being a long-time radio and music fan, who is also a lover of all things London. He was able to open several doors in his vault, and was helpful in putting me in touch with other contributors in the assembly of "A DJ's Spin." James follows in his father's footsteps documenting the London of yesterday and today. What a guy!

Key West Historian Bruce Neff, originator of the Key West Historic Marker Program, who has shared his love of Key West and its history with people all over the world. Thanks, Bruce, for the use of the scripts with which you provided me. Much appreciated.

To Barry Smith, a long-time friend, consummate radio professional, a great Operations Manager, and a man who covered my backside more times than I can count, a thousand huzzas!

I have to also thank Braden Doerr, who has been a big help in refreshing my memory with rafts of information and detail about radio programing and all of the nitty-gritty details about CRTC regulations. Tom Cooke was also invaluable with documentation of some of the "Glory Years" at Q97.5.

Credit is also due to my brother John for his technical advice on all the aviation material. I certainly appreciate his accuracy and attention to detail. It was a pleasure to fly with him and he and his fellow pilots are to be commended on their dedication and skill.

For the arduous task of proof-reading and editing, a special 'word' of thanks to Ron and Betty Eichenberger, Patty Keane, and Marianne Haas.

For his long hours of work on cover art design and graphic content throughout the book, a big salute is due my Key West friend Shane Runde. He added a distinct professional touch of his own, and I really appreciate the effort.

To Will Chapman, my appreciation for a job well done on the interior design.

And special thanks to my editor, Jim Chapman, and the good people at Bettger Books. They helped me turn my musings into a real book. I know it wasn't easy, and your extra efforts along the way are much appreciated.

And in closing, thank *you*, for taking the time to read this sometimes-rambling story. I hope you found a few smiles in these pages, and please feel free to pass these stories on to your friends. Or, better yet, have them order their own copy below!

The final thoughts go to Stan Freberg, from one of the flawless skits delivered on his album Stan Freberg Presents the United States of America:

"Grazie, Arrivederci, Hasta la Vista, Adios, Adios Muchachos (Breaking into song) Adios Muchachos, compañeros de mi Vida ----"

"Will you get outta here!?"

Bye.

Dick Williams, Key West Florida, May, 2015

Published By

Bettger Books

Also available from Bettger books:

Transition Girl, by Sonia Halpern

The Chris Carroll/Heavy Hart Adventures,
by Jim Chapman:
Dead As Can Be
Sad As Can Be
Bad As Can Be
*Coming Winter 2015 - Cruel As Can Be

His Will Be Done, by Jim Chapman

SkyCom: Immortal Deception, by Jim Chapman

Come Back to Life, by Jim Chapman

Visit www.BettgerBooks.com for more information on how
to publish, or to order a book in hard copy!

www.ingramcontent.com/pod-product-compliance
Lightning Source LLC
Chambersburg PA
CBHW071402090426
42737CB00011B/1314